HISTORY'S
PEOPLE

Women of the Raj: The Mothers, Wives, and
Daughters of the British Empire in India

Peacemakers: The Paris Conference of 1919
and Its Attempt to End War

Nixon in China:
The Week That Changed the World

The Uses and Abuses of History

Extraordinary Canadians:
Stephen Leacock

The War That Ended Peace:
How Europe Abandoned Peace for the First World War

MARGARET MacMILLAN

HISTORY'S PEOPLE

PERSONALITIES AND THE PAST

P

PROFILE BOOKS

This edition published in Great Britain in 2016 by
PROFILE BOOKS LTD
3 Holford Yard
Bevin Way
London
WC1X 9HD
www.profilebooks.com

First published in Canada and the USA in 2015
by House of Anansi Press Inc.

1 3 5 7 9 10 8 6 4 2

Printed and bound in Great Britain by
Clays, Bungay, Suffolk

The moral right of the author has been asserted.

A CIP catalogue record for this book is available from the British Library.

ISBN 978 1 78125 512 4
eISBN 978 1 78283 189 1

FSC
www.fsc.org
MIX
Paper from
responsible sources
FSC® C018072

To the memory of my mother Eluned Jane MacMillan,
1921–2015

CONTENTS

INTRODUCTION

HISTORY, I SOMETIMES THINK, is like a rambling, messy and eccentric house. It has been built, added to and renovated repeatedly over the centuries. Its foundations are buried in that conveniently vague place "the mists of time" but some of the spade work was surely done in the Near East by the anonymous author or authors of the *Epic of Gilgamesh*, in Europe's classical world by Herodotus, Thucydides, Tacitus and Livy, or in China by Sima Qian, the great historian of the Han dynasty, while Homer, Virgil, or the Arab traveller Ibn Battuta have added their decorative flourishes. Monkish scribes, Chinese scholars, Arab chroniclers, all painstakingly have placed their bricks and stones. The Renaissance produced some elaborate rooms devoted to understanding princes and popes while the Reformation and Counter-Reformation created some sober undecorated spaces with strongly moral tales. In the nineteenth century the inhabitants added orderly libraries and well-organized files while the twentieth century brought tiled laboratories where the past could be dissected and analysed. There is one wing, the post modernist one, where there appears to be no order at all and no clear style; every room, say those who live there, is as valuable or as meaningful as any other.

It is impossible to discern a single use or a dominant style in history's house. Nor can anyone tell where it begins or ends for it is eternally under construction, and there is always a new corridor to discover or neglected rooms which might be worth cleaning up and letting in the light. Strange noises come from the basement or the attics. Some rooms are like those in Blue Beard's Castle striking dread into anyone who draws near the door much less opens it. Other rooms still open to gardens where it looks like a new spring is coming.

Historians, if I can continue the metaphor just a little bit more, are the house's caretakers. Some of us, like the mediaeval chroniclers, believe in visiting one room after another in the order in which they were built while others prefer to settle on a particular part of the house and get to know it in the round. One group of caretakers thinks it is important to focus on what they deem to be the house's most powerful and influential inhabitants. Yet another insists that we cannot understand the house without gathering as much information as we can on the millions whose toil ensured its construction and upkeep as well as the food and clothing for its inhabitants. Each age brings its own preoccupations which produce an ever-shifting perspective on the past and so we ask different questions when we interrogate the past. Not surprisingly, environmental history or the history of economic booms and busts are increasingly popular subjects today.

Differences among historians sometimes spill over into civil wars which can make us forget that we are all engaged in the same endeavour to unearth and analyse the past. Yet history needs us all, from the material to the intellectual historians. The products of agriculture or of manufacturing can tell as much about past societies as the ideas which animated them. Cultural and social historians help us to understand the values, assumptions and social organization of long gone peoples while political or economic historians bring out the forces that shape societies or have brought change. We also need to compare, to study other histories than the ones we know best. And we should use the insights of other disciplines. Archaeology comes to mind at once but anthropology, sociology, biology, all can and have enriched history.

So does biography although the relationship between historians and biographers is often an uneasy one, marked by mutual suspicions. Historians complain that biographers do not properly understand or short change the context while biographers feel that historians miss out the individuals who help to make history. That tension in turn feeds into the long-standing debate in history over whether events are moved by individuals or the great objective forces such as economic and social changes or technological and scientific advances.

My own view is that there is no right or wrong answer. Individuals are enmeshed in their times. We are all products of our own histories but those in turn are themselves shaped by class, place, ideas, values, institutions and the wider history unfolding around us. Yet, having said that, we have to face the possibility that sometimes a single individual can alter the course of events. If Napoleon had never existed, was there anyone else in France at the time with his combination of talents, intelligence and ruthlessness who could have seized power and taken France to the dominance of Europe? Without Karl Marx to sum up socialist thinking and create of it a powerful and persuasive theory would so much of the twentieth century have been shaped by that particular ideology? Marx himself was aware of the need to find a balance between individuals and their times. As he wrote in 1852: "Men make their own history, but they do not make it as they please; they do not make it under self-selected circumstances, but under circumstances existing already, given and transmitted from the past. The tradition of all dead generations weighs like a nightmare on the brains of the living."

For all of us, and not just historians, there is something exhilarating in becoming aware of other human beings from very different worlds to our own. They will never know us but we can think about them and an individual life can be a way into another time. From villains to saints, with all the great variety humanity is capable of in-between, we can wonder why the figures of the past behaved as they did and what that meant. "The poetry of history", the great British historian G. M. Trevelyan wrote, 'lies in the quasi-miraculous fact that once, on this earth, once, on this familiar spot of ground, walked other men and women, as actual as we are today, thinking their own thoughts, swayed by their own passions, but now all gone, one generation vanishing into another, gone as utterly as we ourselves shall shortly be gone, like ghosts at cockcrow.'

When I started to plan this book, I made a list of personality traits which I felt were important in shaping human affairs. Love, fear, hatred, jealousy, ambition, altruism, loyalty, integrity: we can all add still others to the list. My problem was to narrow those down to a manageable few. In the end too I tried to find a balance between those qualities of personality which could be rightly said to change worlds and those which make it possible for us to have contact with the past. I also wanted to be able to find the people who could best illustrate what I meant. I decided first to look at those leaders who were effective, who managed to persuade sufficient numbers of their contemporaries to support them, and who achieved great ends. I then turned to those who also possessed many of the qualities that make good leaders but who, in the end, threw their position or their people away because they had become convinced that they were invariably right. Perhaps I have been slightly provocative in lumping together Woodrow Wilson, Margaret Thatcher, Adolf Hitler and Joseph Stalin but each in his or her own way fell prey to what the ancient Greeks described as hubris. The third characteristic I chose — that of daring — is again something that leaders often have but I wanted to focus in on the moments when a willingness to take risks had momentous consequences, whether it was Samuel de Champlain venturing across the Atlantic to the New World in the seventeenth century or President Richard Nixon going to Beijing in 1972. Then, in the last two chapters, I considered those who asked the questions and took the notes that make the understanding of others and history itself possible.

This book is the result of my own experiences over many years of reading and writing and, always, enjoying history. I have taken the opportunity offered here to discuss the people from the past I have found most interesting. My choices are highly personal but I hope they will serve to raise some of the important issues we must all think about as we look at the past. History matters and we must do it well. When it is false or one-sided it can be used to mobilize people for evil ends. At its best history can explain others and help us to better understand ourselves and our world. It can also remind us that what we think is normal or the only way of doing things is not necessarily so. There have been other worlds with other values than our own and we need to be reminded of that, if only to give us some sense of humility. In the end I love history because it is such a marvellous combination of enlightening and fun.

ONE

PERSUASION AND THE ART OF LEADERSHIP

OVER THE PAST DECADES, historians have broadened their scope from political, economic, or intellectual history to include the study of emotions, attitudes, tastes, or prejudices. (And in what I find a rather tiresome trend, historians have also been looking increasingly at themselves; how they "created" the past.) And in the house of history are those who think in centuries and those who focus on a single moment. Some historians prefer to deal with the great changes, sometimes over millennia, that have taken place in human society. They look at the shift from hunting to agriculture, for example, or the growth of cities; or they count such things as population growth and migrations or economic output. The great French historian Fernand Braudel argued that the true object of historical research was to look beneath the surface of events and discover the longer-term patterns — what he called the *longue durée*. He saw human history as a great slow-moving river, affected in its course more by geography, the environment, or social and economic factors than by such transient or short-lived events — he called them "froth" — as politics or wars. While biography cannot explain all, it is perhaps no coincidence that Braudel spent the Second World War in a prisoner-of-war camp in Germany. From that perspective the *longue durée* must have offered hope that Nazism would disappear like a bad dream as history moved slowly on.

We cannot dismiss the short term so easily. Ideas and sudden shifts in politics, intellectual fashions, or in ideology or religion matter too. Think of the startling growth in the past two decades in fundamentalism in religions as different as Christianity, Hinduism, or Islam. Historians rightly look at key moments which signalled or set in motion great changes, such as the storming of the Bastille, which marked the French Revolution, or the assassination of the archduke in Sarajevo, which led to the outbreak of the First World War. And historians can take an apparently insignificant incident and use it to illuminate an age, as Natalie Zemon Davis did with sixteenth-century France in her telling of the return of Martin Guerre (who came back to claim his wife and property from an imposter).

Nor can we dismiss the role of individuals, whether thinkers, artists, entrepreneurs, or political leaders. If Albert Einstein had not grasped the nature of the atom early in the twentieth century, could the Allies have developed the atomic bomb during the Second World War? Another question, of course, is what Germany might have done if the Nazis had not driven Einstein and many of his fellow physicists into exile so that they offered their services to the Allies. Without the bomb it is almost certain that the Allied war against Japan would have dragged on for another year or more. And what if the world had never developed nuclear weapons at all? In the nineteenth century, with Europe undergoing the massive changes brought by the Industrial Revolution, Karl Marx took many of the political, economic, and social ideas that were circulating and tied them up into a coherent and apparently irrefutable package that not only explained the past but predicted the future. Generations of men and women around the world believed in Marxism as their ancestors had believed in religion — as a revealed truth — and so tried to change the world in accordance with its precepts.

At certain moments too it really does matter who is in the driver's seat or who is making the plans. The Cold War could have ended very differently — or not ended at all — if someone other than Mikhail Gorbachev had been the Soviet leader. He was not prepared to use force in the 1980s to cling onto the Soviet Empire in Eastern Europe or to keep the Communist Party in power in the Soviet Union itself. The Chinese Communist leadership reacted very differently in the face of dissent, and their crackdown in Tiananmen Square in 1989 was the result. If the Supreme Court decision on the 2000 vote count in Florida had gone differently, George W. Bush would not have been president. President Al Gore would not have surrounded himself with the same hawkish advisers, and it is easy to imagine that he would have resisted the temptation to invade Iraq.

I find in the subjects I have chosen for books — most recently key moments in international history such as the start and the end of the First World War — that I have to pay attention to individuals. If the troubled and erratic man who was Kaiser of Germany in 1914 had been the king of Albania — as his distant relative was — he could not have caused much trouble for Europe. But Wilhelm II was the ruler of a major economic and military power at the heart of the Continent. What is more, under Germany's imperfect constitution he had considerable power, especially over foreign policy and the military. In the end, he was the man who had to sign the order that took Germany to war. So it is impossible to look at the causes of that catastrophic conflict without considering Wilhelm, or his cousin Nicholas, who as tsar of Russia had equally great power and responsibility. And can we write the history of the twentieth century properly without looking at the roles played by democratic leaders such as Margaret Thatcher, Franklin Delano Roosevelt, Winston Churchill, or William Lyon Mackenzie King, and even more so those played by the great tyrants such as Hitler, Mao, Mussolini, or Stalin?

Sadly, biographers themselves, as well as historians who use biography, have too long been regarded with suspicion by much of the historical profession — dismissed as amateurs whose grasp on history is shaky, or accused of ignoring society and focussing too narrowly on individuals in the mistaken assumption that "great men" or "great women" make history. The nineteenth-century writer and intellectual Thomas Carlyle is often hauled out as an exponent of the theory that key figures — he called them heroes — are the shapers of the past. In the academic world, this view is treated with contempt (although, not surprisingly, business leaders find it rather attractive). This does an injustice to Carlyle, whose view of history was more complex. In an early essay he asked, "Which was the greatest innovator, which was the most important personage in man's history, he who first led armies over the Alps, and gained the victories of Cannae and Thrasymene; or the homeless boor who first hammered out for himself an iron spade?" Society itself, he argued, was the product of the work and lives of countless human beings, and history therefore "is the essence of innumerable Biographies." Although he is remembered more for his works on heroes, he saw them less as the makers of history and rather as people who summed up the feelings of a particular age or could see most clearly where society was headed and what it needed.

Carlyle understood that the secret of good biography — and indeed of much good history — is to understand that relationship between individuals and their societies. To understand the people of the past, we must start by respecting the fact that they had their own values and ways of seeing the world. They were shaped by different social and political structures; their ideas came from different sources than our own. Sometimes we have to work hard to understand their thinking. The great British historian James Joll talked of an era's "unspoken assumptions" — the sorts of things people didn't say, just because they were so taken for granted. We ourselves don't usually bother to explain why, for example, we think democracy is the best form of government, because generally, in Western societies, we assume it is.

So we must always locate people in their times and also remind ourselves that we cannot expect them to think things that hadn't yet been discovered or articulated. The Romans, we know thanks to historians, had very different ideas about families and honour than we do. The Byzantines lived in a world where the unseen was as important as what was visible to them. On the other hand, we should never forget that the people of the past were as human as we are. I will be looking at some who were important for what they did, but I also want to tell you about those who speak to us, about themselves, their contemporaries, and the worlds they lived in. The acerbic sketches of Michael Psellus, written in the eleventh century, tell us something of the long-vanished Byzantine Empire and the men and women who ruled over it, thanks in part to the details he includes; for example, the plump, golden-haired Empress Zoe, who ruled with her younger sister in 1042, was clever, passionate, and much more generous than the skinnier Theodora, who was talkative, stingy, and rather dull. The memoirs of Madame de la Tour du Pin help us to understand what it was like to live through the French Revolution and to go, as she did, from being a lady-in-waiting to Marie Antoinette to milking cows on a farm in northern New York State. Or a simple object can bring the past to life. I still remember the first exhibition to come out of China after the Cultural Revolution. We all marvelled at the leopards made of gold and the jade suit made to give a long-dead princess immortality, but it was a dried-up dumpling that moved me most. Just as a labourer would do today, a Chinese working on the tomb centuries ago had brought his lunch — and by mistake had left a bit behind.

Like us, the people of the past faced the challenges posed by life, even if we worry about different things. The Black Death, mercifully, is no longer with us, but then the past centuries did not have to fear nuclear annihilation. Yet while we must acknowledge the differences between then and now, we recognize in the people of the past familiar characteristics; they too had ambitions and fears, loves and hates. We can share in their pleasures and sorrows, and sympathize as they try to deal with problems or decide what is best to do. There is a particular pleasure in hearing a voice which reaches across the decades or centuries and reminds us that we share a common humanity. We read the great diarists — Samuel Pepys, for example, or James Boswell — because we find them such entertaining and interesting individuals.

Michel de Montaigne, a wealthy French nobleman living in the troubled sixteenth century, matters to us, as he has to all the generations between then and now, because his writings are an exploration of what it is to be human. His essays were never finished because their subject was in large part himself, his thoughts, his emotions, and his reactions, and, as he said repeatedly, he and they kept changing. "We are entirely made up of bits and pieces," he once wrote, "woven together so diversely and so shapelessly that each one of them pulls its own way at every moment. And there is as much difference between us and ourselves as there is between us and other people."

At the age of thirty-eight Montaigne retired from public life to run his estates and to ruminate in a tower at one end of his château. (His wife was put a safe distance away in her own tower at the other end.) In his capacious library, he wrote and revised and then wrote some more. He loved to pose questions: Why do we get angry at inanimate objects? Why are we suddenly overcome by emotion? Why, he asks, do our minds wander so much? His certainly did. In his essays he frequently pulls himself up with a "Let's get back to the subject," but it is no good. He starts on one topic then promptly wanders off into highways and byways. In the middle of a long essay on a contemporary theologian, we find Montaigne speculating on what is the best position in sexual intercourse for a woman to get pregnant. An essay titled *On Coaches* starts with the vehicles but includes, among much else, reflections on why monarchs need excessive grandeur, on the recent European discovery of the New World (and some caustic remarks on the folly of the Europeans in thinking they were more civilized than the peoples they found there), and on the fear of death. He also throws in a remark about fashion: "When I was a young man, in default of other glories I gloried in fine clothes. In my case they were quite becoming; but there are folk on whom fine clothes sit down and die." He is funny, sensible, and brisk. "If you do not know how to die," he advises in one of his last writings, "never mind. Nature will tell you how to do it on the spot, plainly and adequately." To read Montaigne, said Sarah Bakewell, who has written so wonderfully about him, "is to experience a series of shocks of familiarity, which makes the centuries between him and the twenty-first-century reader collapse to nothing."

Yet Montaigne also tells us something about his own times and its preoccupations — its fascinated rediscovery of the classical world, for example, or the discovery of the new ones in the Americas or the Far East. Perhaps because his own times were so turbulent, he ponders the question of what makes good government and bad. For much of his life, France was torn apart by wars between Catholics and Protestants, and so he wonders about the ways in which religion can lead to evil. Although he was a good Catholic, Montaigne was horrified at the intolerance of both sides: "Some approach it from this side, some from the other; some make it black, others make it white: all are alike in using religion for their violent and ambitious schemes, so like each other in managing their affairs with excess and injustice, that they make you doubt whether they really do hold different opinions over a matter on which depends the way we conduct and regulate our lives." He notes sadly that the French have got used to cruelty and wickedness.

In their own ways, all the people I have chosen to discuss have added their pieces to history, whether by making it or recording it or both. Leaders such as Franklin Delano Roosevelt or Joseph Stalin are famous for riding the currents of history and diverting them in one direction rather than another. Others, like the intrepid men and women who became explorers and adventurers, went against the current, often at great personal cost. Others still, like Montaigne, are better known as observers, standing on the sidelines. Yet without those who kept the records, wrote their diaries or letters, etched their graffiti, or even buried their garbage, we historians would not have the evidence we need to examine the past.

In the first three chapters I will concentrate on those who might be said to have left their mark on history. What were the qualities that they possessed, and what were the circumstances that made it possible for them to become leaders or merely risk takers. Why did they behave as they did? While all the leaders I am going to be considering had an instinctive understanding of the mood of their times, some proceeded by building consensus while others imposed their will by fiat and force. But both sorts of leaders have choices and the capacity to take history down one path rather than another. Then I will look at the particular quality of daring, where individuals take risks, leap into the unknown. What makes them do it? And what difference has it made? In the last two chapters, I am going to move from those who changed the course of history and turn to the sort of people you might want to have dinner with because they would be so entertaining. (And unlike many leaders, they would not hold forth but listen.) Some did occupy positions of power, like the Indian emperor Babur, while others were middle-class Englishwomen, but all had a great curiosity about the world. They shared a refreshing freedom from the prejudices and judgements of their own times. Some were prepared to travel — often in conditions of great discomfort, even danger — while others stayed where they were and observed what was going on around them.

History's people, for me, are those who stand out in the foreground, like a Madonna in a Renaissance painting, the pop-up figures in a children's book, or the one face a movie camera fixes on when it passes over a crowd. While a single life cannot stand in for a whole era, it can illuminate it and make us want, indeed oblige us, to know more. Catherine the Great was fascinating as a person, a woman of strong passions and equally strong determination, but to properly understand her we need to ask about her times. What was Russia like in the eighteenth century, especially to a young woman who came from a small German court? What values did she bring with her, and what did she acquire in her new life? She was able to survive and thrive in the treacherous and dangerous world of the Russian imperial family and in due course left her stamp on it, on Russia, and on Europe. The size and shape of Russia today owe much to her conquests, as at least in part do its complicated relations with its neighbours to the west. Otto von Bismarck had an outsize personality which would have sent waves through whatever society he found himself in, but he was fortunate, even if much of Europe wasn't, that fate gave him a big stage on which to act. As we follow Bismarck through his life, we learn about the emergence of Germany as an independent state and what that meant for his own times and for posterity.

LEADERSHIP — MY INITIAL topic — is a fashionable subject at present. If you do a search on the Internet you will find literally millions of links to leadership academies. Everyone, it seems, from business schools to Oprah Winfrey, is in on the business of teaching people how to be successful leaders, and often they promise to do so in only a few hours or days. It makes you wonder whether there can be any followers left. As the American historian Garry Wills has pointed out, not everyone wants to be a leader — or can be. Successful leadership depends in part on inherent qualities such as the ability to motivate or inspire others, but we all know people of great talent who never quite live up to their promise.

For years many Democrats hoped that Adlai Stevenson would be another Franklin Delano Roosevelt. He had the same sort of social connections and polish, the charm, and the willingness to make reforms. Yet he was not prepared to work hard to get elected; the voters, he assumed, would recognize his talents without any effort on his part. Nor was he willing to take strong stands. As American ambassador to the United Nations, he had echoed his government's denial of its involvement in the abortive attempts to overthrow Fidel Castro in the Bay of Pigs landing. When he realized he too had been lied to, he was furious with President Kennedy but made it clear to a friend that he had no intention of challenging Kennedy publicly or resigning. "That would be burning my boats," he said. In any case he was enjoying the UN and the diplomatic social round far too much. He died young, and the obituaries made much of the hopes for him that had been left unfulfilled.

The successful leader must have, to start with, ambition, even ruthless ambition. When he was a poor young man in a remote corner of North Wales, the future prime minister, David Lloyd George, wrote to the woman he hoped to marry, "My supreme idea is to get on. To this idea I shall sacrifice everything — except I trust honesty. I am prepared to thrust even love itself under the wheels of my Juggernaut if it obstructs the way..." Today, we would find such openness shocking. While it is considered perfectly all right and indeed admirable to want to succeed in banking or Silicon Valley or in sports, ambition in politicians is seen as somehow reprehensible. The very successful *House of Cards* shows a London (and in its American version a Washington) where politicians lie and cheat and have no limits on what they will do to achieve power. We should remember that in other times and other places, political ambition has been admired. In Republican Rome, as Tom Holland has pointed out in his fascinating *Rubicon,* it was expected of young men who were citizens that they would enter public life and endeavour to serve the republic. Their fellow citizens would be the judges of how well they did. As one observer said, "More than any other nation, the Romans have sought out glory and been greedy for praise." In Latin, the word *honestas* stood for both reputation and moral excellence. Ambition purely for one's own gains was equally a source of shame and condemnation.

Ambition on its own is never enough to make successful leaders. They must be both persistent and resilient. Winston Churchill suffered one setback after another in the course of a long career. In 1915 he was obliged to resign as first lord of the Admiralty in the wake of the failure of the Allied landings at Gallipoli. Although he worked his way back into the government by 1917, his later decision to abandon the Liberals for the Conservatives meant that he was mistrusted on all sides. He spent the 1930s in relative obscurity. While he did not cease to hope for high office, his career seemed over. Without the outbreak of the Second World War, he might well have stayed on the backbenches and be remembered today only by a few specialists in the period.

Perhaps more than anything else, timing and luck make the greatest difference between obscurity in a backwater and success on a larger stage. Napoleon Bonaparte came from a family of modest means on the island of Corsica. They were able to pull enough strings (and somehow claim sufficient noble ancestry) to get him into the École Militaire, where officers were trained. Without the French Revolution, which shattered the old ruling structures, a provincial boy without wealth or connections would have had little hope of becoming a general, much less the ruler of France. The Revolution made Napoleon's rise to power possible. His great cavalry general, Joachim Murat, the son of an innkeeper, would not even have been admitted to train as an officer before 1789. Thanks to the Revolution and his own talents, Murat became a Marshal of France and king of Naples and Sicily.

Napoleon was a dictator who exercised what the great German sociologist Max Weber described as "charismatic leadership." He led not because of the office he held but because of who he was. His charm, his extraordinary memory and equally extraordinary capacity for work, his uncanny ability to size up his enemy in the battle and seize the moment when his lines were wavering — all combined to create someone who could inspire men to fight and die. His great opponent, the Duke of Wellington, who was not given to exaggeration, said his presence on the battlefield was worth forty thousand men.

The three men I want to concentrate on now — Otto von Bismarck, William Lyon Mackenzie King, and Franklin Delano Roosevelt — were unlike Napoleon in many respects, not least in that their times and circumstances were different. But like him, they too were able to manoeuvre between long-term goals and short-term tactics; they too had an ability to sense the moods and currents of their times; and they could, when necessary, learn from failure and change their tactics, if not their minds. Equally important, the course of history gave them their opportunity, and they took it.

WE TEND TO FORGET how young Germany is as a country —
four years younger in fact than Canada — and we assume that,
for all its turbulent and tortured history, it was bound to come
into existence. Nationalism was a strong, perhaps irresistible
force in nineteenth-century Europe, and German nationalism
was among its strongest manifestations. Poets, teachers, politicians had worked, often deliberately, to create a picture of
a German people united by a common language and values.
The Grimm brothers did not collect German fairy stories to
entertain or frighten generations of children but to demon-
strate that there was a unique German culture. Historians
wrote of a distinct nation, one that had endured through the
centuries. What that might mean politically, however, was
still up for grabs in the middle of the nineteenth century. In
the revolutions of 1848, many German nationalists hoped
that the German Confederation that brought together some
thirty-nine German-speaking states and territories (including the German parts of the Austrian Empire) could acquire
a new, more liberal constitution and be made stronger, perhaps under the rule of the king of Prussia or the emperor of
Austria. Others preferred the status quo. It was by no means
inevitable that a single German state would emerge. After
all, English speakers around the world did not and do not see
themselves as belonging to a single political unit. German
nationalism could have coursed in different directions, perhaps amalgamating some of the separate German territories
and leaving in its wake a number of self-governing German
states: Bavaria, Prussia, Saxony, the German lands of the
Austrian Empire (much of which later became the little state
of Austria).

Without Otto von Bismarck, Germany — as the nineteenth and twentieth centuries knew it — would most likely

not have existed. Gordon Craig, one of the most distinguished historians of modern Germany, unapologetically starts his history of the country with Bismarck. "If he had never risen to the top in Prussian politics," says Craig, "the unification of Germany would probably have taken place anyway, but surely not at the same time or in quite the same way as it did." The Austrian Empire had history on its side; it had always been the dominant force among the German states. Its rulers, the Habsburgs, had virtually monopolized the title of Holy Roman emperor for centuries and so had held sway, at least in theory, over all the German lands, as well as much else in Europe. They had strong historic and family ties with many of the German states, particularly in the south, where the ruling families were Catholic like the Habsburgs themselves. And many German states — Bavaria, for example — mistrusted and feared Prussia.

That unification, when it came, was under the aegis of Prussia and not the Austrian Empire had much to do with the man who became Prussia's prime minister. A desperate Wilhelm I of Prussia appointed Bismarck in 1862 in the hopes that he could solve an internal constitutional crisis. The King had no intention of defying Franz Joseph, the Habsburg emperor, of excluding Austria from the German Confederation, or of uniting the remaining German states into one strong nation with himself on the throne. Bismarck had other ideas. His goal was a Germany united under Prussia's leadership and under the Prussian crown. That meant bringing the other German states to heel and eliminating Austria as a player in the German Confederation. To achieve that, he was prepared to use an array of tools, from diplomacy to, as he once famously said in a speech, "blood and iron." He was not a warmonger; rather he would use war to gain his ends if it seemed like the most effective option. He also knew when to seize the moment, just as Helmut Kohl did more than a hundred years later, when he saw a brief window at the end of the Cold War in which he could reunite the two Germanys. From the moment Wilhelm appointed him, to 1890, when Wilhelm's grandson — now Wilhelm II of Germany — dismissed him, Bismarck dominated Prussian and then German politics and was the master of Europe's international relations.

No other German leader of the time came anywhere near his brilliance as a statesman, nor his ruthlessness and cynicism. He was hard on subordinates and brutal to his enemies, and over the years they were many. He lied without hesitation and invariably blamed others for his mistakes. His rages were terrifying, and although he was a Christian, he did not apparently believe in forgiveness or loyalty. If you crossed him or if he simply had no further use for you, he would abandon you without hesitation. "The demonic is stronger in him, than in any man I know," said a British diplomat who knew him well. Yet he could also be, when he chose, charming and amusing. Bismarck achieved much through the sheer force of his personality, which — like almost everything about him, including his energy, his capacity for work, and his appetite — was outsize. (Two guests in his house once stood in awe in front of his chamber pot because it was so much bigger than the usual.)

Bismarck came from an unlikely background for such an extraordinary personality. The Prussian Junker class was known for producing stolid, pious, conventional country gentlemen who took pride in their pedigrees and family connections and in their service to the Prussian state. Predominantly conservative, Junkers were deeply suspicious of the modern world and of anyone who was not like them — that included liberals, capitalists, and Jews. They also distrusted those who were flamboyant and eccentric; their class valued qualities such as modesty, piety, hard work, self-discipline — and self-sacrifice. Throughout his life, Bismarck was a serious hypochondriac and was prone to prolonged fits of self-pity. Young men from Junker families often went into the military and, when necessary, died for Prussia without complaint. Bismarck did his best to get out of the obligatory military service. Later, with the effrontery and self-aggrandizement that marked so much of what he did, he claimed to have been a dedicated soldier and took delight in wearing an officer's uniform — much to the annoyance of Prussia's senior generals.

His early years gave little indication of the phenomenon he was to become. His childhood does not seem to have been a particularly happy one. His parents were ill-matched: his father was weak, good-natured, ineffectual, and dominated by his wife. She was beautiful, intelligent, and cold. Her son came to hate her and any women he thought like her, such as the wife of his king, Wilhelm I. At his boarding school Bismarck showed no particular promise, and at university he appears to have spent much of his time drinking and gambling. In his first career, as a bureaucrat, he was markedly lazy and ran up considerable debts. When he went off to run one of the family estates, he became notorious for his exploits such as riding like a man possessed or firing a pistol at his guests' windows to wake them up. He was known in the neighbourhood as the "Mad Junker."

He was also bored, as he said in a letter to his father, "to the point of hanging myself." Yet his luck (and it plays an important part in his story) was about to change. In 1847, one of the deputies from Bismarck's district to the Prussian parliament suddenly fell ill. His fellow Junkers surprisingly overcame their suspicions of Bismarck and elected him as the replacement. He took to politics with enthusiasm; more importantly he turned out to be brilliant at them. He rapidly made a name for himself as a man to watch — and as someone who had very few political principles. "If I am to proceed through life on the basis of principles," he once said, "it is as if I had to walk down a narrow path in the woods and had to hold a long pole in my mouth." If he had one guiding idea in terms of domestic policy, it was to keep the Prussian state and later the German one strong, and for Bismarck that meant a strong central government in the name of the king. (No matter that it was Bismarck himself who usually exercised the power from behind the throne.)

When he came into office in 1862, he showed himself adept at winning supporters and dividing the opposition by appealing to special interests, by offering inducements, or through intimidation. Prussia's liberals, who had never liked him, came around partly because their nationalism was aroused by the series of victories in the German wars of unification. The growing working classes and socialist movement were kept quiet, at least for a time, by universal manhood suffrage in the elections for the new Reichstag and by the most advanced and comprehensive program of social benefits in Europe. He never managed, however, to build a lasting coalition. Indeed in his values and ways of operating he was out of step with the new modern Germany that was emerging. Instead he relied on the support of the one man in Prussia who really mattered: King Wilhelm 1.

The Prussian king was a conventional and decent man, and not particularly clever or insightful — in other words, the opposite of his minister. He disliked much of what Bismarck did and how he did it — the confrontations and crises, often manufactured; the defeats of first the Austrian Empire and then France; the defiance of much of German public opinion and of Europe. Yet at some level, the king recognized that he and his dynasty needed Bismarck even though, as Wilhelm once mildly complained, "It's hard to be Kaiser under Bismarck." And since, under the Prussian and then the German constitution, the monarch had the final say over foreign and defence policy, and governments answered to him and not the other way around, Bismarck in the name of Wilhelm was able to exert great control over domestic and foreign affairs. The two men's relationship was marked by terrible arguments, doors being slammed, weeping, and shouting. Bismarck would come down with crippling headaches and fits of vomiting and claim that he was dying. He frequently threatened to resign. In the end it was always Wilhelm who backed down. Bismarck mustn't think of resigning, he wrote after one scene: "*It is my greatest happiness* [underlined twice] to live with you and thoroughly agree with you!"

It helped too that the king lived for a very long time, and so Bismarck had his backing for twenty-six years. If Wilhelm had died in his seventies, his successor, Frederick Wilhelm, would almost certainly have dismissed Bismarck and done his best to make Germany into a more liberal and constitutional state. (Frederick Wilhelm's forceful wife, Vicky, who was the eldest daughter of Queen Victoria, loathed Bismarck.) When Wilhelm finally died at the age of ninety-one in 1888, Frederick Wilhelm, who was mortally ill, lasted for only ninety-nine days. His son, the erratic and complicated Wilhelm II, could not tolerate being in Bismarck's shadow and sacked him in 1890. As the caption on a famous *Punch* cartoon put it, "Dropping the Pilot."

Support at home explains part of Bismarck's success, but again he was fortunate in that Europe was undergoing great changes. He once said to a friend that one could not play chess if sixteen out of the sixty-four squares on the board were already blocked. When he started creating Germany, the chessboard was open. His Prussia was on the rise. It already had a strong army (as the old joke had it, Prussia was not a country that happened to have an army, but an army that happened to have a country), and from the 1850s onwards its economy was growing rapidly. That gave Bismarck the gold, as he described it, to enlarge and equip the Prussian army, and the economic leverage to bring the other German states into line. The Austrian Empire, Prussia's great rival, was fading, increasingly troubled by the many nationalisms within its borders. The conservative power of Russia, which might have intervened to prevent sudden and far-reaching changes in Europe, had drawn in on itself following the Crimean War of 1853–56. It was no longer prepared to co-operate with the other powers — France, Britain, and the Austrian Empire — that had joined with its old enemy the Ottoman Empire to attack Russia. France, ruled by the vainglorious Napoleon III after 1848, was slow to notice the challenge from Prussia. The French had welcomed the defeat of the conservative monarchy of Austria but failed to take notice that Prussia and its allies in the German Confederation were turning into a powerful force on France's borders. Britain was, if anything, sympathetic to the rise of a united Germany but, as so often in its history, more interested in its overseas interests than in what was happening on the Continent.

Without German nationalism, Prussian strength, and the changing international scene in Europe, Bismarck could never have become the maker of modern Germany and the master of Europe. He had the great good fortune (even if the rest of Europe didn't) to be born at a time and in circumstances when he could make use of his undoubted talents. If he had been born into his landed gentry family earlier, he might have been, like so many of them, an unremarkable officer in the king's army or a bureaucrat. In a letter he wrote when he was only nineteen, he sketched an Otto von Bismarck who lived out his life on his country estate, terrorizing his peasants, his dogs, and his servants, but who was bullied by his wife; that alternative Bismarck passed his days hunting, drinking too much, and managing his farms. "I shall get pissed on the king's birthday and cheer him vociferously and the rest of the time I shall sound off regularly and my every other word will be; 'Gad what a splendid horse!'"

In 1862 Bismarck, in concert with Austria, provoked a war with Denmark to gain the duchies of Schleswig-Holstein. By the following year he was wondering whether the time was ripe for a surprise attack on his erstwhile ally. Instead he used the question of the disposition of the duchies to pick a series of quarrels with Austria. By the summer of 1866, Bismarck was ready; both Russia and France had agreed to stay neutral, and the Prussian army, which had not performed well against Denmark, had been reorganized and its foot-soldiers equipped with the most effective new rifles in Europe. In a stormy scene, however, Wilhelm refused to move against Franz Joseph, whom he regarded as the senior monarch. The king finally sent Bismarck out of the room, forbidding him to speak of it anymore. Bismarck rushed to a confidant and complained that "he was morally and physically shattered, that his whole life work, the establishment of the German Empire, had that day been wrecked, and that he was going straight home to send in his resignation." His friend calmed him down and begged the king to see him again. Wilhelm capitulated almost at once, and a jubilant Bismarck reappeared and downed half a bottle of brandy, saying, "Thank you with all my heart — it's war."

On the July 3, at Königgrätz (today Hradec Králové in the Czech Republic), the Prussian Army inflicted a decisive defeat on Austria. In the ensuing peace, Austria accepted the end of the German Confederation. In its place was a new North German Confederation under Prussian control. And Prussia itself grew as it annexed the territory of states, such as Hanover, which had supported Austria. The remaining German states in the south, including Bavaria, were obliged to sign treaties with Prussia. Their days as independent bodies were numbered.

In 1870, recognizing that France alone stood in the way of Prussia's consolidation of its dominance over the south, Bismarck again manufactured a quarrel, out of the unpromising material of who should succeed to the Spanish throne. The French objected to a candidate who was a distant relative of Wilhelm of Prussia. Wilhelm accepted the French objections and, in a conversation with the French ambassador at the resort of Bad Ems, agreed that the name should be withdrawn. The ambassador then unwisely pushed for an assurance that the king would never again support such a candidacy. Wilhelm, courteous as always, declined and then sent a telegram to Bismarck with a neutral account of what had happened. "What a stroke of luck," Bismarck later recalled. He edited the telegram to make it sound as though his master had sent the French ambassador packing, and then leaked it to the press. Feelings against Prussia were already running high in France; the Ems Telegram, as it came to be known, virtually ensured there would be a war.

As with Austria, Bismarck had ensured that the

international scene was favourable to Prussia. None of the other powers was likely to intervene on the side of France. And this time Prussia had an even stronger army with better infantry weapons than the French and a much more coherent command structure. On September 2, after a series of defeats, French forces surrendered near the small town of Sedan, close to the Belgian border. Representatives of the South German states who were watching the battle from a hilltop knew that they were seeing the end of their independence as well. On January 18, 1871, the new German Reich was proclaimed in Louis xiv's great Hall of Mirrors at Versailles. Wilhelm was now the emperor of Germany, and beside him stood Bismarck. The Second Reich was above all Bismarck's creation. Inside Germany he kept power in the crown's hands, and therefore his own, and successfully played off the political parties against each other. Abroad he kept France isolated and the other powers friendly to Germany or at least neutral, and he presided for the next two decades over his country's development into the dominant military and economic power in Europe. Thanks to Bismarck, Europe ever since 1871 has had, in one form or another, a German Question.

THE WORLD HAS NOT had a Canadian Question; indeed it does not pay much attention to this country most of the time. In Canadian history, though, William Lyon Mackenzie King is as important as Bismarck is for Germany. Where the latter built a country, the former preserved it — through part of the turbulent 1920s, the aftermath of the Great Depression, the Second World War, and on into the first years of peace. He managed to hold the centre against challenges from the right and the left and crucially kept the deep mutual suspicions and divisions between English- and French-speakers, and among the provinces, from breaking the country apart. And in the course of his twenty-two years in office — he remains Canada's longest-serving prime minister by far — he laid the foundations of its comprehensive social benefits system. He was a consummate politician who built his Liberal Party into a formidable political force. In the days before opinion polls, he had a knack for sensing the mood of the country and how far it would go in a particular direction. He was an idealist who wanted to build a fairer society, but he was also pragmatist who avoided fights he could not win. He had an impressive capacity for hard work and for paying attention to detail. His papers are filled with letters to people across the country, some of them important, others not. He was meticulous about sending congratulations, birthday greetings, or condolences. He was a private man, but he worked well with a great range of colleagues. To his credit, he frequently brought his political opponents into his government or at least tried to win them over.

Yet King does not fascinate or enthral us as other political leaders do. If anything — and this is particularly true if you are Canadian — he rather appals us. We remember him as the great equivocator and obfuscator. Issues did not so much get settled as buried in verbiage and imprecision. "Parliament will decide" was a favourite King formula, but he usually managed to avoid debate or discussion on contentious issues. In the Second World War the conscription issue — where much of English Canada called for mandatory military service while French Canada generally opposed it — threatened to drive the two peoples apart, perhaps irreversibly. In 1942, at the height of the political uproar, King produced his famous (or infamous) formula: "not necessarily conscription, but conscription if necessary."

"He blunted us," said F. R. Scott, intellectual, constitutional lawyer, radical, and poet, in a 1954 poem which still sums up the feelings of many Canadians then and now about King:

> We had no shape
> Because he never took sides,
> And no sides
> Because he never allowed them to take shape.
>
> He skilfully avoided what was wrong
> Without saying what was right,
> And never let his on the one hand
> Know what his on the other hand was doing.

The poem ends with what have become its most famous lines:

> Let us raise up a temple
> To the cult of mediocrity,
> Do nothing by halves
> Which can be done by quarters.

Perhaps we worry that King represents too well what we were then — and secretly fear we may still be: puritanical and sexually repressed, cautious and even timid, concerned about what others say but quick to judge, hard-working and inclined to be parsimonious, proud to be Canadian but pleased when important countries and people in the outside world take notice, and above all, disliking open confrontation. Is he really us — that plump, fussy celibate with his penchant for spiritualism and for prophecies and advice? Do we have superstitions — such as his belief that important decisions were better made when the hands of the clock made a straight line? Would we pray and sing hymns beside dying pet dogs, then talk to them — or our mothers — through mediums or Ouija boards? Do we make a mental record at the end of the day of where we have succeeded and failed? Do we carefully record every slight and every word of praise?

King did. We know this because he kept a daily diary from the early 1890s until he died in 1950, an historical record unmatched by any other modern political leader. He left orders that his diaries were to be burned after his death, but his executors hesitated and then spared them. So we now know much to his disadvantage. The image that remains is that captured by another Canadian poet, Dennis Lee, in a book of rhymes for children:

> William Lyon Mackenzie King
> Sat in the middle & played with string
> And he loved his mother like *any*thing —
> William Lyon Mackenzie King.

King liked to think of himself as a bold radical, a fitting descendant of one of the few rebels in Canadian history. In the 1830s his namesake, William Lyon Mackenzie, had tried, and failed, to overthrow by force the government of Upper Canada, which was controlled by a cosy interlocking group of privileged families known as the Family Compact. The rebellion was hopeless from the start, and Mackenzie fled to the United States, where he and his family lived from hand to mouth. In time the Canadian authorities granted the rebels amnesty, and Mackenzie returned to Canada and became a member of the elected assembly. His daughter, King's mother, married a lawyer, the son of a professional soldier whose regiment had helped to put down the rebellion, and became a member of the establishment in a small Ontario town. She continued to regard her father as a hero and impressed that strongly on her favourite son. King always liked to see himself as carrying on his grandfather's work, speaking for the underdog, for example, or promoting honest, efficient, and fair government.

He was a lot more talented than the hapless rebel, and a lot more cautious. The grandson was not going to waste his energies and opportunities in doomed crusades. If he took a stand, he preferred to be certain that he would win. In 1922, when the British prime minister, David Lloyd George, tried to drag the British Empire into a war with Turkey, King made it clear that Canada would make up its own mind about when it went to war. In this he was in tune with much of Canadian public opinion, which recognized and took pride in Canada's growing independence as a result of its participation in the First World War and the subsequent peace conference. He also had a remarkable ability to sum up a situation and gauge how far he could go in one direction or another without running into firm opposition. Just before he died he said of himself, "An issue exists for me by intuition or not at all. I either see it at once or it means nothing to me...I may spend much time planning how to defend it but I know from the start what I want to do and how to do it."

Unlike his grandfather, who was largely self-educated, King went to some of the best universities in the world. From the University of Toronto, where he was an undergraduate, he went on to the new University of Chicago and studied under the great and iconoclastic economist Thorstein Veblen. In Toronto he had already shown an interest in social ills (including, as his critics love to point out, in prostitution), and while in Chicago he became involved in the pioneering Settlement House movement, which was trying to ameliorate some of the worst ills of unchecked capitalism. After Chicago he moved to Harvard to start a doctorate and then, before he finished it, moved to the London School of Economics. (Harvard finally gave him a doctorate in 1909 on the basis of a report he did for the Canadian government, and he remains the only Canadian prime minister to hold that degree.) In 1900 he returned to Canada to take up a post as a civil servant and rose almost at once to become deputy minister of Labour.

Over the next eight years he made a reputation as a highly effective and skilled conciliator in disputes. And there were many opportunities for him to practise his skills in those years, as labour and business clashed repeatedly. When riots protesting Asian immigration broke out on the west coast of Canada, the young King was the man to send. And when the Canadian government decided it needed to warn the imperial government in London that immigration from other parts of the empire, in particular India, was causing racial tensions in Canada, King was again the obvious choice. As the Canadian government grew concerned about the export of opium from Asia, King was asked to go to the meetings of the International Opium Commission in Shanghai. On his way he stopped in India and Japan to deal with the immigration issue. Not surprisingly, Sir Wilfrid Laurier, the Liberal prime minister, decided that King was just the right sort to run for Parliament.

In 1908 King was duly elected, and the following year he joined the cabinet as Canada's first minister of Labour, where he was going to be responsible for getting key measures on industrial disputes and the investigation of combines (as cartels used to be called) through Parliament. His career faltered briefly when the Liberals were turned out of office in 1911, but by 1914 he had a very well-paid job in the United States as adviser on industrial relations to the Rockefeller family. In the following years he was offered other American plums: a professorship at Harvard and a position as director of Andrew Carnegie's corporation, with responsibility for overseeing its benefactions. All offered tempting prospects and the chance to mix with the rich and the powerful.

Canada and public service proved the stronger call. As he wrote in his diary in 1919, "I should rather serve my own country than any other land, tho' service for humanity would command me anywhere... To live & die honoured and respected there is closer to my heart than any other ambition... My desire, my inclination is all for politics." His mother's teachings that he should live a moral life and strive to do his best for society, his strong Presbyterian faith, and a large ego reinforced his belief that he had a mission, that he could serve God by doing good works, in his case as a politician. Throughout his life he prayed regularly for the strength to try harder and do better.

In 1919 he returned to Canada for good as leader of the Liberal Party. He managed to win over the older generation by vague references to things they held dear, such as free trade and a balanced budget, and since he was known to have opposed conscription in 1917, he had the votes of most of the delegates from Quebec. He never forgot the importance of those votes or the need to keep the French as partners within Confederation. He had the good sense to choose one of the most competent and effective Quebec politicians of his time, Ernest Lapointe, as his lieutenant and trust in his judgement. As he grew in maturity, King had the self-confidence to appoint other strong figures to his cabinet, something many political leaders are often afraid to do.

In 1921 King became prime minister for the first time, at the relatively young age of forty-seven. Most did not expect him to last; he was inexperienced and heading a minority government. In fact he learned quickly on the job and proved himself adroit at outmanoeuvring his opposition. Taking advantage of a constitutional crisis which he had helped to manufacture, King returned to power in 1926 with a Liberal majority government. With the luck that so often shapes the career of successful politicians, he was voted out in 1930, leaving his Conservative successors to bear the blame for failing to deal with the Great Depression. When he returned as prime minister in 1935 (with the slogan "King or Chaos"), things were starting to improve.

Whether or not he had ever seriously entertained hopes of getting married, King had by now given up and settled into life as a bachelor. He treated his loyal servants and subordinates with a mixture of sentimentality and ruthlessness. He might remember their birthdays but also expected them to work long hours. He complained often of being lonely but also grumbled that much social life was a waste of time. Or so he said. His diaries give a rather different picture, of a man who liked a convivial evening with friends. He was also a notably good dancer. He gave frequent dinner parties at Laurier House, where he could entertain on his own terms. He also relaxed by playing with his beloved dogs, reading devotional literature, or summoning up the spirits of the departed with his few trusted intimates. On his sixtieth birthday he was pleased to record that the spirits of, among many others, William Gladstone, Laurier, and Lord Rosebery had dropped by.

Although he claimed, wrongly, that politics had left him poor, he not only saved much of his salary but received gifts from admirers. He was nevertheless, said a civil servant, "a shameless miser and would resort to almost any device to avoid any charge, no matter how minor, to his expense account or, worst of all, to him personally." Still he spent much time and money on embellishing his country house at Kingsmere. Like an eighteenth-century landowner, he had a taste for picturesque ruins that might carry moral tales. In Ottawa he lived in Laurier's old house. Both houses were crammed with Victorian bric-a-brac, with ugly paintings, sculptures, and bas-reliefs collected in Europe. The drawing room at Laurier House, said a journalist, was "crammed with gilt and crimson plush, gigantic vases and glass-covered tables to hold worthless ornaments, in all an assemblage of expensive junk sufficient to stock a high-class secondhand store."

Many people found him unattractive, even repulsive. There was something unwholesome about him, complained a leading Liberal, and it was not just that his breath smelled rank. His manner was over-ingratiating. A British high commissioner in Ottawa in the 1930s reported, "My wife says after a conversation with him she feels as if the cat had licked her all over and she ought to go and have a bath." Yet even those who disliked him admitted there was something impressive about him, certainly as a public figure. His speeches were not great oratory, but they were well-crafted and solid. He knew Canada and Canadians thoroughly, and he had a sound understanding of the country's place in the world as it balanced between the two great powers of the British Empire and the United States. He was respected in both London and Washington, and his wide range of acquaintances included many leading political figures in both capitals. When he went to Washington during the Second World War, he stayed at the White House and had long private conversations with Roosevelt. (When the president died shortly before the war ended, King was comforted by contacting his spirit in séances.)

Because of his many foibles, we tend to overlook just how clever, perceptive, and skilled a political leader King was. He could have had a distinguished, even dazzling career, in the United States or Britain, yet he chose to live and work in Canada. Over the course of his career he took part in history as an observer and a player. He was there in London before the First World War, talking to the British foreign secretary, Sir Edward Grey, and other leading British politicians about the empire; in Berlin in the 1930s, discussing the state of Europe with the Nazis, including Hitler himself; and in Washington during the Second World War, talking about strategy. He led Canada for much of the time as it moved from being a junior part of the British Empire into a self-governing nation, playing a significant role in international affairs.

While he had watched the rise of the dictators in the 1930s with dismay, he had been willing to go a long way to compromise with them. With national unity always in the forefront of his mind, he did his best to avoid taking sides in foreign crises, such as Italy's invasion of Ethiopia or the Spanish Civil War, on which he knew Canadian opinion was strongly divided. When he met senior Nazis and then Hitler in 1937, his wishful thinking led him to say some silly things in his diary: "My sizing up of the man as I sat and talked with him was that he really is one who truly loves his fellow-men, and his country, and would make any sacrifice for their good." And with his five university degrees, King could not help but be patronizing: "To understand Hitler, one has to remember his limited opportunities in his early life, his imprisonment etc. It is truly marvellous what he has attained unto himself through his self education." King also, however, told the Nazis that Canada would come to Britain's aid if Germany attacked it.

He led the country in the war that came, and brought it out at the end still united. Others might not have been able to do that. Because the unity debate has continued ever since, we sometimes fail to recognize how close the country came to a dangerous, perhaps fatal, split during the Second World War. King did not solve those divisions, but he prevented them from destroying Confederation. That in itself was a major achievement. The crucial issue was conscription; its imposition in 1917 had alienated much of Quebec opinion and set Canadians against one another. Canada could not afford a second such crisis. In 1940 a national plebiscite on conscription gave a clear majority in favour but also revealed a deep division in the country. English-speaking Canada voted Yes, while French-speaking Quebec had a majority for No. Although King introduced a bill into Parliament, he made it clear that the legislation would not be enforced for the time being. His "not necessarily but if necessary" formula for conscription bought valuable time. By late 1944 it had become clear that the armed forces needed manpower and that volunteers were not coming forward in sufficient numbers. Although he had ruthlessly sacked the leading advocate of conscription in the cabinet — his defence minister, James Ralston — King reluctantly concluded that he must enforce at least a limited conscription. He was more fortunate than he deserved, for Ralston refused to make political capital out of the reversal and continued loyally to support the government and the war effort.

In the prolonged cabinet crisis that November, King used all the skills he had sharpened over many years in politics. (In his diary he compared himself to Christ in his last sufferings.) He appealed to his colleagues' patriotism and warned that the country might break up — or, perhaps as dreadful, the Liberal Party might be destroyed. He wept, threatened resignation, even hinted that if the government refused to conscript men, the military might carry out a coup. He managed to carry most of his colleagues with him, including, crucially, the key figure from Quebec, Louis St. Laurent. Only one minister resigned. "I felt," wrote King in his diary, "that the day of Crucifixion had passed and that I was reaching the morning of Resurrection." Although many of the Quebec MPs voted for an anti-conscription motion, the Liberal Party itself survived, and in Quebec opposition to conscription was muted.

In 1940 King had told the Conservative house leader that he would not use his majority to impose conscription. He believed, he said, in leading by finding out what people wanted, not telling them what to do. If he, King, had any authority, it was because people trusted that he would respect their wishes and keep his promises. In the long run, he maintained, the public would come to understand what was necessary for the common good. "That they recognized the truth when it was put before them and that a leader can guide as long as he kept to the right lines." King trusted the public less than he maintained, and not just in the matter of conscription. As long as he could get away with it, he preferred to let sleeping dogs lie and only to move, cautiously and circuitously, to deal with problems when he had to. H. S. Ferns, a political scientist who once worked for King, later wrote, "In terms of understanding the political problems of Canada and in knowing what the Canadian people as a whole were willing to accept from a government, Mackenzie King was miles ahead of any of the active participants in politics."

Canada is now seen as a success story. We have, perhaps permanently, averted Quebec separatism and are successfully multicultural. Unlike our turbulent neighbour to the south, this country has built a strong social safety net. Our political divisions have not polarized us, and we can discuss politics without rancour. Canadians like gun control, and most have long since accepted abortion and same-sex marriage. We should remember, though, that what seems normal and permanent now did not always seem so in the past. King, maddening though he could be, stood for conciliation and building consensus. "The extreme man," he believed, "is always more or less dangerous, but nowhere more so than in politics." And, he went on, "In a country like ours it is particularly true that the art of government is largely one of seeking to reconcile rather than exaggerate differences — to come as near as possible to the happy mean." When he retired in 1948, he told his diary, "I feel a sense of the fullness of life, tremendous satisfaction and pride in the fact that all has gone so well."

IN AMERICAN HISTORY, Franklin Delano Roosevelt (FDR, as he is often known, to distinguish him from President Theodore Roosevelt) is as important as King is for Canada. The United States was left deeply damaged and divided by the Depression and, as the international situation worsened, had to grapple with the question of whether to stay aloof or get involved. FDR restored the confidence of Americans in themselves and gave them hope for the future, and he managed to contain their many divisions and hold American society together. He also gradually prepared Americans for the time when they might have to get involved in the wider world. FDR was as adept as King at the arts of persuasion, at reading public opinion and nudging it in a direction he wanted to go. Like King, he was not always easy to read and drove both his friends and his enemies to distraction with his inconsistencies and vagueness.

The two men had other things in common: both shared an intense interest in politics, both were liberals and had strong social consciences, and both hoped to keep their countries out of war. As well, both had been brought up under the watchful eyes of possessive and devoted mothers. (Mrs. King never went as far as Mrs. Roosevelt, who once had a ladder hauled to her son's boarding school window when he was sick so that she could climb up and chat to him.) There were considerable differences as well. In FDR's background was all the privilege that serious money could buy, from country estates to useful contacts. His father's family came from the original Dutch settlers, and an ancestor, as FDR was fond of telling the British, was a captain in the Revolutionary army. President Theodore Roosevelt was a distant cousin. FDR's mother's ancestry went even further back, to the Pilgrim Fathers. The Delanos also claimed to be descended from William the Conqueror. FDR's mother always said firmly that he was a Delano, inheriting his brains and energy from her family.

Perhaps he inherited his great charm as well. Unlike King — or Bismarck, for that matter — FDR was immediately appealing both to individuals and to the wider public. That handsome and open face; with the wide grin, so often captured in photographs; the cigarette holder at a jaunty angle — all gave the impression of someone who liked people and thought the world was a pretty good place. Women always found him attractive, and he them. His marriage, to his intelligent, earnest, and plain cousin Eleanor, never recovered from her discovery of his affair with a woman who had once been her social secretary. He was also a very effective communicator. As president he made great use of the new medium of radio in a series of Fireside Chats. His voice, with its slightly patrician accent, was calm and reassuring and seductive. At a time when the American people needed reassurance, he gave them optimism. And it was not merely a pose; FDR was someone who, even at the darkest of times for himself or his nation, remained hopeful that things would get better.

In his early years he had lived the pleasant and undemanding life of a gilded youth, sailing on what was to be a succession of increasingly larger boats, shooting, building his bird and stamp collections, and joining the right clubs. He went to the best schools — Groton and then Harvard, where he did respectably but not too well. He went to church as much for the form of it than anything else. Not for him the tortured prayers of King. His Christianity was straightforward and uncomplicated. Eleanor once said, "I think he actually felt he could ask God for guidance and receive it." Although his branch of the family were Democrats, FDR had a great admiration for the Republican Theodore and shared his enthusiasm both for social reform in the United States and for building a big navy to assert its influence abroad. Much to his friends' amusement, he tried to imitate his older cousin's way of speaking. He also resolved to follow him into politics, and so in 1911 he ran successfully for the New York Senate. In 1913 the new Democratic president, Woodrow Wilson, made his promising young supporter assistant secretary of the navy, a post he held through the war. Although he performed competently, even at times with ruthless efficiency, many continued to see him as a charming and spoiled lightweight.

In 1921 came the polio attack that left him a paraplegic — and may have been the making of him. So Eleanor, among others, always thought. He tackled his disability with great fortitude and determination, and over time built up his upper body strength so that he could manoeuvre himself about and give the impression that, for a short spell at least, he was walking. He would not accept pity or even sympathy; when he fell, he would simply make a joke. His affable banter became a way of deflecting attention from his condition. He would not allow himself to be photographed in his wheelchair. After 1921 he is always seen sitting or standing where he can hang on to a support or another person. He had already begun to build a devoted and talented team around him and these now became his eyes and ears, taking trips for him and reporting back.

Yet for all his affability and his love of social life, he remained a very private person who only revealed parts of himself even to his intimates. Some, including his last vice president, Harry Truman, found him cold, even inhuman. At the annual dinner of the Washington Press Club in December 1939, an eight-foot-high model of a sphinx wearing glasses with a cigarette holder clenched in its teeth beamed down genially at the room. Roosevelt loved the joke and later acquired the model for his presidential library. He was a puzzle to his contemporaries and remains so for historians. He rarely put his thoughts down on paper, and even with those people he trusted he gave them only a partial glimpse at what he was thinking or planning. At the opening for his library, he was asked why he seemed particularly cheerful.

"I'm thinking," he replied, "of all the historians who will come here thinking they'll find the answers to their questions."

His administration was frequently chaotic, with departments and agencies assigned overlapping responsibilities or people given different and sometimes conflicting tasks. In the State Department, for example, he appointed as secretary and under-secretary two men who loathed each other and who frequently differed. He also used his trusted associate Harry Hopkins to deal with important foreign policy matters. It was a way of ensuring that power remained centred in his office. Usually only FDR himself had the complete picture, and sometimes not even he did. "I am a juggler," he once said. "I never let my right hand know what my left hand does." Or, as the great wartime general Douglas MacArthur put it, FDR "would never tell a truth when a lie would serve him just as well." In his four terms as president, FDR often acted wilfully, inconsistently, even foolishly. In his first months in office he effectively scuppered the London Conference, which was close to coming to an agreement on how to stabilize exchange rates as a measure to fight the Depression. (He later admitted he may have made a mistake.)

Often he seemed to rely solely on his intuition. "He would have flashes," said Frances Perkins, his secretary of labour, "of almost clairvoyant knowledge and understanding of a terrific variety of matters that didn't seem to have any particular relationship to each other." Putting such insights into practice was another matter. Frequently he would try out one policy, then reverse himself, often before he had given the first one time to prove itself. Economic historians still argue about whether he really made a difference or whether the United States gradually righted itself. What is indisputable is that he gave Americans confidence that better times were indeed coming. Perhaps his greatest strength was that he remained calm in moments of great crisis — the Depression itself and the storm that was about to break over the world.

Like King, FDR was not afraid of surrounding himself with strong characters. He also had a talent, like that of Lincoln, for winning over his enemies and building workable coalitions. As the Southern populist Huey Long once said, "You go in there and see FDR wanting to tear him apart. You come out whistling Dixie." In the aftermath of the fall of France in 1940, he brought in two leading Republicans, Henry Stimson and Frank Knox, to head the War Department and the navy.

Other of his appointments were, to put it kindly, odd — such as making the strongly anti-British Joseph Kennedy the ambassador in London or, just as the Nazis had taken over in Germany, appointing to Berlin William Dodd, a leading historian of the American South with no previous diplomatic experience. When the United States established relations with the Soviet Union in 1933, he chose the vainglorious William Bullitt, who had been an advocate for the new Soviet regime ever since he had spent a week there in 1919, eating caviar and meeting with the Bolshevik leaders. Bullitt believed that he could, on his own, bring about a friendship between the two countries. Among other diplomatic overtures, he tried to show Soviet party officials how to play baseball and introduced polo to members of the Red Army's cavalry. Neither sport took. A wild pitch knocked out a Russian, and the cavalry tended to gallop off the field with the ball. Bullitt's contacts with Maxim Litvinov, who was responsible for Soviet foreign policy, were equally unproductive because, so Bullitt concluded, Litvinov was Jewish. By 1936 Bullitt had completely lost his previous enthusiasm and become strongly anti-Communist.

Preoccupied as he inevitably was with domestic issues, FDR understandably paid less attention to foreign affairs at first. His general approach echoed that of his former boss, Woodrow Wilson: that the United States and its democratic values represented a better example for the world than either Soviet Communism or the old imperial powers of Europe. His attitude towards Britain was and remained ambivalent: he mistrusted its ruling classes and profoundly disapproved of its empire. Like Wilson, he believed that the spread of democracy and free trade would bind the nations closer together and make the world a better and safer place. He had been a supporter of the League of Nations in the 1920s, but by the start of the 1930s he was critical of the shape it had taken. In a speech designed to appeal to those many Americans who opposed the League, he said it now was merely the tool of the European powers, which were up to their usual cynical games. (When it came to shaping the post-1945 world, FDR ensured that the new United Nations started off on the right foot by including both the United States and Russia.)

Like Wilson, Roosevelt was elected on a platform that focussed on pressing domestic issues, and like his predecessor, he would have preferred to concentrate on problems at home and, where necessary, deal with the United States' immediate neighbours, but the great and ominous changes happening in the wider world in the 1930s obliged him to take an ever-increasing interest in developments abroad. For much of the decade, his foreign policy evolved by fits and starts. It is easy to criticize many of his actions, such as his decision in 1933, apparently on a whim, to oppose an attempt to stabilize international exchange rates. Without the United States, the agreement fell apart and the world's economic crisis worsened dramatically. His many critics then and now believe that he could have done much more during the 1930s to rally the democracies to oppose the rise of the dictatorships. Yet if he had struck out too forcefully, he might well have stimulated isolationist sentiments in the American population and, crucially, lost the votes of isolationists in Congress, which he needed to get approval for his measures to get the American economy going again. Like the sailor he was, he knew he was sailing in treacherous waters and that shipwreck was likely at any time. That he somehow succeeded and brought a united country, its confidence in itself restored, through the Great Depression and into the Second World War, is testament to his skill and determination.

In his first term, from 1933–36, he was preoccupied with domestic issues and his New Deal and seemed willing to shape his foreign policy to accommodate American public opinion, which was strongly opposed to what George Washington had called "entanglements." Although the term "isolationism" only entered the American political vocabulary during the First World War, it represented a strong, long-standing strain in American thinking. Based on an assumption of American moral superiority — and a grateful recognition that geography had given the United States great resources and strong defences against the wider world in the shape of two oceans — isolationists took the view that what went on elsewhere (except perhaps among America's immediate neighbours to the south and north) was of no concern. If the rest of the world wanted to tear itself apart in national rivalries, it was not up to the United States to act as policeman. The isolationists of the 1930s were also reacting against the recent American involvement in the First World War: American lives and American resources had been spent, and to what end? From the isolationist point of view, the Europeans had lured the United States into their bloody conflicts, and Wilson for his part had manipulated and deceived the American public into the declaration of war. Fuelled by the work of historians and promoted by prominent Americans, such as Henry Ford and the great aviator Charles Lindbergh, isolationism won widespread support among the public and in Congress. The grimmer the international scene became in the 1930s — with the Japanese invasion of Manchuria and then of China itself in 1937, Mussolini's seizure of Ethiopia, and Hitler's aggressive foreign policy in Europe — the more strongly Americans longed to stay neutral. An early public opinion poll in 1937 showed that 95 percent of Americans thought their country should stay out of any future war.

To ensure that no president could again use his office to get the United States into a war, Congress passed a series of Neutrality Acts from 1935 onwards. Most importantly, these imposed an embargo on financial support or the shipments of arms to belligerent nations and tried to ensure that the president could not wriggle around the provisions by refusing to recognize that a state of war existed. Congress also reflected public resistance to increased defence spending. When FDR asked for a modest $1.1 billion defence budget in 1935 (out of a total of $81.1 billion), there were widespread public protests. "We are rapidly sinking to the level of Hitler and Mussolini in our bowing down before the God of War," said the influential weekly the *Nation*.

In his first term, FDR nevertheless managed to make two important steps towards greater American involvement in the world. By recognizing the Soviet Union, he made possible a relationship, admittedly a turbulent one, with a future ally. And, closer to home, he inaugurated a new era in the United States' relations with its Latin American neighbours.

The Good Neighbor Policy renounced the use of American force in the region and urged co-operation for the benefit of all nations in the Western hemisphere. At the 1936 Buenos Aires Conference, Roosevelt made a speech which was as much directed at his home audience as at the assembled delegates. He warned outside powers that they would meet strong resistance if they tried to interfere in the Western hemisphere, but he also made the point that war in other parts of the world must necessarily threaten the New World "in a hundred ways."

By the start of FDR's second term in 1936, events in the wider world were increasingly threatening, but he had always to be conscious of American public opinion and the unfinished business of dealing with the Great Depression. He also undermined his own position in 1937 by getting into a conflict with Congress over what was probably a doomed attempt to pack the Supreme Court with justices who would be sympathetic to his New Deal. Nevertheless his critics both at home and abroad said, then and later, that he should have taken the lead in the democracies' opposition and resistance to the dictatorships. When Japan invaded China in 1937, FDR's response was to invite the British prime minister, Neville Chamberlain, to visit the United States for discussions. Chamberlain declined, saying to his colleagues, "It is always best and safest to count on *nothing* from the Americans except words."

FDR's great fear was taking actions or stances that might break apart the coalition that kept him in office. He had to take account of the fact that many of his compatriots opposed anything that looked like collusion with Britain and France.

If he had admitted more of the desperate Jewish refugees who were trying to leave Germany and Austria, he might have lost the Southern Democrats and much of the public, which did not understand why the United States should be letting in more immigrants when there were still so many Americans without jobs. These were not easy choices, and perhaps not always defensible ones. Like King in Canada, FDR made national unity a guiding principle. Yet, as even sympathetic biographers argue, he could have used more of his political capital to articulate more forcefully the menaces which were growing in strength, and attempted to gather public support in his battle with Congress over more concrete aid to the countries menaced by Germany. And American opinion was shifting markedly by 1939 as the situation in Europe and Asia deteriorated. A poll showed that 37 percent of Americans now favoured help to Britain, France, and Poland, while 30 percent were undecided. At most FDR was prepared to use his office, very carefully, to educate the American people in the perils which faced the world and which could well face them. Where he could, without risking too much, he would move the United States towards greater preparedness.

In speeches, Fireside Chats, and press conferences, he masterfully floated ideas. He underlined to the American people that geography no longer kept them as safe as it once had; advances in air power meant that the oceans were no longer a secure barrier, and long-range bombers would sooner or later be able to reach the continent from Europe or the Far East. If he roused too vehement a response, he artfully backtracked. In a famous 1937 speech in Chicago, home to some of the most diehard isolationists, he warned against the aggressive nations who were threatening the peace of the world and committing atrocities against innocent civilians. Although he did not mention Japan, which was taking large swaths of China; Germany, which was rearming rapidly; or Italy, which had invaded Ethiopia, his audience can have been in no doubt as to whom he meant. Society, he said, quarantined sick patients to prevent epidemics spreading; the world should do the same with dangerous nations. Yet when reporters asked him what action he intended to take, he airily said that was merely expressing an "attitude" and that he had certainly not meant the use of sanctions, "a terrible word to use."

When Japan invaded China in 1937, he managed to avoid invoking the Neutrality Acts and allowed the United States to sell arms to both sides. In reality his administration tilted towards China. In December 1938, the United States gave a $25 million loan to the embattled Chinese Nationalists, the first of many. At the same time, FDR's own views, like those of many Americans, had hardened on Hitler and his fascist allies in Italy. In November 1938, Kristallnacht, when the Nazi-controlled state encouraged the destruction of Jewish businesses and the beatings of Jews, convinced FDR that Hitler was a "nut," motivated by paranoia. He continued to search for ways to bypass and then amend the Neutrality Acts. Already, in 1937, he had signed an executive order which would substitute a policy of "cash and carry" for an arms embargo on both sides. And the president would have considerable latitude as to where the United States would sell its products. FDR intended the policy to help Britain and France more than Germany or Japan. In 1938 his administration successfully got a new Naval Expansion Act through Congress, and the army and navy updated their plans for a war with Japan should it come.

In his public pronouncements he made clear that he now saw what was happening in Europe and in Asia as a clash of values between liberal democracy and totalitarianism, that the American way of life was itself under threat as a result of developments elsewhere. As he said in his 1939 State of the Union address: "Storms from abroad directly challenge three institutions indispensable to Americans. The first is religion. It is the source of the other two — democracy and international good faith." In April 1939, after Mussolini had wantonly invaded Albania and Hitler had broken the promises he had made only six months earlier to respect the integrity of what was left of Czechoslovakia, Roosevelt described their actions as being like those of the Huns and the Vandals. In a move which was met with crude derision in Berlin and Rome, he publicly asked Germany and Italy to promise that they would not attack thirty-one countries in Europe and the Middle East. FDR had few illusions that either Germany or Italy would accept his proposal, but as he said to King, "If we are turned down the issue becomes clearer and public opinion in your country and mine will be helped."

On September 1 the Second World War started in Europe with Germany's unprovoked attack on Poland. Britain and France, which had guaranteed Poland, in turn declared war on Germany. Two days later FDR took to the radio for a Fireside Chat. "I have said not once," he told the American people, "but many times, that I have seen war and that I hate war. I say that again and again. I hope the United States will keep out of this war. I believe that it will. And I give you assurance and reassurance that every effort of your Government will be directed toward that end." There was little in what he said to encourage the Allies except for one passage near the end: "This nation will remain a neutral nation, but I cannot ask that every American remain neutral in thought as well. Even a neutral has a right to take account of facts. Even a neutral cannot be asked to close his mind or his conscience."

In fact he moved quickly a few weeks later to introduce

what he cunningly called the Peace Bill; in it he proposed the repeal of the arms embargo on belligerents and the extension of "cash and carry." For the first time in his administration, he and his supporters went all out on a foreign policy issue. It helped that public opinion was shifting still faster to the Allies; one poll showed 84 percent of Americans were in favour of an Allied victory. FDR worked from behind the scenes to persuade representatives and senators and, where necessary, buy them off with offices for their friends or economic inducements which would benefit their districts. His office encouraged the public to make its feelings known. The veteran muckraking journalist William Allen White ran a highly successful public campaign which added to the pressure. The bill passed with a comfortable majority. But there was to be little comfort in the months to come.

In May 1940, as the German invasion swept through France with appalling rapidity, FDR broadcast another Fireside Chat. He called attention to the horrors being suffered by civilians in France and Belgium and asked the American people to donate to the Red Cross. He also laid out a challenge to the dwindling number of committed isolationists: "To those who have closed their eyes for any of these many reasons, to those who would not admit the possibility of the approaching storm — to all of them the past two weeks have meant the shattering of many illusions. They have lost the illusion that we are remote and isolated and, therefore, secure against the dangers from which no other land is free."

He went to Congress for a further $10.5 billion to arm the United States, and he agreed to run for an unprecedented third term. He also moved decisively to arrange for more war equipment to be sold to Britain. It was not at all clear, however, in those first anxious months, that Britain, even under the vigorous new leadership of Winston Churchill, would continue to fight on — or be able to. By August Churchill had made it clear to the British people and the world that there would be no surrender. Moreover the German air force appeared to be losing in its attempt to destroy Britain's air defences. FDR pushed the limits of his powers. He allowed secret military talks between the Americans and the British, and, using executive authority, he signed off on a deal which gave the British American destroyers in return for long leases on British bases in the Americas. (He persuaded the navy to declare perfectly good destroyers obsolete so that there would not be a political outcry.) He also took steps to protect the Western hemisphere, meeting King near the border with Canada to sign a defence agreement. A further agreement, signed at Roosevelt's country estate of Hyde Park the following year, served to integrate Canadian and American war production.

In the election campaign, FDR undercut the Republicans by promising the voters that "Your boys are not going to be sent into any foreign wars." He deliberately left out the phrase "except in case of foreign attack," which was in the Democrat platform. When a speechwriter asked him what he intended, FDR replied, "Of course we fight if we're attacked." The election safely behind him, he moved to extend American aid to Britain. The British were running short of funds, and "cash and carry" was no longer an option. In a press conference in December 1940, he asserted that helping Britain defend itself was the best way of defending the United States. What was the point, he asked, of keeping war materials in storage at home when they could be put to good use across the Atlantic? And now was not the time to worry about how the British would pay; eventually they would pay up or make good what

they had been lent. He suspected that pretty much everyone at the press conference agreed with him: now was not
the time to worry about money. Let's, he said, "get rid of the
silly, foolish old dollar sign." And, as he did with such skill,
he used a homespun analogy: "Suppose my neighbor's home
catches fire, and I have a length of garden hose four or five
hundred feet away. If he can take my garden hose and con-
nect it up with his hydrant, I may help him to put out his fire.
Now, what do I do? I don't say to him before that operation,
'Neighbor, my garden hose cost me $15; you have to pay me
$15 for it.' What is the transaction that goes on? I don't want
$15 — I want my garden hose back after the fire is over."

In a Fireside Chat a couple of weeks later, he fleshed out
his ideas. He started by talking about security for Americans,
their children, and their grandchildren. He warned of the
danger that was creeping ever closer to them. Their very way
of life was threatened by the Nazis and their allies. If Britain
fell, the United States could not count on the Atlantic Ocean
to be a secure barrier to that threat. The new long-range
bombers had made sure of that: "The width of those oceans
is not what it was in the days of clipper ships." The Azores,
which might well fall to Germany, were closer to the con-
tinental United States than Hawaii was. The United States
must look to its own defences, but it must also do more for
Britain: "We must be the great arsenal of democracy."

The legislation he laid before Congress had another clever
title: "An Act to Promote the Defense of the United States."
The debate was a difficult and passionate one, but FDR prevailed and the bill passed by big majorities in March 1941. It
gave the president sweeping powers to give, lend, or sell war
material to any nation whose defence was vital to the United
States. That spring, FDR also gradually expanded the area

deemed necessary to defend the Western hemisphere, including the Azores, most of Greenland, and Iceland, moving the Western hemisphere's defensive perimeter well out into the Atlantic. In June, when Germany invaded the Soviet Union, the United States moved still closer in support of Britain. FDR gave the go-ahead to the U.S. Navy to start discussions with the British about Atlantic convoys for the crucial supplies to Britain. In August, off the coast of Newfoundland, FDR and Churchill met for the first time since 1918 and agreed, largely at FDR's insistence, on a common set of principles — the Atlantic Charter, as it came to be known. The following month, a German submarine fired on the *Greer*, an American destroyer, off Iceland. FDR used the incident in a Fireside Chat to announce that the United States' forces would not only defend themselves in the part of the Atlantic that the States deemed its defensive perimeter, but they would also protect all merchant ships there. Although he did not say so specifically, this was the start of shared responsibility for convoys with the British and the Canadians. Nor did he mention that the *Greer*, along with British aircraft, had been trailing the U-boat and had attacked first. As FDR cheerfully said of himself the following year, "I may be entirely inconsistent, and furthermore I am perfectly willing to mislead and tell untruths if it will help win the war."

On December 7, 1941, the time for such subterfuge ended with the surprise attack by Japan on the American Pacific base at Pearl Harbor, which brought the American people united into the war. A few days later, Hitler removed any lingering doubts about whether the Americans should fight in the European conflict by declaring war on the United States, a nation he despised as having a "mongrel" population. Thanks in large part to FDR, the United States was already prepared both psychologically and materially for the great struggle it now faced. Americans were clearer than they had been five years previously about what was at stake.

In the years to come, FDR was to rise to the challenge of providing strong and inspiring leadership for his country, and he was to do much to shape the postwar world. It is hard to imagine that his Republican opponents in the presidential elections of 1936 and 1940, Alf Landon and Wendell Willkie, could have done the same. And if you want to consider an even more worrying alternative, read the Philip Roth novel *The Plot Against America,* in which Charles Lindbergh, anti-Semite and pro-German, becomes president in 1940. FDR came to office at a dark time for the United States — how dark, we now sometimes forget. Even sober commentators talked of the possibility of widespread and violent civil unrest, even civil war. The Depression had thrown one in four Americans out of work, and there were voices, often powerful ones, to argue that capitalism and democracy no longer worked, that new forms of economic or political organization were needed. The world of the time provided all too many examples of societies collapsing and new authoritarian regimes emerging. Without FDR the United States might have gone down other paths. And without him the Second World War would have taken a different shape. Our world, the one shaped by the post-1945 institutions which FDR played such a crucial role in setting up, would be quite another one too.

BISMARCK WAS A PRUSSIAN Junker with many of the values and attitudes of his class and times. While King and FDR were both the products of liberal and democratic worlds, the former came from the middle classes in a part of the British

Empire, while the latter from the upper classes in one of the most powerful countries in the world. Yet, for all their dissimilarities, the three men were favoured by time and circumstance, each was prepared to seize the opportunities he was offered, and all three shared the key characteristics which made them such effective leaders: they had great goals they wanted to achieve, and they had the talent, skills, and determination to persist and bring their countries with them. That does not mean that they did not make mistakes. All did, but they were able to learn from those mistakes, and most importantly of all, they knew when to make compromises. They managed, for the most part, to avoid the trap that powerful leaders can so easily fall into — and that is the one of thinking that they were always right.

TWO

HUBRIS

WHEN I WAS GROWING up in Canada, there would always come a moment in a conversation about friends or neighbours when someone would say reprovingly, "But we mustn't gossip." And we have had the equivalent — perhaps for different reasons — in history, where it was felt somehow inappropriate or unnecessary to be interested in the individuals who stood out in their times for what they had said or done. But I want to gossip. And there is such an extraordinary range of subjects to gossip about. How can you make up someone like Catherine the Great or her Chinese equivalent, the Empress Wu? Or explorers such as David Livingstone or Alexander Mackenzie, who walked across continents? The people of the past, their stories and personalities, are what first drew me to history. Surely we all like stories.

Like many of us, I enjoy hearing the voices from the past, whether belonging to the players or the observers. I like the details of long-gone people: what they wore or ate, who they loved and hated. When I was a child, I liked the stories my parents and grandparents told of their pasts: of my Canadian grandfather walking three miles to school near

London, Ontario, or the Welsh one going to a boarding school in England without knowing a word of English; my mother playing with a hoop in a London park, or my father's adventures in the Canadian navy during the Second World War. I also liked the stories of people I would never know. Whether it's Samuel Pepys complaining about how dull his wife's friends are or Michel de Montaigne probing his own psychology, we are reminded that people who looked very different to us, who often had quite different values and ways of seeing the world, also had emotions we feel too, from boredom to curiosity to passion.

Possibly because history, like the other social sciences and humanities, has been influenced by economics, historians are sometimes uneasy with the role of personality and emotions in shaping events. In my view we have to take both into account. If someone other than Hitler had been in charge of Germany in the 1930s, would he or she have risked all in a war against Britain and France, and then the Soviet Union and the United States? If the Japanese militarists had not been obsessed with the prospect that the United States was getting too strong for them to defeat, would Japan have gone to war in 1941, while the odds were still favourable? Fear, pride, anger: such emotions shape attitudes and decisions as much and perhaps more than rational calculations.

And that leads to the What If questions. What if Hitler had been killed in the trenches in the First World War? What if Winston Churchill had been fatally injured when a car knocked him down on New York's Fifth Avenue in 1931? Or what if Stalin had died during his appendix operation in 1921? Can we really consider the history of the twentieth century without placing such figures somewhere in the story? It is striking how historians such as Ian Kershaw or Stephen

Kotkin, who started out describing and writing about Nazi or Soviet society, have moved on to writing biographies of the two men who stood at the apex of those societies. Political scientists have been reluctant to grapple with the role of the individual, but articles are now appearing in their journals with titles such as "Let Us Now Praise Great Men: Bringing the Statesman Back In."

As soon as we try to assess the impact of individuals or single events on history, we are, whether we realize it or not, thinking of an alternative outcome in the past. Let us imagine how things might have turned out differently on that sunny summer day in June 1914 in Sarajevo. The heir to the Austrian throne, Archduke Franz Ferdinand, had been foolish to visit the Bosnian town. Many Serbian nationalists, among them those living in Bosnia, were still furious that only six years before, Austria-Hungary had annexed Bosnia from the Ottoman Empire. The province, so they thought, belonged with Serbia. And June 28 was a particularly bad day for the Archduke to visit, since it was the Serbian national holiday, the day they commemorate their great defeat in the Battle of Kosovo. It did not help that the Austrian security was lax in spite of warnings about plots by shadowy terrorist organizations. That morning, determined young men, armed with pistols and bombs, had stationed themselves around the town to lie in wait for the Archduke. One had managed to hurl a bomb at the procession as it arrived but had missed. Police had managed to round up some of the would-be assassins, and others had lost their nerve. Only one — Gavrilo Princip — remained at large and ready to act. He had wandered along the main street beside the river, hoping to find a chance to carry out his mission and come to rest beside a well-known local café. His chances were slim, until suddenly the Archduke's open touring car appeared. Its chauffeur had made a mistake and turned up a small street right in front of Princip. As the chauffeur struggled to reverse, Princip stepped up and shot the imperial couple at point-blank range. The death of the Archduke became the excuse that the Austrian government needed to either bring Serbia under control or destroy it. That in turn precipitated Germany's decision to back Austria-Hungary, and Russia's to back Serbia. Without that assassination it is unlikely that Europe would have gone to war in 1914. It might never have had a general war. We will never know, but we can wonder.

Counterfactuals are useful tools of history because they help us to understand how consequences can flow from a single action or decision. Julius Caesar defied his own government when he decided to cross the Rubicon with his troops in 49 B.C. and head for Rome. The river marked the boundary between the province where he was governor and the Italian territories ruled directly by Rome. His act was treason, punishable by death or exile. His success meant the death of the Roman Republic and the birth of imperial Rome. In 1519 Hernando Cortés took an almost unimaginable gamble when he marched into the interior of Mexico. He had six hundred soldiers, fifteen horsemen, and fifteen cannon to face well-organized and powerful local kingdoms. What if the inhabitants had united against the tiny band of invaders instead of allowing themselves to be divided and conquered? It is just possible that Mexico could have survived as an independent state, as Japan did when it faced similar challenges from outside in the 1860s and in the period of the Meiji Restoration, when it successfully transformed itself to deal with the foreigners. The history of North America would have been very different if there had been a strong and independent indigenous power.

Counterfactuals help to remind us that contingency and accidents matter in history. Having said that, they must be used with care. If we change too many things in the past, alternative versions of history become less and less plausible. Nor can we expect the unthinkable or even the unlikely to have occurred. The ancient Greek playwrights may have been able to resolve impossible situations by introducing the *deus ex machina*; we cannot do that in history. Nor can we expect figures in the past to think and react in ways that are improbable given their own characters and times. We cannot expect, for example, Queen Elizabeth I of Britain to have behaved like a twenty-first-century feminist. And when we are trying to understand why historical figures behaved as they did, we must always try to gauge what they themselves could plausibly have seen as the alternatives before them.

I want to look now at four people who changed history, or so I believe. Margaret Thatcher, Woodrow Wilson, Joseph Stalin, and Adolf Hitler operated, of course, within very different contexts. The first two were democratic leaders, while the latter were dictators of a particularly twentieth-century type, for they not only had great power but aspired to control their subjects both body and soul. A new term — totalitarianism — had to be invented to distinguish them from the older-style dictators who wanted mere obedience rather than enthusiastic consent.

What all four have in common, however, is something I have already referred to, and that is driving ambition. Equally important, they had the good fortune to live in times when changes were taking place that gave them opportunities, which they seized. Wilson rode the Progressive Movement into the White House in 1912, when millions of Americans were ready for change and reform. Thatcher tapped into the widespread discontent in 1970s Britain with the state of British society and the economy — high unemployment, economic stagnation, and then the crippling strikes in the winter of 1978–79 — to become first leader of the Conservative Party and then prime minister. Stalin and Hitler took advantage of the collapse and discrediting of the old order caused by the First World War and the Great Depression to present themselves as the agents of radical change.

All four also had a firm conviction that they were right and that they spoke for much greater forces, whether the people, the race, or the flow of history. Like Bismarck, Mackenzie King, and Franklin Delano Roosevelt, they had a clear and compelling vision of the sort of society and world they wanted. They were less prepared, however, to compromise to gain their ends, and over time became convinced that they alone knew what was best. Of course, I do not want to suggest that Thatcher, Wilson, Stalin, and Hitler were of the same order. The first two had to work within the limits of democratic societies with constitutions, rules of law, a free press, and strong civil organizations. While Wilson and Thatcher wielded, with enthusiasm and a conviction of their own correctitude, such power as they had, they respected and were constrained by those limits. Hitler and Stalin, on the other hand, had unlimited power, and, thanks to modern technology, the means to apply it more thoroughly than any of the dictators of the past. What I see as a common characteristic among all four is that success and power went to their heads. Each, in his or her own way, fell prey to what the ancient Greeks called hubris — that supreme arrogance which leads humans to think they are infallible — and they or their unfortunate people were punished for it.

OF WOODROW WILSON, WHO became the American president in 1912, the French ambassador in Washington once said he was "a man who, had he lived a couple of centuries ago, would have been the greatest tyrant in the world, because he does not seem to have the slightest conception that he can ever be wrong." And Wilson, unlike Thatcher, was presiding over a country on its way to world power. When he first entered politics just before the First World War, the United States economy was expanding rapidly, its population was growing, and under President Theodore Roosevelt it had taken its first steps to building a strong navy. The war itself was going to hasten the transformation of the United States into a major diplomatic and military power. At the Paris Peace Conference of 1919, Wilson was able to insist on the creation of the League of Nations. Yet his career ended in a grievous disappointment when he was unable to get Congress to approve it. The failure, as we shall see, was in large part the result of the flaws in his own character, the stubbornness which turned too easily to a refusal to compromise or the conviction that he was absolutely right and his opponents absolutely wrong.

Wilson was born to a Presbyterian minister in Virginia, and his earliest memories were of the Civil War. Although he always believed that the Union had to be maintained, he remained a Southerner, not least in his attitudes to race. His background also left him with a profound Christian faith, coloured by Calvinism and its belief in sin and a stern God. His childhood and upbringing were nevertheless happy; his devoted parents encouraged rather than forced his education. They were as pleased as he was when he told them: "I've found I have an intellect and a first class mind." He was also highly ambitious, not for wealth, but to make a mark and to do good.

He shone as a student, first at Princeton and then later

at Johns Hopkins, where he did a Ph.D. He had briefly tried the law but gravitated naturally towards the academic world, where again he stood out. By the time he was forty-six, he was president of Princeton University, where he set about transforming what had been an undemanding finishing school for young men into a leading academic institution. He also made a name for himself as a well-respected political scientist and historian and as an impressive orator. By 1910, people, including key figures in the Democrat establishment, were talking of him as a possible candidate for governor of New Jersey and perhaps, eventually, for national office.

The timing was good for Wilson. The turn of the twentieth century was a time of considerable political and social ferment as a growing Progressive Movement — which drew in Republicans like Theodore Roosevelt as well as Democrats — attacked corruption in government, monopolies and cartels in business, and the inequality and poverty in American society. The public wanted new leaders, untainted by the old order, and Wilson, with a well-deserved reputation for rectitude, idealism, and efficiency, fitted the bill.

By now in his early fifties, Wilson looked and sounded like a leader. He was handsome (although some felt he looked like an undertaker), dignified, and reserved. Not for him either Roosevelt president's easy affability and ability to talk to complete strangers. Beneath the control lay a sensitive and passionate man who was capable of great love. He could be warm and engaging with his family, his few trusted intimates, and the women he loved in the course of his life, including his two wives. He loved to read out loud in the evenings or tell jokes, admittedly not very good ones.

He had a darker side and failures as well. He never lacked courage for a struggle, but he sometimes failed to achieve his goals because he was too rigid. Colonel Edward House, who for a time was one of Wilson's most trusted advisers, said, apparently in admiration: "Whenever a question is presented he keeps an absolutely open mind and welcomes all suggestion or advice which will lead to a correct decision. But he is receptive only during the period that he is weighing the question and preparing to make his decision. Once the decision is made it is final and there is an absolute end to all advice and suggestion. There is no moving him after that." In his last years at Princeton he got involved in a complicated and unnecessary dispute with many of his colleagues and alumni over his plans for new student residences. If he had consulted more widely and shown a willingness to compromise, he might well have succeeded, at least partly. As it was, he suffered an unwelcome and unexpected defeat and briefly considered resigning.

He was not good at working with strong colleagues, either then or later. Nor did he deal well with opposition. Instead of trying to come to terms with it or co-opt opponents, he cast them into the outer darkness. When he was convinced, as he often was, of the rightness of his cause, he regarded those who disagreed with him as not just wrong but wicked. His career was marked by episodes when he felt that he had been betrayed. In the Princeton dispute, Jack Hibben, a close friend and colleague, sided with the opposition. "Why is it," Wilson asked, "that I was blind and stupid enough to love the people, who proved false to me..." He never forgave Hibben and never talked to him again. Wilson was to do the same in 1919 to House, who, he felt, had betrayed him by not pushing sufficiently strongly for Wilson's dream of a fair peace and a new world order. In a pattern that was also to be repeated in 1919, he collapsed while he was at Princeton, possibly with a stroke, and was left with recurring headaches, temporary blindness in one eye, and emotional imbalances.

Defeat at Princeton made him ready for the move into politics. When he was approached to run for governor of New Jersey, he promptly agreed. He held out the promise of a progressive, clean, and efficient administration which would bring powerful bodies such as corporations under control. He was swept into office with 54 percent of the popular vote. His two years as governor were marked by a series of reforms, and by 1912 he was for many, both in the North and his own South, the obvious Democratic candidate for president. In the election campaign, luck was with him. The Republicans were divided among themselves because Theodore Roosevelt had bolted to run as the head of the new Progressive Party. Although Wilson got only 43 percent of the popular vote, it was more than enough to give him a commanding majority in the Electoral College.

As president he showed the same energy and determination as when he was governor, and he also proved to be a formidable communicator, holding more than sixty press conferences in his first year alone. In his first term he focussed on domestic issues, bringing in a whole series of progressive measures, including lowering tariffs and setting up the Federal Reserve and the Federal Trade Commission. "It would be the irony of fate," he said to a friend in 1913, "if my administration had to deal chiefly with foreign affairs." Yet he could not entirely ignore the outside world, especially those parts closest to the United States.

Wilson's views about foreign policy were moralistic and straightforward. The United States was a force for good, and it should be an example to the rest of the world. As he once said when he was campaigning, "America is an idea, America is an ideal, America is a vision." Where necessary, he was prepared to promote that ideal (and, even if he did not always admit it, to protect American interests) by forcefully intervening in the affairs of America's neighbours. As he once said to a British diplomat, "I am going to teach the South American republics to elect good men!" When he sent American troops into Mexico on a flimsy excuse, he defended it as serving humanity.

When the First World War broke out in Europe, Wilson, like many Americans, was horrified at what he saw as folly and a lapse into barbarism. He tore himself away from the bedside of his first wife, who was dying, to offer his services as a mediator. Initially he was convinced that his country had no interest and no need to get involved in the struggle. The United States, he said in a message to Congress in 1914, "must be neutral in fact, as well as in name, during these days that are to try men's souls. We must be impartial in thought, as well as action..." As the war went on, however, the United States tilted towards the Allies, and Wilson did little to stop that. His own sympathies and those of a significant number of Americans were with the Allies, particularly Britain and France, which were fellow democracies. American banks lent increasing sums of money to the Allies, and American factories benefitted from Allied orders. In February 1917, when the first Russian Revolution overthrew the tsarist autocracy, one of the chief objections to the Allies was removed. In the end, though, it was German folly that persuaded Wilson that the United States must enter the war: German submarines were sinking American ships and killing American citizens, and in early 1917 the German government tried to persuade Mexico to attack the United States. That was the final straw, and Wilson went to Congress and got a declaration of war on April 2.

From the start he was clear that the United States was entering the war on different terms and for different goals than the other belligerents. Unlike the imperialistic powers in Europe, the U.S. wanted nothing for itself, either in terms of possessions or indemnities. (Like many of his fellow Americans, Wilson was perfectly happy to see American trade and investment growing around the world.) To make the point, the United States never referred to itself as an Ally but rather an "associated power." Wilson aimed at using American power to bring the fighting to an end and destroy German militarism, which he, like many, felt was responsible for the war. There must, however, be peace without victory. More, the opportunity must be seized to build an international society where nations came together in a "community of power" to replace the old, discredited balance of power. In a series of speeches and statements Wilson elaborated on his vision, most famously in his Fourteen Points of January 1918, which sketched out a new world order with a new open diplomacy, free trade, disarmament, respect for the sovereignty and integrity of nations, and, for national groups who were not yet independent, "autonomy." The keystone that would sustain and strengthen the whole was a "general association of nations" — in other words, the League of Nations.

Wilson's words resonated throughout a war-weary world. When the war finally ended in November 1918, he decided to attend the coming peace conference. Huge and enthusiastic crowds turned out to welcome him in Europe. On the voyage over, he had already told the American delegation, as one of them noted, that "the men whom we were about to deal with did not represent their own people." His reception served to confirm his belief that he understood the masses of the world and spoke for them in a way that their own leaders could not.

It was a curious assumption for a democrat, and he was at least partly wrong. While many of those who greeted him shared his vision of a better world order, others were motivated by the hope that he would give them and their countries recompense for their sufferings and punish their enemies. Yet Wilson was to persist in believing that he, alone among the world's statesmen gathered in Paris and the politicians back home, knew what the world wanted and needed. That conviction was to destroy his chances of getting the League approved by Congress.

When he arrived in Paris in January 1919, he insisted that the first item of business before the conference must be the League. It would then matter less if the conference made bad decisions on matters such as borders or reparations: the new League would be able to sort things out. Unfortunately he was also storing up trouble for the future. In the November 1918 elections, he made the war and the coming peace a partisan issue when he urged voters to show that they approved of his leadership by voting for a Democratic Congress. This understandably infuriated Republicans who had loyally supported the war effort. He refused as well to make the American delegation to the peace conference a bipartisan one, as he could have done by appointing, for example, former president William Taft, or Elihu Root, who had served with distinction in two Republican administrations. Since the Senate had to approve treaties, he could also have appointed the chair of its Foreign Relations Committee, Henry Cabot Lodge. Instead Wilson appointed Democrats and nonentities. The slight, for that is how Lodge saw it, served to increase the animosity of a powerful politician who already disliked and distrusted Wilson. (FDR wisely learned a lesson from this and made sure that he had Republican support for his peace aims.)

While there were some diehard Republicans — the irreconcilables — who wanted no part of a league, many would have accepted an organization which safeguarded the right of the United States to decide when it went to war, or which accepted that it had a special position, as defined by the Monroe Doctrine, in its relations with the countries in the Western hemisphere. American public opinion, as much as one could tell in the days before opinion polls, was also in favour of some form of league. When a prominent American journal asked its readers for their views, more than two-thirds were in support. Wilson did little, however, to try to win over the moderates, much less his opponents. Between February and March 1919, when he was back in the United States on a rapid visit, he managed to offend Lodge still further. He gave a rousing speech in favour of the League in Boston, Lodge's home territory. Equally foolishly, he irritated even sympathetic senators, always conscious of their dignity, by distributing copies of the draft League Covenant before they had been given a chance to see it. In Washington Wilson refused to lay himself out to conciliate even the wavering members of his own party; he would not talk to one particular Southern Democrat whom he despised. At House's urging he held a dinner party for key senators, including Lodge and the other members of the Foreign Relations Committee. It was a conspicuous failure: Wilson, said one, treated them "as though they were being reproved for neglect of their lessons by a very frigid teacher in a Sunday School class." Even Wilson's sour little joke when he first saw a newborn grandson struck the wrong note: "With his mouth open and his eyes shut, I predict he will make a Senator when he grows up." Wilson was starting to wonder if he could bypass the Senate altogether and somehow commit the United States to the League.

Once back in Paris, he turned on House, who he felt was lukewarm in his support for the League. In April Wilson had another of his physical collapses. It may have been an attack of the influenza, which was now making the rounds, or a small stroke, a harbinger of the much more serious one which was going to come four months later. Whatever the cause, his illness left him with a permanent tic in his face and had the effect of making him more emotional, more erratic, and more easily irritated. He also became even more self-righteous and stubborn.

The key peace treaty, the one with Germany, with the League Covenant as its first clauses, was finally signed on June 28, 1919. Wilson set sail immediately for the United States to wage the struggle for its approval by the Senate. He was determined that he would accept no compromise on its clauses. If the Senate chose to exert its rights to make amendments or attach "reservations" — modifications of the terms — he would reject them all. He might have been able to cobble together a coalition of his own Democrats and those sympathetic Republicans who wanted only a few mild reservations, but he refused to consider it. When he presented the treaty to the Senate that July, his speech was defiant. The League was "the only hope for mankind." He laid down a challenge to the senators: "Dare we reject it and break the heart of the world?" His appearance in August before Lodge's committee, which was holding hearings on the treaty, was marked by angry exchanges. Lodge himself still supported some form of league, but he argued that it should not be embedded in the treaty with Germany but should be negotiated separately later, when things were calmer. Whatever his motives, and hatred for Wilson may have played a part, his objections were not unreasonable.

Wilson decided to take the treaty fight to the people, who, he was sure, were with him. On September 3 he left Washington for a three-week tour of the West, home to key "irreconcilables." It was still very warm, and Wilson was looking tired and ill. His second wife, his friends, and his doctor urged him not to undertake what would be an exhausting trip. "I will gladly make any sacrifice to save the Treaty," he said. As he moved west, giving two to three speeches a day, increasing crowds came out to hear him. Support for the treaty appeared to be growing, and his colleagues began to hope that it might pass the Senate, if Wilson would be prepared to accept some mild reservations. On the night of September 25, he suffered a major stroke from which he never fully recovered. As had happened during his battles at Princeton or in Paris, he became emotionally fragile and unreasonably stubborn. From his sickbed in the White House, he issued instructions that there must be no compromise over the treaty.

When Lodge put forward a motion to ratify the treaty with the modifications that had emerged from his committee, it was defeated by a combination of Republican irreconcilables and Democrats who still followed Wilson's orders. In March 1920 moderates in both parties made a final attempt to get the treaty, with only mild reservations, approved. Twenty-three Democrats defied Wilson and voted in favour, but their votes, combined with those of the Republican moderates, were not enough to ensure its passage. The United States later made a separate treaty with Germany, but it did not join the League.

If Wilson had been a different sort of man, things might have turned out differently. We can imagine how the subsequent decades might have gone if there had been a stronger international organization to confront Hitler's Germany,

Mussolini's Italy, or the Japan of the militarists. Wilson left the world with a grand vision; it is a pity his own flaws prevented him from making it a reality in his lifetime.

LIKE WILSON, MARGARET THATCHER'S inner conviction that she could see more clearly than anyone else had been reinforced beyond reason by a string of successes. Like him, she had unexpectedly won the party leadership and had then been elected to office. Like him, she had carried out a series of bold reforms that had helped to transform society. And she, like him, had presided over military victory. For Thatcher, the Falklands War of 1982 was both her defining moment and contained within it the seeds of her downfall. Her belief that she could and should prevail in any struggle led her to adopt and then stay with a disastrous policy when the many warning signs showed that she should abandon it. The issue was apparently trivial — to replace the tax on houses, which financed local government, with a head tax, payable by all adults — but, as we will see, it ended her career.

Thatcher was a most unlikely Conservative prime minister. Unlike her predecessors and indeed the overwhelming majority of Tory MPs, she was an outsider. In a party dominated by men, she was a woman. She had to fight within her own party and against her political opponents to be taken seriously. When she first got up to speak, the Labour backbenchers would make mocking "female" noises. She made up for it by working harder than anyone else; in later years her mastery of detail would astonish and frequently intimidate others. Moreover the Tory establishment was overwhelmingly upper class. She came from the lower middle classes; her father was a grocer, and in her childhood the family had lived above the shop. She had gone to a state school; most Tory men had been educated in expensive private schools. At Oxford she studied chemistry; most of her colleagues had done arts subjects. She did not much like travel or foreigners; the other Tories had grown up accustomed to holidays abroad. As her career advanced, she acquired a more genteel accent and married a well-to-do businessman, but unlike her predecessor, Edward Heath, who came from a similar background, she never chose to become part of the upper classes. Indeed she revelled in being an outsider. It served to stiffen her already formidable backbone. "You make up your own mind," she said. "You do not do something or want something because your friends are doing it."

Anthony King, a distinguished Canadian political scientist who has made it his business to study British politics, has remarked: "There was always about Thatcher the air of a gatecrasher at a party being given by people she disliked." He argues that like other "outsider" politicians — Richard Nixon, for example, or Stephen Harper — she found that status both psychologically satisfying and a good tactic. She could feel morally superior to those around her while at the same time ignoring their conventions and rules. In fact, says King, outsiders may calculate that their confrontational approach is the best way to achieve success. Thatcher could be charming when she chose, but she never hesitated to shout and bang on the table, whether at European Council meetings or with her colleagues. As she said proudly of herself, "I offended on many accounts."

Thatcher brought to her political career simple but strongly held convictions. She had little time for the politics of inclusion and compromise. That, she felt, was what had got Britain into trouble: governments, even Tory ones, had made too many concessions to non-elected bodies, such as unions. As she once remarked: "The Old Testament prophets did not say, 'Brothers, I want a consensus.' They said: 'This is my faith. This is what I passionately believe.'" In 1979, during her first campaign as Tory leader, she told a newspaper that if she was elected she didn't want a pragmatic or consensual cabinet: "It must be a conviction government."

"She wasn't a woman of ideas," said one of her closest advisers, "she was a woman of beliefs, and beliefs are better than ideas." She was never a great reader and nor did she pay much attention to think tanks; she drew more on her own background and experience and the opinions of a few trusted colleagues. She valued highly such qualities as thrift, hard work, and self-reliance, and she was deeply patriotic. When she was having lunch with the historian Andrew Roberts after her forced retirement, a waiter made the mistake of asking if she wanted English or French mustard. She cried "English!" as if there could be no doubt.

As a young woman she had watched, as she saw it, social-ism sapping the initiative of a once-proud people. The power of the state had increased at the expense of the individual. Successive governments had interfered with the economy, spent recklessly, and piled tax burdens onto the hard-work-ing middle classes. Her own background gave her an instinc-tive understanding of the resentment felt by such groups as small businesspeople, the self-employed, or pensioners, who felt the Tories under the influence of moderates such as Harold Macmillan had abandoned them and that Labour was always going to be their foe. As she said proudly of her-self in 1975 as she was standing for the Tory leadership, "All my ideas about [Britain] were formed before I was seven-teen or eighteen." The late 1960s and early 1970s had not been kind to Britain, and Thatcher, like others on the right wing of the Conservative Party, feared that the country faced economic collapse. Yet, said one businessman who talked to her at length in 1976, she had no clear policy prescriptions beyond a belief that the current situation was shaming and that something had to be done.

Luck and good timing were on her side. Being one of the few women in the Commons was often a disadvantage, but when Heath, the prime minister of the time, was looking for a woman for his cabinet she was an obvious choice. She also benefitted from many of the Tories' disaffection with Heath as a leader. In their view, he had been weak at dealing with the unions, especially the militant miners, and this had led to the Tory defeat by Labour in the 1974 election. Within the party, a radical free-market group was emerging which was also dedicated to rolling back the power of government over society, and Thatcher gravitated towards it. Its leading figure, Keith Joseph, decided against challenging Heath for the party leadership, which left the field open to Thatcher. It also helped that Heath refused to go quietly, which damaged the chances of any likely moderate successors. In 1975 Thatcher was elected as leader.

She had by this point developed what were to become her trademarks: her smooth helmet of blonde hair; the simple, well-cut suits and dresses; the string of pearls; and the menacing handbag. A television producer had taught her to lower her voice so that she did not sound quite so shrill. A surprising range of men — hardbitten journalists, junior ministers in her government, or political antagonists — found her quite sexy. As France's president, François Mitterrand, famously said, she had "the eyes of Caligula and the mouth of Marilyn Monroe." She also accepted advice on her speeches, which had tended to be long and rambling, and became a master of the one-liner. She even memorized a few spontaneous jokes, something of a challenge for someone with no sense of humour. Her staff learned to dread her unwitting double entendres: the time she told a young apprentice, "I've never seen a tool as big as that!"; or when she declined to fire a field gun with "Won't it jerk me off?"

Her next piece of luck was the turbulent Winter of Discontent of 1978–79. A series of strikes in the public sector, some marked by violence, persuaded many voters that the time had come to bring the unions under control. Labour, so it seemed clear, was incapable of doing that. Margaret Thatcher was a fresh face who promised a fresh start. In the general election of 1979, the Tories won 339 seats to Labour's 269. As she stood outside 10 Downing Street, Thatcher quoted a prayer she had carefully memorized for the occasion: "Where there is discord, may we bring harmony." Irony, like humour, was not something she did.

Her first years as prime minister were not easy ones. To be sure, the opposition was badly divided, and in 1981 a dissident group split from the Labour Party to form a new Social Democratic Party. Yet the unions were still challenging the government, the British economy went from bad to worse, and her own party was unsure of what to make of her. A group of influential Tories, some within her cabinet, strongly opposed Thatcher's plans to cut public expenditure sharply. Their opposition — she contemptuously called them the "wets" — only strengthened her resolve. She was convinced that she knew what was right for Britain, and she had no intention of altering her course. "You turn if you want to," she said with icy calm at the Party Conference in the autumn of 1980. "The lady's not for turning." The rank and file loved it, but in the country at large her popularity plummeted as unemployment continued to grow rapidly — by a million in 1981 — and businesses collapsed. In a poll taken at the end of the year, only 23 percent of voters thought Thatcher was doing a good job.

What saved her, and ensured that she would be re-elected with a comfortable majority, was again luck — in this case, a war far from British shores. At the start of April 1982 the Argentine junta invaded the Falkland Islands, which Argentina had long claimed as its own. The generals assumed that Britain, especially headed by a woman prime minister, would not respond. Thatcher made up her mind from the start and never shifted: Britain was going to take the islands back. Interviewed on television about what would happen if the British expeditionary force which had been hastily dispatched across the Atlantic failed, she replied, "Failure? . . . Failure — the possibilities do not exist." In fact the possibilities did exist, and yet again luck played a role. The Argentine leaders were weak and divided and, in the case of the junta's head, General Galtieri, frequently drunk. Their troops were not expecting a battle and were poorly equipped. Several of the shells which hit the British ships failed to explode. Thatcher remained calm and resolute and was absolutely clear that there would be no peace until Argentina had given back the islands. By the time the war ended in a British victory on June 14, her overall approval ratings stood at 51 percent, over twice as high as six months earlier.

The Falklands War always remained for Thatcher the most significant moment of her career and a turning point in modern British history. The long, drawn-out quarrel between Britain and Argentina over possession of the islands had suddenly escalated with the invasion. Although many of her own

advisers told Thatcher that it was impossible to mount a coun-
terattack over a great distance, she overruled them. It was a
terrific gamble, but she won both the war and a political victory. The doubters in her own party were silenced, and even
her opponents were impressed and admiring. To the public,
she became "our Maggie," proof that Britain still mattered
and that it was dangerous to pull the lion's tail. In the victory
over Argentina, she told the party faithful during a speech at
the Cheltenham Racecourse, she could see the rebirth of the
nation: "We have ceased to be a nation in retreat. We have
instead a new found confidence — born in the economic battles at home and tested and found true 8,000 miles away." The
Falklands War became the touchstone by which she judged
her own actions and policies and those of others, and she
never forgave those who had not supported her. And victory
also made her virtually unassailable, or so it seemed. Alan
Clark, the charming reprobate who was one of her greatest
admirers, told a close associate shortly after the war ended:
"The Prime Minister has complete freedom of action now."
And, he went on, "no other Leader has enjoyed such freedom
since Churchill, and even with him it did not last very long."
The following year the Conservatives were re-elected with
an even larger parliamentary majority.

Thatcher's self-confidence was now unshakeable. The war
had shown, or so she concluded, that she succeeded best when
she acted on her own and listened to her heart. Her already
well-developed tendency to self-righteousness was now ada-
mantine. Victory, said one minister, "fortifies her conviction
that she is right on every subject." Thatcher now held forth
to her cabinet far more than she listened to its members.
She would present policies that she had already decided and
demand approval. She reshuffled her cabinet, and those who

were left were her creatures and appropriately submissive. Usually, as the Borg used to say in *Star Trek*, resistance was futile. "I must prevail," she once said to Nigel Lawson, her chancellor of the exchequer. Anyone who disagreed with her was likely to be labelled a wet — or, more ominously, a "traitor." Her nickname, not to be used when she was in earshot, was by now Attila the Hen.

By the time of the next election, there were signs that the public was running out of enthusiasm for Mrs. Thatcher, if not for Thatcherism itself. She was perceived, found one survey, to be "harsh" and "uncaring," and under her leadership the government appeared to be drifting. This only served to put her back up and stiffen her resolve to continue the great task of remaking British society — or, as one chapter of her memoirs was entitled, "Putting the World to Rights." She won again in 1987 (although the party lost twenty-one seats) and set to work with renewed determination and vigour — and a conviction of her own rightness. One of her targets was education, which she had long felt was dominated by left-wing teachers' unions which promoted a wishy-washy and largely useless curriculum. History, she liked to say, should be about facts and not what she dismissed as trends, and it should focus on Britain and not the rest of the world. She moved to prise state schools out of the control of the unions and the local politicians, two groups she felt could not be trusted.

More ambitiously still, she decided to take on local government itself, trimming the powers of local councils and bringing them more firmly under central control. This would rein in their spending, which she saw as profligate; somehow increase efficiency; and remove alternative power centres to Westminster. One of the key instruments she intended to use was a new form of local tax; instead of taxes on the value of houses — the "rates," as they are called in the United Kingdom — every adult would pay a flat charge on the basis that everyone drew on local services equally. Her government called this the "community charge"; everyone else called it the "poll tax," after those imposed by kings in the past, which had usually been deeply unpopular.

Thatcher had been committed to the idea long before the 1987 election. To her, it had two great advantages: it was simple, and it would appease the many Tory homeowners who complained bitterly when increases in the value of their houses sent their rates up. In marginal seats — in Scotland, for example, where the Tories were not doing well — a move that capped taxes would, or so she thought, be popular and helpful in getting votes. In retrospect the government might have got away with the poll tax if they had chosen to phase it in over a number of years, and perhaps had a number of bands so that the well-off paid larger amounts than the poor. Thatcher was not in a mood to be cautious. The 1987 Conservative Party Conference appeared to show solid grassroots enthusiasm for a uniform tax to be introduced, and as soon as possible. Thatcher, who always liked the big and dramatic gesture, agreed.

Criticism and opposition began to gather momentum. The poll tax was going to be expensive to collect. It was regressive and unfair, since it represented a greater burden to the poor. Heath, who had never forgiven Thatcher for ousting him, publicly asked, "Are we to change the philosophy of our party for the past century?" The party itself grew uneasy. A number of studies between 1988 and early 1990 showed that the new charge would be higher than the old property tax for many homeowners, including Tory supporters in key seats. In Scotland, where the poll tax was introduced early, Tory support was eroding fast — and has never recovered to thisday. In 1990 the poll tax came to England and Wales and provoked widespread protests. Some seventeen million people in England alone refused to pay, and in London a mass demonstration produced some of the worst scenes of civil violence in living memory.

Thatcher refused to back down, even though the 1989 polls showed her to be the most unpopular British prime minister since the start of polling in 1939. Standing up for principle, showing leadership, being tough — these had served her well in the past. And she had driven away almost anyone who would dare to tell her she was making a huge mistake, and over an issue that was not worth the fight. In the end it was her long-suffering and much-bullied foreign secretary, Sir Geoffrey Howe, who finally brought matters to a head by submitting his resignation. In his letter he focussed on her antagonistic and unproductive relations with the European Council, but it was his phrase in his speech to the Commons about her "nightmare image" of the European Community which struck a chord with the Tory party, which was now increasingly desperate to avert what it saw as the coming wreckage. The prime minister, Howe said tellingly, did not listen to anyone, and in her frequently offhand approach to important issues was risking the nation itself. By November that year, Margaret Thatcher was out, obliged to resign when it became clear that her own party no longer wanted her as leader. In an interview with *Vanity Fair* in 1991, she insisted that she had never been defeated in an election, by a vote of confidence or by the people. She compared herself to a broken piece of glass. As one close aide said, "She never had a happy day after being ousted from office." She never showed a sign, however, that she understood the part she played in her own downfall.

WILSON AND THATCHER WERE elected leaders, and although their power at times was great, it was limited in duration and constrained by the values and institutions of constitutional democracy. The twentieth century has also seen dictators, often for life, with enormous powers. Apart from Atatürk, the creator of modern Turkey, it is hard to think of many who imposed limits on themselves or accepted that they might be wrong. The twentieth century (and perhaps the twenty-first) was an age of ideologies which seized their adherents body and soul. Marxism, fascism, or ethnic nationalism — for those who believed in them, these ideologies were the only truth. Each demanded sacrifice if it was to triumph, and each was far more important and lasting than individuals. What brought the horrors of the twentieth century was the combination of such ideologies with industrialization, science, technology, and the mass media, which made it possible to engineer human societies and human souls — and remove those people and classes and ethnicities who stood in the way. The horrors did not happen on their own, however; they needed someone or some people to set them in motion. And so we come back to the role of the individual leader.

Take China, for example. If Deng Xiaoping had been head of the Communist Party rather than Mao Zedong when the Communists won the Civil War in 1949 and so gained control of China, he would have undoubtedly set up the one-party state. It is unlikely, however, that he would have exacted the price that China paid in the succeeding years: Mao's hurried land reforms and then his push for collectivization, in which many millions were killed deliberately or died of starvation; the Great Leap Forward, which wrecked much of the Chinese economy; or the mad frenzy of destruction of the Cultural Revolution. When Deng gained the leadership after

Mao's death, he loosened the controls on the economy, made reforms, and set in motion the great changes which have peacefully transformed China.

Like Wilson and Thatcher, Stalin and Hitler had a vision for their societies, and the ambition and will to attempt to achieve it. They too were favoured by luck and circumstance. Hitler survived the First World War, although he was wounded in the German trenches. Stalin managed to escape execution in tsarist Russia and survived the Civil War. Hitler's career might have ended with his abortive attempt to seize power in Munich in 1924, which could have made him a criminal rather than a hero. Stalin's might have come to an end at the same time if the senior members of what was now known as the Communist Party had been fully aware of what Lenin had said about him in one of his last letters. Stalin, said the dying Lenin, had concentrated unlimited power in his hands: "I am not convinced that he will always manage to use that power with sufficient care." More damningly still, Lenin urged the Party to get rid of Stalin and replace him with someone "more tolerant." Stalin managed to ensure that these views did not become public.

Hitler rose to power in a deeply troubled Germany, its confidence shattered by its loss in the First World War, and its society divided between the right and the left and between those who accepted the Weimar Republic and those who did not. Still, if it had not been for the Great Depression, which hit Germany particularly hard and persuaded many Germans that radical new measures and a strong, decisive leader were what they needed, he would never have achieved power. Stalin's opening came with the collapse of the old regime in Russia during the First World War and the seizure of power in the autumn of 1917 by the Bolsheviks (later to call themselves the Communists). An obscure revolutionary at once became part of the inner circle in charge of a great country. When the Party's leader, Vladimir Lenin, died suddenly at the age of fifty-four, his colleagues were divided over the succession and Stalin was able to patiently manoeuvre among them until he emerged supreme.

Their successful consolidation of power made Hitler and Stalin increasingly impervious to criticism or disagreement and enhanced their inner conviction that they saw more clearly than anyone else which way history was flowing, and that they were infallible. They were surrounded by adoring or obsequious followers who were unwilling to risk their lives by saying something the great leader did not agree with or want to hear. "One thing is certain," said Hitler's favourite architect, Albert Speer, after the war, "all his associates who had worked closely with him for a long time were entirely dependent and obedient to him." In the great purges of the 1930s, many of Stalin's closest associates lost family members; none dared complain. Vyacheslav Molotov had to divorce his Jewish wife to prove his loyalty. She was later arrested, and probably only survived because Stalin died. (She and Molotov then remarried.)

Both men persisted in trying to achieve their ends even as disastrous consequences became abundantly clear. Unlike Wilson or Thatcher, however, Stalin and Hitler did not want merely to change society; they believed they could transform humanity itself. They were prepared to sacrifice lives, as many as they deemed necessary, for the idea. Millions died as Hitler waged war against a growing number of enemies to fulfil his dream of making the German race supreme in the world. And millions died in Stalin's attempt to create the perfect socialist society. As Stalin once said during the siege of a key city in the early-1920s Civil War between his Communists and their opponents, he would sacrifice 49 percent of the inhabitants if he could save the remaining 51 percent, "that is, save the revolution." Both men chose to avoid seeing for themselves what such schemes meant for their own people, much less any others. Stalin did not travel to the famine-stricken areas in the Soviet Union in the 1930s, and Hitler refused to tour the bomb-damaged cities of Germany during the Second World War.

I want to look specifically both at Hitler's decisions for war — which led to the destruction of his country, and of much of the world — and at Stalin's forced collectivization of Soviet farms and his Great Terror in the 1930s, which so damaged the Soviet economy and society and left it weakened in the face of growing German and Japanese power. Without Hitler, Germany might have had a conservative nationalist government which wanted to reassert the country's power and status, including by revising the terms of the Treaty of Versailles, but it may well have decided to do this through peaceful means rather than war. Even Nazi leaders such as Hermann Goering or Heinrich Himmler might have tried to achieve their ends peacefully or settled for partial victories. In the Soviet Union, another Communist leader might have let Lenin's New Economic Policy, which allowed for limited capitalism to continue and attempted to move gradually and incrementally towards socialism. Neither Hitler nor Stalin was prepared to compromise in such a fashion.

Their own histories, their beliefs, and their personalities are therefore key to understanding what happened. Their early lives had been similar in some respects, but the differences between them were also great. Both had unhappy childhoods with authoritarian fathers; both were closer to their mothers. Stalin ate meat and drank moderately; Hitler was a vegetarian, non-smoker, and drank very little. Stalin had close relationships with women; Hitler's sexual relations, even with his mistress, Eva Braun, were always a mystery. Both men were outsiders in the worlds to which they wished to belong: Stalin came from Georgia and always spoke Russian with a Georgian accent, while Hitler was an Austrian who longed to be part of Germany. Both were, at least at first, socially awkward, even vulgar. Hitler, said one upper-class German in 1920, looked and behaved like a head waiter; Stalin liked to swear like a peasant. Both men could be brutally rude, yet charming when they chose. Their eyes, Hitler's large blue ones and Stalin's amber — like a tiger's, some said — were compelling. Hitler loved to hold the stage, even in social situations, strutting about, talking in a monologue, with his voice rising to a shout when he was excited. Stalin was a poor orator and preferred to sit quietly in a corner, simply dressed and apparently too modest to put himself forward. He had a great capacity for hard work, whereas Hitler was lazy and slapdash.

The two men were shaped and moved by similar impulses — mastery, revenge, or hatred — but by quite different ideas. Hitler, as a young, aimless drifter in Vienna before the First World War, had picked up and embraced the racist and Social Darwinist ideas floating around Europe at the time. The belief that the human race could be divided into separate species of varying qualities, and that the different races or nations were condemned by nature to struggle against each other for survival, became a deep-rooted conviction. For Hitler, the German race was at the top of the evolutionary tree and ought to be able to impose its will on lesser peoples. As he said in a speech to Erlangen University in 1930, the Germans had more right than any other people to fight and gain control of the world. He never wavered in this view and in his passionate German nationalism.

Stalin's vision came from another source: socialist ideas, especially Marx's, which put all the ills of society down to capitalism. Stalin never doubted that socialism — defined in various ways but including the sharing of property and the elimination of classes — would create not just a new and better society but a new human nature. And he believed that history was moving ineluctably in that direction, towards that Utopia. Once their environment was changed, human beings would become socialist men and women, thinking, feeling, and working collectively. If necessary, enemies of socialism, or those who refused to adapt — members of the upper and middle classes, or the peasants in the countryside who clung to the old, pernicious ideas and values — would have to be eliminated. For Hitler, the characteristics of what he saw as different human races could never be changed; races could be purified and strengthened, however, through selective breeding, including the elimination of the unfit and the inferior. Each man embraced his guiding ideas early on and never altered his conviction that they explained all and justified all.

While both dominated their parties and through them the institutions of the state, they also aimed to control society totally. They used the old and well-tried methods of earlier dictators — censorship, repression, and violence — but on a massive, industrialized scale. Where the Terror in the French Revolution lasted for under a year and killed some 42,000, the Communist war against the Soviet people lasted from the Russian Revolution until Stalin's death in 1953. In Stalin's Great Terror between 1934 and 1940, as many as one million were shot. Millions were sent to jail or the forced labour camps — the gulag — and many never returned. While it is impossible to know the numbers for certain, Robert Conquest, the leading historian of the Great Terror, estimates that ten million died in that period. The Nazis killed ten thousand of their fellow citizens between 1933 and 1939; the war then gave Hitler his opportunity for murder on a much greater scale throughout Europe.

The twentieth-century dictators — and they include not just Hitler and Stalin but a host of imitators, from Mao in China to Enver Hoxha in tiny Albania — relied as well on modern techniques of mass marketing, mass persuasion, and the mass lie. In 1940, when Nazi Germany and the Soviet Union were temporarily on the same side thanks to their non-aggression pact of 1939, a Soviet interpreter was sent to work in Berlin. He found there much to remind him of home: "The same idolization of the 'leader,' the same mass rallies and parades...Very similar, ostentatious architecture, heroic themes depicted in art much like our socialist realism...massive ideological brainwashing." Both regimes were hostile to Christianity, but they drew freely on its iconography to elevate their leaders into Christ-like figures who lived austerely, toiled selflessly for their people, and could perform miracles.

Hitler and Stalin both allowed and fed on the cult of their personalities. Hitler, as Ian Kershaw, his pre-eminent biographer, argues, had virtually no life outside of politics; playing the role of the great leader — the führer — before an admiring audience served to reflect him back to himself and became his essence. Stalin seemed more reluctant to be at the centre of such adoration, at least in his early years in power, although his close associate Molotov felt he came to enjoy the adulation rather too much as time went by. Stalin was able to justify the cult in Marxist terms: the Party was the vanguard of the revolution because it possessed a monopoly of the truth, but in moments of crisis all the threads had to be gathered together into one spot — or one set of hands.

It is a mistake though to see the German or the Soviet people as inert masses, swayed this way and that by skilled communicators at the top. The cult of personality in both countries reflected real feelings and a longing for a strong, decisive leader who would make the world right again. The Germans and the Soviets — like many others in Europe — had seen their societies disintegrate around them. The First World War, revolution, violent civil conflict — and in the case of Russia, all-out civil war and economic and social collapse — had left peoples adrift. Old, apparently solid institutions, from monarchies to the state, had suddenly vanished, leaving a bewildering and disturbing new world. Millions of Germans and Soviets were psychologically ready to accept strong, even dictatorial leadership. Hitler and Stalin, precisely because they were not conventional leaders whose solutions seemed stale and ineffectual, offered reassurance, inspiration, and the promise of a new dawn. Their followers adored them uncritically, as children adore their parents. One of Stalin's closest colleagues called him Father. Women at Hitler's mountain home of Berchtesgaden, in Bavaria, apparently ate the gravel he had just walked on. When Stalin died in 1953, people across the Soviet Union wept in genuine grief.

Max Weber's definition of charismatic rule, where the leader is important not for the office he holds but because of his personality, helps to explain the power of both men. Hitler in particular grasped this instinctively. As early as 1920 he declared, "We need a dictator who is a genius." A constant theme in his writings and speeches is the way in which the fracturing of society allowed someone like him, "a higher personality," to gain power. He only ever wanted to be called führer, not chancellor or president, since those suggested posts with limits on the holder's power. Both he and Stalin made free use of terror, but they by no means relied on that alone; they had many willing collaborators. Kershaw quotes a Nazi Party member who says that it was the duty of every person in Germany "to work towards the Führer along the lines he would wish." They should not wait for orders but anticipate them. When Stalin forced collectivization on an unwilling peasant population, eager young Communists poured into the countryside from the cities and towns, prepared to do anything, including murder, to please him.

Soviet collectivization made no sense economically and indeed so damaged Soviet agriculture that it has not recovered to this day. However, to Stalin and those who thought like him, the policy was imperative if the new socialist society was to be built. That is what the theory said, and the theory had to be right. To admit otherwise was to question the very foundations of the Communists' right to rule the Soviet Union. The limited capitalism of the New Economic Policy, which brought economic recovery in the 1920s and benefitted small traders and the peasant farmers, was anathema to Stalin and his followers, a tactical retreat on the road to socialism which might postpone its achievement indefinitely. More, the hopes of international revolution had faded, and that left the Soviet Union on its own to build socialism in one country. The essential building block in the shape of a large industrial working class did not yet exist. So, to make reality fit theory, the Soviet Union had to industrialize and that required capital and a work force. The countryside could provide both, in the form of grain exports and peasants forced off their land. Stalin seems to have assumed that collectivization would not only remove or reshape a class that was an obstacle, but that it would be efficient, increasing food production dramatically. He was driven by fear as well, of a hostile capitalist world which was waiting to strangle the revolution by helping to subvert it from within or by invading the Soviet Union. Collectivization and industrialization — in his mind, at least — served the further goal of strengthening the Soviet Union against its many enemies.

In 1928, when he had subdued his opponents within the Communist Party, Stalin announced a crash plan of development: the first Five Year Plan. Peasants would sign away their land, willingly or not, to the collective farms, become workers as though they were in factories, or migrate to the cities. He had a particular animus against peasants — especially the more prosperous ones, the kulaks — perhaps because he came from a peasant background himself. Everything they owned, from animals to equipment, would belong to the state, which then would also be able to ensure that it laid its hands on the output of agriculture. Stalin never wavered as he set out to make the future happen, even as the costs mounted higher and higher. Would his defeated opponents have done the same? We can never know, but it is highly likely that they would have backed off. None of the rest of them had Stalin's will. Leon Trotsky had allowed himself to be removed from the Party and sent into exile; Nikolai Bukharin, who had once been seen as Lenin's successor, had been outmanoeuvred and had acquiesced in Stalin's seizure of power.

Between 1928 and 1932, Stalin forced through a revolution in the countryside. Farmers whose ancestors had been serfs only two or three generations ago signed away their land and found themselves tied to new collective farms. Many tried to resist, but their weapons were no match for those of the state. Many burned their crops and killed their animals rather than hand them over to the collective farms. In all, it is estimated that 32 million cattle out of 70 million died, nearly two-thirds of the sheep and goats, and about half the horses. Stalin responded by sending party members from the cities and the army to enforce his will. He also purged the lower ranks of local parties, where there might be sympathy for peasants, and he recruited new members from the cities and towns, who came to the countryside motivated by a vision of the future and a firm belief that they were waging war on real enemies. In each region, panels determined who was a kulak and who was not (often the difference was as insignificant as owning a cow). To be declared a kulak was usually the equivalent of a death sentence. Some five million men, women, and children were sent to the gulag, where they became slave labour. Eventually eighteen million peasants or other enemies of the state from all over the Soviet Union were deported.

Agricultural production dropped like a stone, but Stalin still insisted that quotas for grain and other foods be met. It was "imperative to export." By 1931 the state was expropriating seed grain so that there was nothing to sow the next year. Reports of famine were coming in from all over. Over a million had starved to death in Kazakhstan by 1932. Ukraine, which with its rich black soil had always been the breadbasket of Russia, was equally hard hit. Now its villages were deserted, corpses lay unburied, orphaned children begged along the railways, and reports circulated of cannibalism. Stalin, who seems to have had a particular hatred for Ukraine, persuaded himself that any trouble there was the result of

the disloyalty of the Ukrainian Communists in collabora-
tion with the peasants to sabotage his plan. He complained
that the starving Ukrainian peasants were upsetting others
by their "whining." They were also, he was convinced, trying
to help the Soviet Union's enemy, Poland, by weakening the
borderlands. So they were traitors too. (Stalin had a lifelong
pattern of blaming anything that went wrong in the Soviet
Union on foreign powers and their saboteur agents inside the
country.) In 1933 he laid to rest his fear of attack by his neighbours, at least temporarily, by signing non-aggression pacts
with Poland and Japan. This gave him an even freer hand to
bring the peasants completely to heel. The government now
declared that all food was state property. People were shot to
death for picking up a rotting potato in a field or scrabbling
in the dirt for grains of wheat.

As far as is known, Stalin never had any doubts about
what he had done. If anything, he had become even harder
and self-contained after his second wife, whom he seems to
have genuinely loved, shot herself in the autumn of 1932. He
dismissed the reports of famine as a "fairy tale" and claimed
those who were starving had brought it on themselves to dis-
credit the revolution. In 1934 he declared a stunning victory.
One of his faithful henchmen said Stalin had brought about
"the greatest revolution history has ever known."

Having exerted his will over the countryside, Stalin now
turned his attention to those institutions which still had some
autonomy: the Party itself, the military, and the state police,
the NKVD. He used the murder of a popular party leader in
Leningrad, as St. Petersburg was now known, to start a series
of purges of what he claimed were thousands, possibly millions, of traitors and saboteurs at the heart of the state. He
replaced the head of the NKVD with Nikolai Yezhov, a tiny,

murderous loyalist, who carried out a series of "investigations" which roped in ever-larger numbers of servants of the state and members of the general public. In 1936 leading Communists who had been trusted subordinates of Lenin and key figures in the Revolution were tried in a series of show trials on absurd and unsubstantiated charges. They had always been traitors, it was said, and had plotted to murder Stalin. By 1937 the accusations were even more fantastical and terrifying in their scope. Yezhov now claimed that he had discovered a widespread and co-ordinated conspiracy throughout the state's institutions and the Soviet Union. Its purpose was to restore capitalism, and it had already carried out massive sabotage, including, it was solemnly noted, the castration of prize sheep.

Stalin genuinely seems to have believed that the revolution was threatened from both within and without. His ideological position led him to think in such terms, for he accepted completely the view that the struggle between classes was inevitable and continuing. Capitalism and capitalist countries were bound by the laws of history to seek to destroy socialism. "Is it not clear," he asked in a dramatic speech to the Party's Central Committee, "that as long as capitalist encirclement exists we will have wreckers, spies, diversionists and murderers sent to the interior by agents of foreign states?" So, with Yezhov's willing support, he announced a policy of the "direct physical elimination of the counter-revolution." In a toast on the twentieth anniversary of the Bolshevik revolution, Stalin said, "We will mercilessly destroy anyone who, by his deeds or his thoughts — yes, his thoughts! — threatens the unity of the socialist state. To the complete destruction of all enemies, themselves and their kin!"

The ensuing purges did not spare the elites or ordinary

people: 98 members of the Central Committee out of a total of
139 were shot, as well as hundreds of thousands of Soviet citizens who happened to be deemed the wrong class or the wrong
ethnicity. Poles, Ukrainians, kulaks, children of kulaks, anyone who believed in a religion — all these were now enemies
of the revolution. So eventually was Yezhov himself. Local
NKVD offices were told to set quotas for arrest and execution.
If they failed to produce enough names, they too were suspected of sabotage, and paid the price. Soviet citizens were
turned in by their neighbours or by the omnipresent inform-
ers for crimes such as telling a joke about Stalin — or failing
to report someone else who had told a joke. By the end of 1938
alone, the zealous NKVD had executed 386,000.

The leadership of the armed forces was devastated. The
defence minister, Marshal M. N. Tukhachevsky, one of the
leading military thinkers of his time, was accused of con-
spiring with Hitler's Germany against the Soviet Union. He
was shot in 1937 along with seven other top generals. In the
ensuing purges, thirty-four thousand officers were arrested.
Two-thirds died, including 3 marshals, 16 generals, 15 admi-
rals, and 264 colonels. In 1938 Stalin said jovially to his new
defence minister, "Klim, do you still have some lieutenants
capable of taking command of divisions?" Marshal Georgy
Zhukov, who became the Soviet Union's leading general in
the Second World War, later said of Stalin: "He destroyed,
destroyed the army's whole top echelon. We entered the war
without the army's top echelon. There wasn't anybody."

While Stalin was destroying agriculture and killing or
imprisoning many of his most skilled and productive compatriots, the enemies of the Soviet Union were gaining strength.
In Japan firmly anti-Communist militarists were now in control, and in 1939 there was a brief, undeclared war between

the Soviet Union and Japan in the Far East. It ended in a non-aggression agreement, but Stalin could not be sure it would last. In the West, Germany was rearming rapidly and moving to dominate its neighbours. Hitler had made no secret of his conviction that Communism was a Jewish plot. In August 1939 Germany and the Soviet Union signed a non-aggression pact, but again it was doubtful that it would last. Stalin's next and nearly final act of folly was to trust Hitler and refuse to believe the many warning signs that Germany was planning to attack in the summer of 1941. His regime came close to collapsing, and much of the reason for that can be attributed to his obdurate and unflinching determination in the 1930s to continue with his revolution in his way.

JUST AS IT IS impossible to conceive of what happened in the Soviet Union without taking Stalin into account, so it is impossible to separate the policies of the Nazi regime from Hitler. Each man was able to so thoroughly shape and lead his regime that his wishes and thoughts determined the path his nation took. Just as Stalin's colleagues in the Communist Party underestimated him until it was too late, so did the conservatives who made Hitler Chancellor in 1933 fail to understand that they were dealing with a man whose drive for power was limitless, even if it meant his own destruction. An observer described him in 1940 as "the potential suicide *par excellence.* He owns no ties outside his own 'ego'... He is in the privileged position of one who loves nothing and no one but himself... So he can dare all to preserve or magnify his own power... which alone stands between him and speedy death."

Once in power Hitler moved quickly to eliminate the

opposition and bring the German state and German society under control. A month after he had been appointed, a convenient fire in the German parliament, the Reichstag, enabled him to gain the right to rule by decree. He and the Nazi Party moved quickly and ruthlessly to destroy the other political parties, unions, and any other institutions that might stand in their way. In 1934, in the Night of the Long Knives, he turned the secret police, the Gestapo, and his loyal security unit on leading anti-Nazis and on the Nazis' own paramilitaries, whose leader had shown unwelcome independence. Hundreds may have died, and thousands were arrested. Finally, in 1938, two fortuitous scandals removed the top army leadership. The defence minister married a much younger woman with a dubious past; within days, Berlin prostitutes were saying — truthfully — that one of their number had done well for herself. Rumours were also circulating — false, in this case — that the head of the army was homosexual. Both men had to step down, and Hitler announced that he would personally take over control of the armed forces. In the ensuing reshuffle much of the top leadership was removed. The military, which had regarded Hitler as a jumped-up corporal whom they could easily manipulate, acquiesced mutely. Although the military continued to worry about Hitler's reckless foreign policy — and from time to time dreamed of removing him — they were going to follow him down the path to great crimes and the ultimate catastrophe for Germany.

As Stalin accepted as incontrovertible truth the existence of the class struggle throughout history, so Hitler saw a racial struggle. In Stalin's world view the capitalists were plotting against socialism; in Hitler's the inferior races, in particular the Jews, were bent on the destruction of the German race. Hitler's view, like Stalin's, was terrifyingly simple and could be used to explain — and justify — everything and anything. "The impact of Jewry," he said in a speech in 1920, "will never pass away, and the poisoning of the people will not end, as long as the causal agent, the Jew, is not removed from our midst." He never changed his mind. His other key ideas and goals were set equally early: the need to get rid of the weaker members of the German race — those with physical or mental disabilities — and the imperative to satisfy the inexorable march of the German people by providing them with proper living space, *Lebensraum,* which when the time was right would have to be seized from less worthy peoples, such as Poles, Ukrainians, or Russians. The Second World War made it all possible. The Final Solution to kill all of Europe's Jews emerged in its final form when conquest made it possible to set up the death camps in the east. In Germany, the war brought the opportunity for the German state to use euthanasia on its own citizens, including those who had been wounded in the fighting. And the cleansing of the conquered lands in Poland and the Soviet Union of their indigenous inhabitants to make way for German settlers was now possible too.

For Hitler war was not just a tool to be used by the German people; it was the highest and noblest expression of their struggle for survival. He had fought joyfully for Germany in the First World War and suffered an agonizing humiliation when the war ended in German defeat and the signing of the Treaty of Versailles. He was determined on undoing that outcome and that treaty, and did not want to settle for anything less than a war of revenge on Germany's enemies. From the moment he gained power he gave priority to a large-scale program of rearmament and to breaking what he saw as the chains of the Treaty of Versailles. In open defiance of its terms, he established an air force and introduced conscription as well as markedly increasing the size of the German army. In 1936 he marched troops into the Rhineland, which had been demilitarized under the treaty. In Germany there was widespread approval, and the outside world took no action. It is at this point, according to Ian Kershaw, that Hitler became the foremost believer in his own cult. In a speech in Munich he said, "I go with the certainty of a sleepwalker along the path laid out for me by Providence." Hubris had taken him firmly in tow.

The successes continued to mount. In March 1938 he incorporated Austria into Germany. Again the Germans exulted and the world did nothing. Then, in the summer of 1938, he turned his attention to neighbouring Czechoslovakia, demanding that it cede the Sudetenland, which had a majority of German speakers. The Czechs appealed to Britain and France for support. Hitler was ready for war, even if his generals were not, but at the last minute, at Munich in September, the British and the French prevailed on the Czech government to hand over the Sudetenland. Hitler had won a bloodless victory, but he was furious at being deprived of his war and ever after regarded the Munich Agreement as one of his biggest mistakes. What also worried him was that his German people had not shown the right warlike spirit and enthusiasm. At a meeting with a crowd of German editors and journalists, he spoke about the need to get the Germans ready so that "the inner voice of the people itself slowly begins to cry out for the use of force."

By this stage his plans were well developed. He foresaw a series of wars, each providing a springboard for the next. He would start with Britain and France, then move on to the Soviet Union, after that to the United States, which he saw as the great geostrategic threat to German dominance of the globe, and finally on to the rest of the world. He had already thought out what benefits each victory would bring. In Europe, Germany would annex those territories occupied by Germanic-type peoples: Alsace and Lorraine, Belgium and the Netherlands, and possibly the north of France and the Scandinavian countries. Southern European countries would become satellites of Germany or of its ally Italy. In the east the Ural Mountains would be a convenient dividing line between the German Empire and that of Japan, another ally. The Japanese Empire would, for the time being, control Asia. Africa was to be divided into three parts, with Italy controlling the north, Germany much of sub-Saharan Africa, and possibly a friendly South Africa in charge of the southern zone. When it came to the far-off future, after the defeat of the United States, Hitler was less clear on the details. He expected, however, that the German race would eventually have to fight the Japanese.

The newly acquired lands in the east would be stocked with Germans, who would be given farms. The existing inhabitants would be killed or driven out. They might be spared to be used as cheap or slave labour, but in that case they would be sterilized. In October 1939, shortly after the start of the Second World War, Hitler appointed Heinrich Himmler as Reich Commissioner for the Strengthening of Germandom to put these plans into effect.

The war itself initially unfolded as Hitler had hoped. In the late summer, he and Stalin signed their non-aggression pact which included a secret deal to divide up the countries that lay between them. With the Soviet Union conveniently neutralized, Hitler moved quickly to invade Poland at the start of September. Although Britain and France declared war on Germany, they could do little but watch as Poland was overrun, first by Germany and then by the Soviet Union. His rapid victory in Poland confirmed — if confirmation were needed — Hitler's view that he knew better than any of his generals. As he said in a speech to some two hundred senior officers that November: "I must in all modesty describe my own person: irreplaceable. Neither a military man nor a civilian could replace me...I shall strike and not capitulate. The fate of the Reich depends only on me."

The following spring, he gave the order to invade France, and six weeks later the French capitulated. The British under Churchill refused to make peace, and Hitler gave half-hearted orders to prepare an invasion. When the head of his air force, Hermann Goering, suggested bombing the British as a prelude, or even to bring about their submission, Hitler accepted with alacrity. He was already turning his attention to his next great enemy, the Soviet Union. In any case, he thought a bombing campaign in Britain would be much easier than a seaborne invasion. When his generals demurred at the prospect of a two-front war, Hitler swept aside their objections. Once the Soviet Union had surrendered, Britain would have no choice but to do the same. He ignored the evidence that President Franklin Delano Roosevelt was slowly positioning the United States to support Britain and that the British showed no signs of wanting to sue for peace.

On June 22, 1941, Hitler invaded the Soviet Union. Although his forces swept the ill-prepared Soviet troops aside and advanced hundreds of miles eastwards, they did not reach their targets, which included Leningrad and Moscow, before the snows set in. It is said that several of the German generals sent letters to their booksellers in Berlin to ask for copies of the memoirs of Napoleon's generals from 1812, when the French armies had come to grief in Russia. The Soviet forces pulled themselves together and fought a dogged retreat while partisans harassed the ever-lengthening German supply lines. Although it was not fully apparent at the time, the invasion of the Soviet Union paved the way for Hitler's downfall.

His second great mistake came in December that year, when his ally Japan attacked the United States at Pearl Harbor. That brought the United States, with all its manpower and resources, into war in Asia. It was not yet involved militarily in Europe, however, and might never have been if Hitler, in a show of bravado, had not declared war on it.

By late 1943 Hitler was coming to realize that Germany might not win the great victory he had envisaged. At least not this time. So he placed his hopes in a separate peace with the Soviet Union or just possibly with the United States and Britain, which would leave him free to deal with one enemy at a time. In the spring of 1945, even as Allied forces advanced from both east and west on Berlin, he still continued to hope for a miracle. He also issued orders to destroy all remaining German infrastructure to slow the advance. When Speer pointed out that this would also grievously harm the German people, Hitler said they were lost anyway if the war was lost, and that they would not need to survive. By April 1945 the reality of Germany's total defeat had at last made its way into his bunker. On the 30th he committed suicide. The war, he said in his last testament, would be remembered as "the most glorious and valiant manifestation of a nation's will to existence."

ALL FOUR LEADERS I have considered here — Wilson,

Thatcher, Hitler, and Stalin — lived in times that gave them great opportunities, and all four had the inner drive and conviction to seize them. Their successes hardened their self-confidence to the point where it became unshakeable, and it was from that point that they plunged wilfully ahead. The Greeks believed that hubris was usually punished by a dramatic reversal of fortune. Wilson and Thatcher did pay a penalty in the humiliation of political defeat. Hitler committed suicide when it became clear that his dreams to dominate the world had come to nothing. Stalin, alone among the four, did not pay the price for his hubris in his lifetime. But if there is an afterlife, perhaps he has seen the end of everything he worked for with the collapse of Communism worldwide, the end of the Soviet Union, and the dismantling of its empire in Eastern Europe.

THREE

DARING

ON DECEMBER 1, 1783, four of France's leading aristocrats escorted a large, gaily striped red-and-yellow balloon into its launching place in the Tuileries Garden, in the heart of Paris. A huge crowd of nearly half a million, many of whom had contributed to the balloon's cost, watched as Dr. Alexandre Charles and his assistant, Nicolas-Louis Robert, climbed into a wicker basket filled with ballast, fur coats, and a light meal of cold chicken and champagne; the ropes were cast off and the balloon ascended into the skies. "What's the use of a balloon?" someone asked Benjamin Franklin, who was among the onlookers. He replied: "What's the use of a new-born baby?"

Although the Montgolfier brothers had already experimented with hot air balloons, this was the first manned flight using the more efficient hydrogen. The balloon sailed off towards the northwest and came to rest some twenty-eight miles outside Paris. Robert climbed down to lighten the load, and Charles sailed off again, going up to ten thousand feet, where he was amazed to see the sun set for a second time that day. His ears began to ache, and he manoeuvred the balloon back towards the earth. "Nothing," he later said, "will ever quite equal that moment of total hilarity that filled my whole body at the moment of take-off. I felt we were flying away from the Earth and all its troubles and persecutions for ever. It was not mere delight. It was a sort of physical rapture…I exclaimed to my companion Monsieur Robert, 'I'm finished with the Earth. From now on our place is in the sky!'"

The next decade saw dozens of manned balloons sailing across the skies in Europe and in North America. In 1785 came the first successful balloon crossing of the English Channel (and the first death in another attempt). Four years afterwards, Jeanne-Geneviève Garnerin made the first recorded parachute jump from a balloon by a woman. Two decades later, Sophie Blanchard was the Royal Aeronaut under the restored monarchy in France. The fragile and fearless Sophie, who had been a favourite of Napoleon's as well, was famous for solo flights when, dressed in tight white dresses and wonderful hats with coloured feathers, she carried out acrobatics and set off fireworks. She died in 1819, during a dazzling display, when the hydrogen in her balloon caught fire and she plummeted to earth. The dangers have not stopped balloonists to this day.

Sometimes the daring only risk their own lives, but sometimes the stakes are much higher. In 1940 Winston Churchill took over the leadership of the United Kingdom at a moment when the very survival of the British people was at stake. On May 10 he drove away from Buckingham Palace, where he had just been sworn in as prime minister. "I hope it is not too late," he told his bodyguard. "I am very much afraid it is. We can only do our best." The situation was grim indeed. German forces were racing through France, driving wedges between the Allied armies. The Belgian forces were collapsing, and it was becoming clear that the French will to fight was vanishing. The British and some of the French were falling back to the coastal ports. By May 20 the British were starting to plan for a mass evacuation from the port of Dunkirk, where over three hundred thousand men were now gathered. It was not clear that they could be rescued. At home Churchill faced a cabinet divided over whether Britain should sound out Hitler about peace terms. Churchill's own view was that Britain had nothing to gain, since it would be negotiating from a position of weakness. "We should get no worse terms," he told his colleagues, "if we went on fighting, even if we were beaten, than were open to us now."

Knowing what we now know about Hitler, Churchill was right to choose to fight on. What the new prime minister could not know, but may have guessed, is that Hitler was determined on the complete defeat and subjugation of Britain. For two days, however, the decision hung in the balance in the cabinet. Neville Chamberlain, Churchill's predecessor, and Lord Halifax, the foreign secretary, were for making an overture to Germany through Italy. Churchill managed to win Chamberlain over to his view, leaving Halifax isolated. On May 28 Churchill told the cabinet: "We shall go on and we shall fight it out, here or elsewhere, and if at last the long story is to end, it were better it should end, not through surrender, but only when we are rolling senseless on the ground." He was not sure that either he or Britain would survive; as he told a close aide, he would not be surprised if he was dead in three months. As his own career had shown, however, Churchill was at his best when he faced long odds.

Let us imagine for a moment an alternative version of history. If Britain had come to terms with Germany, Hitler's domination of Europe would have been virtually unchallengeable. Germany would probably still have attacked the Soviet Union — that was part of Hitler's long-term plan — but there would have been no British air force to bomb Germany, no British supplies for the Soviet forces, and no ally left in Europe and the Far East for the United States as it confronted the Axis powers. More, there would have been no independent Britain to act as a base for the invasion of Europe in 1944. Our world would have been very different indeed.

What is it that makes some people more daring than others? Launch themselves into the atmosphere — or into space; climb mountains or squeeze into dark caverns under the earth; risk their lives in extreme sports? And daring is not confined to particular professions. History gives us many examples of inventors and scientists — Alexander Graham Bell or Marie Curie — who staked their futures and their happiness on their work, or of entrepreneurs who have gambled everything they had on a particular investment. As researchers find out more and more about the genetic makeup of human beings they are able to pick out genes that underlie particular traits, whether it be a propensity to be happy or violent — or to take risks. Increasingly, however, scientists are also arguing that environment plays a key role in triggering certain characteristics which might otherwise lie dormant. Professor Tim Spector at King's College, London, who specializes in studying identical twins, believes environment may be even more important in developing personality than genes. To date, the scientific jury is still out.

When we try to pick out the characteristics that risk-takers share, we almost invariably find curiosity — about what lies over the horizon, for example — and the determination to find out. Sheer endurance helps too. Think of the first sea-borne adventurers from Europe, who set off into uncharted oceans not knowing whether or not they would fall off the edge of the world. In what now seem like impossibly small and fragile sailing boats, they faced storms, privations, disease, and often hostile shores around the globe. They were followed by the explorers who then criss-crossed the Americas or Africa by foot and boat, struggling through thick forests, across vast open plains, down rapid rivers, or over high mountain passes.

The first expeditions from the outside world for Everest in the 1920s were looking for a mountain which was almost entirely a mystery, from its approaches to its structure. The first two expeditions were necessarily reconnaissance ones through a largely unknown Tibet, with its deep valleys, plateaus, and high mountain passes. Everything from equipment to food had to be carried in by horse or mule and, at the higher altitudes, by local porters or the members of the expedition. The men struggled on, for months on end, their feet sore, their breathing short, frequently weakened by fever or dysentery as they tried to find a route to Everest. That was finally achieved when Oliver Wheeler, a young Canadian surveyor, discovered the way onto the high North Col underneath the summit. A skilled climber from his youth in the Canadian Rockies, he worked away from the rest of the expedition for much of the time to map some two hundred square miles around Everest, climbing from one peak to another to set up his observation points and take photographs for mapmaking. He and his porters, all of them heavily laden, often camped on heights above twenty thousand feet, in howling winds, while rain, sleet, snow, or falling rocks crashed around their tents. Most of the rest of the expedition were British, survivors of the Great War, which had just ended. George Mallory, the greatest climber of his generation before the war, had left a wife and children behind. He wrote his last letter, on May 24, 1924, to his beloved Ruth, from a tent high on Everest: "The candle is burning out and I must stop. Darling I wish you the best I can — that your anxiety will be at an end before you get this — with the best news, which will also be the quickest. It is 50 to 1 against us but we'll have a whack yet and do ourselves proud." On June 9 he and his climbing partner, the younger Sandy Irvine, were seen for the last time from below, some eight hundred vertical feet below the summit and apparently moving up towards it. It will never be known whether they made it. Mallory's mummified corpse was discovered in 1999.

Mallory was once asked why he wanted to climb Everest, and he replied simply, "Because it's there." For scientists, the challenges are different but the curiosity and the motivation to find a solution are the same. Dr. Barry Marshall was a modest, little-known internal medicine specialist in Perth, on the west coast of Australia, when he became convinced in the 1980s that stomach ulcers and indeed most stomach cancers were caused by bacteria. The prevailing view in the medical establishment was that the causes lay in such factors as stress, excessive alcohol, or spicy foods. The standard prescription was, as it had been for decades, for the patients to calm down, take antacids, eat bland food, and drink lots of milk. Additional cures ranged from antidepressants to surgery to remove part of the stomach. If Marshall was right, a course of antibiotics could cure ulcers, and there was some evidence to support his view. The medical establishment remained highly skeptical, as did the drug companies, which were doing very well with their antacids and antidepressants. Marshall got little support for his research and, for ethical reasons, could not test his theory on healthy patients. So he used himself.

Marshall swallowed a mix made with bacteria from the stomach of a patient with ulcers. He remembers his stomach gurgling slightly. Five days later he was vomiting regularly, he was exhausted, and his appetite had gone. Five days after that, he had a biopsy on his stomach, which showed that the suspect bacteria were everywhere and that he was suffering from serious inflammation and gastritis, the underlying cause of stomach cancer. At this point he told his wife about his experiment. She was understandably furious but agreed to let him continue without antibiotics for a couple of days more. As soon as he started taking the drugs, he began to recover. In 2005, his theory now widely accepted, he won the Nobel Prize for medicine. It is reassuring to know that today he is working on flu vaccines.

Risk-takers are often optimists too, believing that this time the airplane they have built will get off the ground or the new company they have set up will work. A British journalist in Hong Kong once asked a local why he kept going to the casino when the odds of winning were so bad. The man flatly disagreed with him: the odds were fifty-fifty, because either he won or he lost. Age can play a part as well in a willingness to take risks: the young tend to think they will live forever, or at least have many second chances, while their elders know that is not true. When I was a teenager, I could go on roller coasters; now I could not do it for love or money. I am too aware of what might go wrong.

Not all risk-takers, however, are heedless of the dangers they might face. Rather, many both understand and choose to accept the possibility that they might fail and so bring trouble, even disaster, on themselves and perhaps their families and societies. Yet for them the challenge and the hope of succeeding are worth the risk. The knowledge that failure, even death, are possible can add spice to the risk. I once interviewed a Canadian general about peacekeeping. He was perceptive and thoughtful, but what I remember most now is what he said when I had turned off the tape recorder. Few soldiers, he said, would ever admit it publicly, but part of the attraction of the profession was that edge that came from knowing you could be killed. It was the sort of feeling you got, he said, riding a motorcycle fast or bungee jumping.

Lord Reith, the creator and long-time director of the British Broadcasting Corporation, was quite open about it in his memoir about his time on the Western Front in the First World War. He was in charge of a transport unit, which is not as mundane as it sounds, for he and his men had to drive carts loaded with supplies up to the lines, along roads that were raked by enemy machine-gun fire and artillery. He was nevertheless happy and indeed thrilled. "Interesting to walk across a turnip field," he remarked, "knowing that at any moment one will stop walking for the most conclusive of all reasons." When he was quite badly wounded and sent back to Britain, his main reaction was one of anger and impatience to get back to the front. "I'm more disgusted than I can say," he wrote home. "I was getting on so well and enjoying the work and everything." And, he added, "I've spoilt my best uniform." (His memoir was not published until the 1960s, perhaps because it was out of tune with the increasingly popular anti-war literature of writers such as Siegfried Sassoon or Wilfred Owen.)

For whatever reason, some people will willingly seek out risk; others have it forced upon them and may surprise themselves by how they deal with it. Libussa Fritz-Krockow came from an old landed family in Pomerania, then in the east of Germany. (Today, thanks to the fortunes of war, it is in

Poland.) She was married, in the last old-style Junker wedding ever to be held on the family estate, in the summer of 1944, as the Allies were spreading out towards Germany from their landings in Normandy and the Soviet armies were advancing from the east. Old families such as hers had always sent their men into the Prussian army, and the values they held dear were masculine and military — discipline, order, obedience to superiors and to the state, and a readiness to sacrifice oneself. In what was about to come, such values had little use.

In her memoir, *Hour of the Women*, Fritz-Krockow describes how she learned to deal with the occupying Russian soldiers, bribe officials, scavenge for useful items, and steal food. She and her mother took over responsibility for the family, which included her newborn daughter, from her stepfather, who had crumpled as his world collapsed. The men of her world, she remarked without bitterness, were brave, ready to die nobly in battle. "When it came to ducking your head and crawling on all fours to pick the spinach you needed so as not to starve — with no room for honor and duty — that was where they failed. Such tasks they left to us." After a harrowing journey in and out of Allied-occupied Germany, she managed to bring her small party of women, which included her own newborn baby and her mother, safely to the West. Her beloved stepfather, they discovered, was in a camp in the Russian zone. Fritz-Krockow made one last trip eastwards across the border. She reconnoitred the camp and found a spot, out of sight of the Russian guards, where the fence was only wooden slats. She managed to whisper through the cracks to a passing prisoner to get word to her stepfather to meet her there when it got dark. Somehow she got her hands on a pry bar and crept back to the rendezvous. To her dismay, her stepfather refused to leave: it was too difficult and too dangerous, and he did not want to risk her life. It was only when she exclaimed that she would not know what to do or where to go without his help that he agreed to come.

Sometimes people take risks because honour demands it or because they are unwilling or unable to contemplate alternatives. Many of the generals in charge of Europe's armies before the First World War were well aware of the mounting evidence that changes in technology were making it more and more difficult — and costly — to carry out attacks on well-defended positions. Wars around the world — the American Civil War or the more recent Russo-Japanese War of 1904–5 — as well as those in Europe itself, such as the Balkan Wars of 1912 and 1913, showed the impact of the dramatic increase in firepower. Long-range artillery, the new machine guns, and more accurate and rapid-firing infantry rifles combined to create a deadly zone of fire, often a thousand yards or more, across which attackers were meant to advance. Yet the men making the plans still assumed that their armies would go on the offensive when war broke out. Better-trained and motivated soldiers in greater numbers than the defenders would, so they hoped, overwhelm the enemy and win decisive victories. In any case, it was almost unthinkable for the military leaders to go to the civilians and admit that they could no longer guarantee victory. When the crisis of 1914 came, they were in the position of gamblers who had to risk an all-or-nothing bet. Moreover, honour demanded it. "It will be a hopeless struggle," the chief of the Austrian General Staff wrote to his mistress, "but it must be pursued, because so old a Monarchy and so glorious an army cannot go down ingloriously."

Like the general staffs before the First World War, groups can hold values that encourage risk-taking. There has been much debate among historians about whether the spread of Protestantism, with its insistence on individual responsibility and rewards for hard work and sobriety, fostered the rise of capitalism. More recently, keen observers such as Gillian Tett, Michael Lewis, and Andrew Sorkin have tried to explain the crash of 2008 in terms of the values of the bankers involved, where risking more and more for greater returns was the norm and caution was seen as cowardice (and moreover did not bring big rewards in the form of bonuses). Many of the traders who were creating and marketing more and more dangerous financial instruments were like bands of brothers (and they were almost all men). At Morgan Guaranty in London, for example, the special highly paid unit which dealt in the arcane and highly profitable "credit default swaps" prided itself as being quite different from the rest of the bank. "We had this sense of being special, of being detached from everyone else, a little team that was very tightly bound together," said one member. As their successes, and their rewards, mounted up, they and others like them came to believe that they could never lose.

Conversely collective values may discourage risk-taking. There is a long-standing discussion among scholars about whether or not classical Chinese civilization, with its stress on harmony and a literary culture, militated against innovation. To take just one example, a civil servant who once invented a pump to keep fresh air flowing into mines — thus making it possible to dig deeper — received praise from the emperor for the poem he wrote describing his invention, not for the thing itself. Can that difference in values help to explain why Britain took off in the Industrial Revolution and China, for all its previous advances in technology, did not? In our own century, innovation is seen as one of the

keys, perhaps the most important one, to continuing economic health. Canadian scholars at Montreal's Concordia
University published an interesting study in 2015 on a brain-
storming exercise they had done with groups of students
in Canada and Taiwan. Both had to come up with creative
answers to problems; for example, what would be the practical benefits of a second thumb? The Canadian students, cat-
egorized as products of a more individualistic culture, came
up with twice as many ideas. They were also more prepared
to promote their own ideas and criticize those of their colleagues than the Taiwanese, who came from a more collec-
tivist culture. (On the quality of the ideas, the Asian team
scored slightly higher, so we may wonder what it is precisely
the study showed.)

Perhaps history can help us by providing examples as we
search for answers. I want to look at people from several different times and societies who in their own ways took great
risks, and who in so doing changed their worlds, and perhaps ours too. Max Aitken was an entrepreneur who helped
to transform Canadian business before the First World War
and then went on to play an important role in British public life. Richard Nixon took a huge political risk and perhaps
even a personal one when he visited Beijing in 1972. His visit
marked the end of the deep freeze in relations between the
United States and China and the start of a new era. Samuel de
Champlain, the great explorer, not only extended the knowledge Europeans had of the New World, but he established the
first permanent French settlement in Canada.

WHEN CANADIANS COMPARE THEMSELVES to Americans, they
often worry about whether they are individualistic enough.

Where, we sometimes ask, is Canada's Bill Gates or Steve Jobs or Henry Ford? Are Canadians too cautious? A constant theme in the speeches of Stephen Harper, the prime minister, has been that Canadians do in fact make good entrepreneurs. Yet he also points out that his government does much to encourage innovation and risk-taking. In 2011 he announced the Year of the Entrepreneur, "to raise public awareness of the importance of entrepreneurs to Canada's economy and pay tribute to their drive and dedication." Roger Martin, the long-time dean of the Rotman School of Management at the University of Toronto, has spent much of his career exhorting his fellow Canadians to think more boldly, with dozens of articles and speeches and books such as *Playing to Win: How Strategy Really Works*. Should Canadians be worried that they are somehow falling down in the international race for success?

Perhaps history can offer some comfort. We do not remember him much today, but Max Aitken, who is known best by his later title of Lord Beaverbrook, is one of Canada's greatest and most successful entrepreneurs. He took huge chances in business, in politics, and in the newspaper business, and gained riches, power, and influence in both Canada and the United Kingdom. Beaverbrook came from a background that was, if anything, antithetical to the making of vast fortunes. Although he later painted a picture of an impoverished childhood in which he had to go barefoot, his family was comfortable by the standards of the time (and if Beaverbrook did not wear shoes, it was by choice). His father was a Presbyterian clergyman who hoped his sons would go to university and into respectable professions. That was not for Max.

Born in 1879, he was a scrawny, unprepossessing boy with a wide grin and large ears, and he was to grow into a short and ugly man. A "wicked Buddha" was how one of his biographers described him. As a child, Beaverbrook was restless and impatient with routine. That never changed. "Nothing," he said in 1922, "is so bad as consistency." He was clever but did not like school; he skipped classes and got poor grades. He disliked following orders and repeatedly defied his parents. His mother, who was a tougher character than his father, beat him, but it never stopped him from offending again. When things got too hot at home, he would take off, sometimes hiding out at a sympathetic neighbour's. He was always able to make useful friends — partly because of his undoubted charm, but he also had an ability to sum up others, both their strengths and their weaknesses. Early on he demonstrated too a keen interest in business and an eye for opportunities. He took on a big newspaper route and subcontracted the deliveries. At the age of fourteen he borrowed the press of the local newspaper, his employer at the time, to start his own, short-lived newspaper. To boost circulation, he announced prizes for the best essays. It was one of his rare unsuccessful ventures, closing after three issues.

At the age of sixteen he abandoned formal education for good and with the help of an early patron — the future prime minister of Canada, R. B. Bennett — managed to get himself hired as a law clerk and articling student in the small New Brunswick town of Chatham. The law bored him as much as school, and he was so lackadaisical that he was fired after a year. He drifted to Halifax, the capital of Nova Scotia and the business centre of the Maritimes, and for a time eked out a living by selling insurance door to door. When that palled, he made his way out west to Calgary, where Bennett was now established as a successful lawyer and fledgling politician. Bennett was unable or unwilling to hire him on at his firm, so Beaverbrook threw himself into various low-grade business ventures, such as a bowling alley. An attempt to sell meat to railway work camps failed when the meat spoiled. He was obliged to skip town, leaving his debts unpaid. He was now twenty years old, a failure, but with a hunger for success and all the good things that life could offer, from money to women.

Back in the Maritimes, Beaverbrook had a moment he later called his "conversion." He resolved, he claimed, to stop wasting time. He was going to give up gambling — at least at cards — and take up instead hard work and thrift. He chose a good moment in Canada's development, and he had the qualities, from ruthless ambition to a knack for business, to take advantage of that. In the 1890s the country was booming, and there was plenty of scope for bold entrepreneurs, whether in mining, manufacturing, or finance. The newly determined Beaverbrook started by selling blocks of bonds for some of the utility companies that were emerging, but he soon realized that the big money lay in becoming the promoter who underwrote the whole issue of new stocks or bonds. With another stroke of luck, he caught the eye of John Stairs, a highly successful and respected Halifax businessman. Beaverbrook, so one story goes, turned up in Stairs's office telling everyone there he had been hired as his personal secretary. Whatever the truth, Stairs was certainly impressed by Beaverbrook's audacity and abilities, and involved the younger man in his expanding business ventures.

Beaverbrook had at last found his métier. He proved a formidable deal-maker and started to lay the basis of his great fortune. In 1903 he became one of the founders of the Royal Securities Corporation, which was going to play a significant role in creating massive new Canadian companies which would dominate their sectors of the economy, among them the Montreal Engineering Company and the controversial Canada Cement Company. He had a talent for picking good and competent men, but he was never easy to work for. While he could be charming when he chose, and outrageously flattering to those he needed, he bullied his subordinates. Waste of any sort infuriated him; one of his bugbears was the excessive use of company stationery, and he spent much energy trying to get railway companies to pay up when he had not used the return half of a ticket. He was, however, reasonably generous to his family, although he preferred to see little of them.

As he moved up into the Canadian establishment, Beaverbrook acquired his own tailor, learned to play golf, and joined respectable clubs. In 1906 he married Gladys Drury, who was from a distinguished Halifax family. She was a redhead, taller than him, and far more beautiful. In a passage for his autobiography which he left out of the published version, he claimed that he only married because he had reached the stage in his life and career where a wife seemed useful and expected. "And so I had made what I thought to be the best marriage. I do not say that I made her life easier for her but I can claim that I made it more interesting and exciting." She was a good and loyal wife, bringing up their children and managing the family's increasingly grand houses. Nor did she complain when Beaverbrook proved to be as great a seducer of women as he was persuasive in business or politics. Many women found him irresistible, from actresses to society beauties, and, possibly, his wife's younger sister. He charmed and amused them and lavished fur coats and diamonds on them. Yet when Gladys died suddenly at the age of thirty-nine of a brain tumour, he was — for a time — overcome with grief and perhaps guilt. (He also took good care to burn almost all of her papers.)

By 1907 Beaverbrook was a millionaire in an age when that was still rare, and his wealth continued to grow as he took one risk after another. As he later wrote in a treatise on "Success," "Examine your profit and loss account before you go out to conquer the financial world, and then go for conquest — if the account justifies the enterprise." It was not as simple as he made it sound. In those years before the First World War, Beaverbrook was frequently on the edge of success or failure, his mood swinging between elation and gloom. He was a dedicated and lifelong hypochondriac, but he did suffer real physical misery as a result of the strain he subjected himself to. As a deal reached its crisis point, he suffered from insomnia, nightmares, and stomach upsets. When he had pulled off yet another successful deal, he would collapse. Once he had created a company, he tended to lose interest in it, preferring to draw off his profits and move on to fresh challenges.

The rules of business were looser then in Canada, and Beaverbrook stretched and ignored even those. His prospectuses for new ventures were works of art that often bore little relation to reality. His companies routinely issued securities for sale worth more than the properties backing them. He was also expert at driving up the price of stock and making sure that he and his associates skimmed off their profits first. He made his name, however, in merging companies — three huge ones in one year alone — and each time he came out richer. His many enemies, who included former associates, claimed that he did so at the expense of his partners.

There was a major public uproar when a white-bearded and widely respected Canadian entrepreneur and inventor, Sir Sandford Fleming, publicly accused Beaverbrook of

stealing millions of dollars from Canada Cement, the product
of Beaverbrook's last big Canadian merger of smaller companies. The charges may have been unfair (and Beaverbrook
had not done anything that other respected business figures of the day had not), but they came at a time when public anger at unscrupulous and rapacious businessmen was
growing. From farmers in the West, resentful of the power
of Eastern banks, to progressive reformers across the country, Beaverbrook came to represent all that was wrong with
capitalism. The conclusions of a Canadian historian who has
studied Beaverbrook's Canadian business career in detail are
that "although he often resorted to deception and puffery
to reap the largest possible profit in every transaction, his
actions were never criminally fraudulent."

The whispers of shady dealings were to cling to
Beaverbrook for the rest of his life, even though he became
a respected and influential figure in both Canada and Britain.
He occasionally tried to deal with the charges directly. As
he said to his new friend Winston Churchill in 1911, "There
is an objection to me you must know about. I created all the
big trusts in Canada. None of them are bad trusts but the
Western Farmers attack me very often and sometimes very
offensively." Churchill, who was amused by Beaverbrook,
took him at his word. Others were less forgiving, including
Churchill's wife, Clementine, who once urged her husband:
"Exorcise this bottle Imp." As the leading Labour politician J. H. Thomas once remarked, "Max Aitken came from
Newcastle, New Brunswick. Newcastle wasn't big enough for
Max so he went to Halifax. But Halifax wasn't big enough
either so he went to Montreal. Montreal wasn't big enough so
he went to London. Even London isn't big enough. So he'll go
to hell." Over his long career, many people were to conclude

that Beaverbrook was a wicked man who took a malicious delight in making mischief. "The more I saw of him," wrote General Alan Brooke, Churchill's chief military adviser in the Second World War, "the more I disliked and mistrusted him. An evil genius who exercised the very worst of influence on Winston." Beaverbrook may well have suspected Brooke's antipathy, but he would have shrugged it off. Like many great risk-takers, including Churchill, he did not worry about what other people thought.

In 1910, with his wife in tow, Beaverbrook decided to try life in London. He was only thirty-one and had lots of money and quantities of nerve. The move to Britain was natural enough for an ambitious man, or woman, from the colonies. London lay at the heart of the world's greatest empire and offered greater opportunities for wealth, power, and influence. Beaverbrook already had plenty of the first, but he wanted more of the rest. And he was running out of challenges in Canada (and his fellow Canadians were taking an increasingly dim view of his wheeling and dealing). He rented a flat in London, did some desultory sightseeing, which bored him, and on a whim bought the Rolls-Royce Motor Car company. He continued to manage his Canadian businesses (and opened a London office for Royal Securities) but increasingly found the worlds of politics and newspapers more congenial.

He charmed his way into British society with impressive rapidity. Through his initial introductions he met a wide range of people, from Rudyard Kipling, who became a friend, to Bonar Law, already a leading Conservative politician, who persuaded him to run for Parliament in the autumn of 1910. The seat, near Manchester, was by no means a sure thing for the Conservatives, and especially for a little-known young man from the colonies. Beaverbrook went at it as he would have one of his business ventures, pouring in resources and organizing his campaign meticulously. Ashton-under-Lyne had never seen anything like it; the Beaverbrook campaign divided the whole constituency into districts and assigned a canvasser to each one. In his campaign literature, Beaverbrook typically played with the facts to his advantage, claiming, for example, that he had studied law. He knew that he was a bad speaker, and so his wife did most of the public speaking for him. He won by 196 votes, and his brief career as an elected politician was launched.

It did not start auspiciously. Beaverbrook was an indifferent member of Parliament and rarely spoke. Not surprisingly, he did not pay much attention to party discipline; the party whips found themselves urging him to show up in the House of Commons. For no very clear reason, he was nevertheless made a knight. (His enemies back in Canada suggested it was because he had made large donations to the Conservative Party.) At the same time, he was embarking on a parallel career as a newspaper magnate. In 1911 he made his first investment in the *Daily Express*, the newspaper that he was soon to own and from which he was to campaign for his favourite causes, from Empire Free Trade to appeasement in the 1930s.

In the same year, Beaverbrook found himself in one of his favourite positions, in the middle of a complex struggle and set of negotiations. It was not business this time but politics. Arthur Balfour's resignation had left open the leadership of the Conservative Party, and Beaverbrook backed his close friend, Bonar Law, against the other contenders. Law was inclined to hesitate, even back down, if he felt his candidacy was damaging the party, and much of Beaverbrook's efforts were devoted to keeping him set on course. Beaverbrook also worked behind the scenes to stir up what was intended to look like a spontaneous press campaign in favour of Law. A year after he had arrived in London, Beaverbrook had the satisfaction of being a kingmaker; the other two leading candidates withdrew, and Law became the new leader of the Conservative Party. In a private letter, Balfour's secretary described Beaverbrook as "the little Canadian adventurer" who had manipulated the outcome from behind the scenes in an underhanded fashion. In the years to come it was a charge that was often repeated. There was much truth in it. In the great political crisis of 1916, when Henry Asquith was forced out as prime minister over his running of the war and replaced by David Lloyd George, Beaverbrook played a key role (if not perhaps as great as he later claimed) both in undermining Asquith and in bringing Bonar Law and Lloyd George together so that the latter would have the support of the Conservatives for his coalition government. Lloyd George rewarded Beaverbrook with a title, and a year later brought him into the cabinet as minister of information.

In 1922, as Lloyd George's support in turn fell away, Beaverbrook successfully helped to bring about the downfall of his government and bring back a Conservative government with Law as prime minister. By 1924 Law was dead, and Beaverbrook was never to enjoy quite such extended influence again. He still mattered a great deal in British life and politics, of course, and through his wide circle of friends and his stable of newspapers — the *Daily Express* had now been joined by the *Sunday Express* and the *Evening Standard* — continued to cause waves. In 1929 he tried to remove Law's successor, Stanley Baldwin, as leader of the Conservative Party, which led Baldwin to his famous comment on "power without responsibility — the prerogative of the harlot throughout the ages." Baldwin did not forgive Beaverbrook for the attempt, and for much of the 1930s the latter remained on the outer fringes of power.

With the coming of the Second World War and Churchill's subsequent ascent to the prime ministership, Beaverbrook was on the inside again. Churchill, who had been attacked by the Beaverbrook press for his firm stance against Germany before the war, was more forgiving than Baldwin and made him minister of aircraft production. Beaverbrook took it on with his usual vigour (although General Brooke was by no means alone in thinking his methods chaotic) and helped to cheer Churchill up during the darkest days of the war. He could never resist an intrigue, though, and even imagined that he might supplant Churchill. In the postwar years, Beaverbrook continued to stir things up — campaigning against British entry into the Common Market, for example — but his influence was no longer what it had been. He died in 1964 in his huge house in Surrey. It had been a long voyage from the manse in New Brunswick, and in his wake he had left many enemies, some friends, and much change.

FOR BEAVERBROOK BUSINESS WAS where he risked his wealth and his reputation; politics was a game which he could play, or not, as he chose. For full-time politicians the stakes are different. They are in a profession where they can be dismissed, like Bismarck by his monarch or Margaret Thatcher by her colleagues, from one day to the next. In democracies politicians live too with the knowledge that in any election, the voters can reject them.

Richard Nixon was in certain respects a most unlikely

politician, especially in an age when image mattered. In his famous television debates with John F. Kennedy, he came over as shifty and sweaty even though he had the better of the arguments. He was not good at patting children on the head or slapping strangers on the back. "It doesn't come naturally to me to be a buddy-buddy boy," he once complained to a journalist. "I can't really let my hair down with anyone." His attempts to put his visitors at ease often had the opposite effect. His awkward jokes usually fell flat. "He was a man totally lacking in personal grace," said a senior colleague, "with no sense of the proper distance to keep in human relations." Nixon envied much about his contemporary and predecessor John F. Kennedy: the relaxed informality, the wide grin and ruffled hair, the ease with which he tossed a football around or sailed his dinghy off Hyannis Port. Nixon could never pull it off. When he went for what was said to be a spontaneous walk along the beach in California, the press snickered at his polished leather shoes and formal trousers. When his staff persuaded him to get a dog to help his image, it had to be given a trail of biscuits to come near its master. Yet when Nixon tried to bring style and dignity to the office of the president, as Kennedy had also done successfully, that too went awry. After a visit to the French president Charles de Gaulle, Nixon ordered elaborate new uniforms in white and gold for the White House police. The press talked about comic operas, and the uniforms vanished, although pieces turned up later at a rock concert.

In other and important ways, however, Nixon was made for politics. He was highly ambitious and a gambler by nature; indeed, as a young officer in the South Pacific during the Second World War, he had made a lot of money playing poker. Although he loved to dramatize the impossible odds he had faced in his life, he also believed that determination and willpower could overcome the obstacles in his path. "If you are reasonably intelligent," he told an old friend, "and if your anger is deep enough and strong enough, you learn that you can change those attitudes by excellence, personal gut performance, while those who have everything are sitting on their fat butts." At college he had turned out for the football team even though he was much too small. "I'd have to knock the little guy for a loop," a much bigger player remembered about the practices. "Oh, my gosh did he take it." When he was a mature politician, one of Nixon's favourite movies (along with *Around the World in 80 Days*) was *Patton*. In the 1970 film, the Second World War general is shown as a bold and resolute outsider who is, importantly, in control and usually right when those around him are losing their heads and wrong to boot.

That did not stop Nixon from also seeing himself as an unlucky victim. Travelling in Asia before he was president, he told a diplomat waiting with him at the airport in Saigon that the plane was bound to be late. "If anything bad can happen to me, it will." And in his career bad things did happen to him, culminating with Watergate. Yet today we also remember him for his achievements, especially the opening to China.

In 1952 General Dwight Eisenhower agreed to have the young Senator Nixon as his vice-presidential candidate without knowing anything much about him. In the run-up to the presidential election, Nixon's career nearly ended when rumours circulated of a secret slush fund used to support him and his family while he was a senator. Eisenhower remained conspicuously silent, but word came down from Olympus that the general's top advisers wanted his vice-presidential candidate to resign. In the absence of a direct request, Nixon refused and went public with became known as the Checkers speech. In one of the best performances of his life, he talked about his family and their struggles to get by on his salary. Pat did not have luxuries like a mink coat — only a respectable Republican cloth one. Yes, he said, a donor had given them a pet dog — Checkers — but he was not going to give it back because his little daughters loved it. The speech was a triumph, and Nixon went on to become vice president when the Republicans won the presidential election.

Eisenhower was stuck with him but never came to like him or trust him. Nixon tried in vain to become part of the older man's inner circle, even taking up golf and fly-fishing, not sports for someone so naturally clumsy. In 1956 Eisenhower suggested that Nixon take a cabinet post and let someone else run as his vice president. Nixon again refused — he was aiming at the presidency and thought being vice president provided a better springboard. Eisenhower did not press the point, but when the time came he did little to help Nixon get the nomination. When someone asked the outgoing president in 1960 what major thing Nixon had contributed to his administration, Eisenhower replied, "If you give me a week, I might think of one." Kennedy carried the election by the narrowest of margins. Nixon tried to start his comeback by running for governor of California in 1962 and was humiliated by a defeat yet again. He gave a bitter and rambling talk to reporters in which he famously said, "You won't have Nixon to kick around anymore, because, gentlemen, this is my last press conference…"

It wasn't, of course, because Nixon could not abandon politics. While he took a job in a New York law firm, he continued to work towards the presidency, speaking across the country and travelling abroad to keep up to date with the international situation. In 1968 the man who many had written off was elected president. Nixon's presidency is now overshadowed by memories of Vietnam, Cambodia, Chile, and above all Watergate, when he tried to use the power of the presidency to obstruct justice. But it had its successes, in achieving détente with the Soviet Union and, perhaps above all, in re-establishing relations between the United States and the People's Republic of China.

Now that the two countries have a normal, if at times strained, relationship, it is difficult to remember just how different things were in 1968. The two countries had had virtually nothing to do with each other since the Communists took over in 1949. The Korean War, which started in 1950 and ended in a truce in 1953, saw the two fighting each other directly. Memories of that conflict and of the thousands of dead on each side stood in the way of peace being made. The gulf between the two powers was seemingly unbridgeable as each hurled insults and accusations across it at the other. The United States obdurately continued to recognize the Nationalists on Taiwan as the legitimate government of the whole of China, and Mao and his Communist government made it clear that their China was firmly committed to the Soviet bloc.

The Republican Party had taken an unrelentingly hostile stance to what it called "Red China" and had hurled charges at the Democrats that they had somehow lost China to the Communists and were in general dangerously soft on Communism. And Nixon had been among the most vociferous of anti-Communists. Early on in his political career, he had successfully smeared his liberal Democrat opponent, Helen Gahagan Douglas, as being "pink right down to her underwear." In Congress, he had made a name for himself as a diligent "Red-hunter," even if he was more restrained than his colleague Senator Joe McCarthy. In the famous Kitchen Debate at the American National Exhibition in Moscow in 1959, Nixon garnered much favourable comment back home when he confronted Premier Nikita Khrushchev in front of a life-sized model of an American kitchen.

Yet there was another Nixon: the internationalist who believed that the United States needed to be engaged in the world, even with powers representing very different values from those of his own country. He thought the United States should have joined the League of Nations, and he supported its membership in the United Nations after the Second World War. He thought the Marshall Plan, which helped to rebuild Europe, had been the right thing to do and in the United States' interest, as was the American commitment to the North Atlantic Treaty Organization (NATO). When he assumed office in 1969, he knew that he did not have to like the Soviets, but he was prepared to work with them to bring the arms race under control and establish a more general understanding, or détente.

As far as China was concerned, he had been thinking for some years that it had to be brought out of its "angry isolation" and into the community of nations. That would be better for world order but also, crucially, for the United States. Nixon believed, wrongly as it turned out, that he could get the United States out of its increasingly unpopular and costly quagmire in Vietnam if only China, the patron and supplier of the Vietnamese Communists, would agree to put pressure on them to make peace with the United States. He also saw (and here he was correct) that a rapprochement between the United States and China would shake the Soviet leadership and put pressure on them to be more reasonable in the arms limitation negotiations, which had become stalled. Above all, relations with both the Soviet Union and China would serve to put the United States, whose prestige and credibility had been so badly damaged by Vietnam, back in the centre of world affairs.

To the considerable surprise of his National Security Adviser, Henry Kissinger, Nixon on assuming office started to talk about making contact with the government in Beijing, even recognizing it. Like all effective gamblers, Nixon had calculated the odds carefully. His well-known anti-Communist stance meant that he was considerably less vulnerable than a Democrat president would have been to charges of being soft. The China lobby, once a powerful and well-connected group opposed to any dealings with Mao and his government, was running out of steam as time carried away many of its most prominent members. A younger generation in the United States no longer shared the same visceral antipathy to Communists. After all, the United States had been dealing with the Soviet variety for years. Nixon counted on the conservative wing of American public opinion trusting that he could deal with the Chinese as effectively and firmly, and he hoped that liberals would welcome his move as leading towards a more peaceful world. With Kissinger now firmly onside, the United States initiated a series of highly secret probes through Pakistan and Rumania, both of which had good relations with China.

Nixon was lucky in his timing. The Chinese, and most crucially Mao, who still made the key decisions, were feeling particularly friendless at the start of 1970s. They were on bad terms with virtually all their neighbours except for little North Korea and North Vietnam, neither of which were reliable partners. China had no relations at all with Japan or

Taiwan and was on bad terms with India, with which it had fought a war in 1960. Most worryingly of all for the leadership in Beijing, the powerful Soviet Union on its northern border was increasingly hostile. The two Communist powers had fallen out in spectacular and public fashion in the early 1960s. In the course of the decade, the Soviet Union had markedly increased its military forces in the Far East, while Mao had talked openly about how the Chinese people stood ready to fight a guerrilla war against invaders. In 1969 there were armed clashes between Soviet and Chinese soldiers along the common border, and in Moscow there was talk of a pre-emptive nuclear strike on China. Intimations of a possible surprise attack reached the Chinese leadership and helped to bring about a dramatic turnabout in Mao's thinking — that the time had come to mend fences with the United States. And where Mao turned, so did China.

Nixon could not know this, although the Americans were well aware of the tensions between the Soviets and the Chinese, so he was still risking public humiliation if his careful overtures to Beijing became public and if the Chinese leadership turned them down. A complicated exchange of secret messages went on for much of 1970 and the first half of 1971, and there were increasingly open public hints that attitudes on both sides were easing. Nixon dropped all references to "Red China" in favour of "the People's Republic," and in April 1971 the Chinese table tennis team at an international tournament in Japan suddenly invited their American counterparts to visit China for some friendly games. (The Chinese even let the much inferior American players win.) On June 2, after a further exchange of secret messages and more public gestures of goodwill, a warm invitation arrived in Washington from Zhou Enlai, the Chinese premier, inviting Nixon to send Kissinger to China to discuss a visit by Nixon himself. It was, as both men later said, like going to the other side of the moon. Especially since the great convulsions of the Cultural Revolution of the late 1960s, China had largely cut itself off from the outside world; only a handful of foreign journalists were allowed, under tight restrictions, in Beijing. Americans had not been able to visit since 1949.

The visit, which Kissinger made that July, was kept top secret until the American party was safely on its way home again. Nixon and Kissinger always defended the secrecy on the reasonable grounds that it was essential to carry out highly delicate negotiations away from the public glare and, as well, so that hard-liners in the United States would not have time to mount a widespread opposition. They also hoped to keep the State Department, which both men despised, in the dark, and take the credit for a major breakthrough for themselves and enhance their subsequent place in history. They may have been self-serving, but they were also brave. Going to China was risky on several levels. American public opinion and the reactions of American allies were hard to predict. It was impossible to guess what the Chinese might do. Would they humiliate Kissinger and send him packing? After all, only a few years ago China had seemed in the grip of madness as Mao had egged on the young students — organizing themselves as Red Guards — to brutalize and kill authority figures, whether in the factories, the party, the schools, or the universities. Foreigners and any Chinese with foreign connections had been regarded with particular venom and had been singled out for attack as enemies of the Chinese people. Howling mobs of Red Guards had ransacked and burned down the British mission in Beijing and beaten Soviet diplomats and their families, forcing them to crawl on the ground beneath portraits of Mao. Kissinger's visit went off smoothly, but the risk was still there for Nixon's visit, scheduled for February 1972. As we now know, there was opposition among some of China's top Communist leaders to mending fences with the Great Satan, as it had been usual to call the United States. In September 1971, the defence minister, Lin Biao, suddenly disappeared in circumstances which remain mysterious. One theory that has since emerged is that he was plotting against Mao, partly because of the unfolding rapprochement with the United States.

In February 1972, when Nixon boarded the presidential airplane outside Washington, he apparently had little fear for his physical safety in China, perhaps because little was known about the Lin Biao affair. What concerned Nixon and his advisers was that they still had not received word from Beijing about whether he would have a meeting with Mao. If the American president — moreover the first one ever to visit China — came back without having met its most powerful leader, he would look like a fool, and worse, weak. America's many enemies abroad would be delighted. When the Americans finally landed in Beijing, Zhou Enlai, who was at the airport to greet them, was noncommittal about a meeting. What the Americans did not know, among much else about China at the time, was that Mao was seriously ill in early 1972, and it was not at all clear that he could be made fit enough to greet his visitors. His doctors had worked on him intensively, and by the time Nixon arrived he was able to sit up by himself and walk a few steps. The decision about a meeting rested, however, with Mao himself. The afternoon of Nixon's arrival, as the Americans were settling into their quarters, Zhou suddenly got a call from Mao; he would see Nixon right away. To the alarm of the rest of the American party, including the Secret Service, a relieved and delighted Nixon, with Kissinger in tow, jumped into a Chinese limousine and disappeared to see Mao. The meeting was momentous not for what was said — the remarks made by both sides were largely banal — but for the fact that it took place. It symbolized the start of a new relationship and a revolution in international affairs.

It was to take several years for the visit to bear fruit. Nixon was driven out of office in 1974 as a result of the Watergate scandal, and his successor, Gerald Ford, had little interest in pushing ahead the normalization of relations while in China Mao's death in 1976 led to a prolonged power struggle. It was not until 1979 that China and the United States established full diplomatic relations, and not until the 1980s that the trickle of trade and investment and exchange of people started to swell to the flood it is today. Without Nixon's determination and bold initiative, would that have happened? Some would argue that it was inevitable that the two great powers would mend fences, because they had so much to gain by doing so, but you could make the same argument about Iran and the United States. Yet it is now over thirty-six years since the two cut relations, a period much longer than that of the deep freeze between China and the United States. Without Nixon, I believe, we would not have seen a thaw for years, even right up to the present. Nixon went to his grave thinking his opening to China was his greatest achievement, even though it was overshadowed, perhaps forever, by Watergate, "that silly, silly thing."

FROM THE SPARTANS TO the urban gangs of today, and from mining villages to fishing ports around the world, certain groups have valued courage even in the face of death. In a nightclub near Delhi, the bouncers all come from a nearby village with a strong tradition of fighting to protect their homes from outsiders. Its young men train from childhood as wrestlers, learning stories from the Hindu epics. In Prussia and then Germany, the landed Junker class, from which Bismarck came and which dominated the upper ranks of the German army, brought up its children to be brave and uncomplaining. Manfred von Nostitz, a friend of mine from the University of Toronto who is a descendant of Bismarck, remembers the last moments of that now-vanished world. He was a little boy during the Second World War, on the Bismarck estate in the eastern part of Germany. His great-grandmother, whom he and his cousins had to address as *Excellenz*, made the boys learn to use their knives and forks with either hand. When you grow up, she told them, you will be soldiers and may lose an arm, but you will always need to eat politely. As the Soviet troops advanced ever closer, she refused to leave with the rest of the family and the estate workers. She made her preparations: she gave orders that her grave should be dug in the grounds, because once the Soviets arrived "there would be nobody left to do this job," and she shot her beloved dogs with her hunting rifle. She waited only to show the Soviet commander around the house before she killed herself.

Across much of Europe before the First World War, duelling among officers was regarded favourably by the military authorities as a way of enhancing the proper military qualities. As the Prussian war minister protested to the head of the government when there was talk of outlawing the practice, "The roots of the duel are embedded and grow in our code of honor. This code of honor is a valuable, and for the Officer Corps, an irreplaceable treasure." The British were looked down upon because they had long since outlawed the practice, but the British upper classes exhibited many of the same characteristics as their counterparts on the other side of the Channel. Julian Grenfell, from an old aristocratic family, wrote home after his first experience of combat in 1914: "I *adore* war. It is like a big picnic without the objectlessness of a picnic. I've never been so well or so happy." He died the next year, followed two months later by his younger brother. In her wonderful novels, Molly Keane, who came from the Protestant Anglo-Irish landowners, shows them riding to the hounds and going to war with the same reckless abandon. Attitudes such as these help to explain why so many in Europe before the First World War thought that it would be exciting, and that the war would bring victory.

Geography, like culture, can foster an adventurous spirit. Those who live along sea coasts have tended from the time of the Phoenicians to look outwards. The great seafaring explorers of the Renaissance came, not surprisingly, from Genoa or Venice, the coasts of Portugal, or the British Isles. They were driven by curiosity and greed. If they could find a quick sea-route to Asia, they could bring its riches back at great profit to Europe. While Columbus continued to hope that he was about to reach Asia by going westwards, those who followed in his footsteps, such as Cortés and Pizarro, realized that there were riches closer to hand than Asia. Through a combination of daring, luck, and ruthlessness, the conquistadors overthrew great empires, plundered their rich gold and silver mines, and enslaved their peoples. Where ambition had once been seen in Europe as a vice, the Renaissance neatly adjusted its thinking by the mid-sixteenth century to make it a virtue.

Certain types of societies may produce more or fewer

risk-takers, but across time and space it is possible to pick out certain common characteristics among such people. Ambition, of course, but also a capacity to see opportunities where the rest of us might merely see insurmountable obstacles. It surely also helps to be determined and resilient, like Churchill, in the face of setbacks or failure. Nor should we underestimate sheer endurance.

Samuel de Champlain, explorer, ethnographer, botanist, map-maker, and colonizer, made some twenty-seven crossings of the Atlantic between 1599 and 1635. Sailing out from France, often in the late winter, he and his crews braved the Atlantic in boats which were no longer than two modern buses laid end to end. They encountered wild storms (one in 1603 lasted for seventeen days), icebergs that towered above them, and thick fogs, all in largely unknown and uncharted waters. On more than one occasion Champlain's voyages nearly ended on hidden shoals or dashed against rocky shores. Painstakingly he explored the coasts of North America and made his way up the great St. Lawrence River towards what became the cities of Quebec and Montreal. Here too the hazards were great — rapids, dangerous currents, native peoples who might or might not be hostile, and English freebooters.

Then there was the vast continent itself; Champlain may have dreamed of salt seas just out of reach and China somewhere not too far away, but no one knew, not even his Indian guides, what might lie over the far horizons. And exploring ran the risk of encounters with dangerous animals or hostile peoples. The land was itself a constant test, with its thick, tangled forests, its lakes and rivers beckoning to ever more unexplored territories, its extremes of weather, from oppressive summer heat, when the clouds of mosquitoes and black flies circled travellers, to the long winters, when the snows

came and food ran short. Champlain travelled hundreds of
miles through it by canoe and by foot. He learned how to
shoot rapids or portage around them. Once, when he was
helping to drag the canoes up through a dangerous part of
the Ottawa River, he lost control of his own vessel and was
dragged into the roiling waters among the rocks. The rope,
wrapped around his hand, nearly pulled it off. "I cried aloud
to God," he later wrote, "and began to pull my canoe toward
me, when it was sent back to me by an eddy such as occurs in
this rapids...I nearly lost my life." Sailing back to France in
the autumn brought fresh dangers as the weather turned win-
tery, but staying through the North American winter meant
possible starvation and almost certain disease.

The first winter of the colony he established at Quebec, in
1608–9, nearly destroyed it. The winter started early, with
snow in mid-November. The rivers and lakes froze in the bitter cold, but less snow fell than usual. This was not a bless-
ing but a disaster. The colonists could not bank the walls
of their newly built houses with snow, and the Indians, on
whom the French depended for help in getting game, found
it difficult to move on snowshoes across frozen ridges. To
add to the misery, the usual autumn eel and beaver hunts
had come up short. Desperate, emaciated Indians from the
Montagnais tribe begged the French for food. Champlain
gave them what he could, but as the winter dragged on, supplies ran very short. The colonists started to fall sick of dysentery or scurvy. By the time spring came, only eight of the
original twenty-eight French were still alive. Champlain was
nevertheless determined to persist.

This extraordinary man could have had a successful
career without ever leaving France, but he chose instead to
devote his life to exploring and to his dream of establishing

a French colony in North America. As he wrote in 1613 in a book he was dedicating to the powerful Queen Mother of France: "MADAM. Among all the most useful and admirable arts, that of navigating has always seemed to me to hold first place; for the more hazardous it is and the more attended by innumerable perils and shipwrecks, so much the more is it esteemed and exalted above all others, being in no way suited to those who lack courage and resolution. Through this art, we gain knowledge of diverse lands, regions, and kingdoms; through it, we attract and bring into our lands all kinds of wealth; through it, the idolatry of paganism is overthrown and Christianity proclaimed in all parts of the earth." Champlain's life and career are an important part of the complex encounter between the Old World and the New, and of the story of New France, which has left a legacy which has helped to shape the modern nation of Canada.

We cannot be sure what he looked like. The portrait which was widely believed to show him has turned out to be that of a famous swindler, done in the nineteenth century. The only one that may show the real man is in an engraving of a battle in which he and his Huron allies fought the Iroquois near what is now known as Lake Champlain, in the northeastern United States. It shows a small figure of a European, possibly taken from a sketch done by Champlain himself. Dressed in breastplate and helmet, the bearded man is firing an early type of gun. Since the picture also contains palm trees, it is hard to have complete confidence in the scene.

We also do not have much detail about Champlain's early years. We know that he was born around 1570 in southwestern France, at the time a strongly Protestant region. Perhaps some of his family were themselves Protestants, but his own parents were Catholic. Tensions between the two branches of the Christian faith had already set off civil war in 1562, which would smoulder on, with atrocities on both sides, throughout Champlain's childhood. In 1598, peace came when King Henry IV conspicuously abandoned Protestantism for Catholicism while also proclaiming religious tolerance for the Protestants. Champlain, so his most recent biographer argues, developed, perhaps as a result of his own experiences, a strong commitment to understanding and tolerance among peoples of different faiths and cultures. Champlain's own religious faith was strong, but he hoped and believed that the peoples he encountered in the New World would come to Christianity of their own accord.

Columbus's discovery of the New World in 1492 had shaken many of the fundamental beliefs of the Europeans. Not only did it rapidly become apparent that the Americas were much vaster than Europeans had first realized, but they were filled with peoples with their own, often very different, customs, religions, and codes. This set off a long debate, which was still intense as Champlain reached manhood, about whether these Americans were part of the same human race as Europeans. (We would feel a similar sense of shock and uncertainty if we found life elsewhere in the cosmos.) Reactions in Europe to the discovery of these previously unknown peoples took one of two forms: they were either innocent and noble savages living in harmony with each other and with nature, or they were bestial creatures devoid of morality and given to licentiousness in sexual relations and such horrors as cannibalism. In either case they must be converted to Christianity.

Over time a third view emerged, fostered paradoxically by the presence of missionaries who settled among the indigenous peoples and learned their languages: that the natives of the Americas had societies every bit as complex as those in Europe, with their own ways of organizing themselves, their own values, and their own religions. Even Cortés, the destroyer of the Aztec Empire, was moved to comment: "I will say only that these people live almost like those in Spain, and in as much harmony and order as there, and considering that they are barbarous and so far from the knowledge of God and cut off from civilised nations, it is truly remarkable to see what they have achieved in all things..." In his essay *On Coaches*, published in 1588, the French essayist Montaigne mocks the Europeans' unfounded belief that they deserved to conquer these newly discovered peoples. The Aztecs, he says, did not fall before a superior civilization: "As for their piety, observance of the laws, goodness, liberality and frankness: well, it served us well that we had less of that than they did; their superiority in that ruined them, sold them and betrayed them."

Champlain's views seem to have fallen somewhere between that growing understanding and even admiration for the native societies of the Americas and a fervent hope that they would be converted to Christianity. On his first voyage to the New World, in 1599, he sailed south, to the Caribbean and Central America. He made the first of what were to be a series of detailed and accurate maps of the New World. In what was to be characteristic fashion, he made copious notes on everything he saw. On the road to Mexico City, he was struck by the beauty of his surroundings: "I marvelled at the great forests of palm trees, cedars, laurels, orange and lemon trees, cabbage-palms, guavas, avocadoes, ebony, Brazil and Campeachy wood..." He listed the many varieties of birds and the types of crops grown by the locals. They mixed cacao berries, honey, and spices to make a nourishing drink, and from the locust tree they made a healing oil for cuts. He noted some "very foolish" local customs and beliefs but was critical of the Spaniards' mistreatment of their new subjects and the severity of the Inquisition. Eventually, he believed, the Spanish would have to allow liberty of conscience.

His interest was drawn further north, up to the region that is today the east coast of the United States and Canada's Maritime provinces, where the territory had not yet been fully claimed or explored. Between 1604 and 1607, he surveyed and mapped much of the coast from what is now Nova Scotia southwards down to Cape Cod. Increasingly, however, he became convinced that the St. Lawrence River was the key both to Asia and to the future of French power in the New World. French and British merchants were already making annual voyages partway up the river to acquire the beaver pelts that hat-makers in London and Paris used in their most expensive products. Champlain himself showed little interest in commerce; his main goals were to find lands and resources that the French could settle and develop and where they could bring missionaries to convert the indigenous peoples. In addition he hoped to find a route to Asia and its riches. As a friend wrote about him, he was dedicated "to travel still further, convert the peoples, and discover the East, whether by North or South, so as to get to China." He never found his route to Asia, although he repeatedly questioned the natives he met further inland about whether they had come across a salt sea. A remnant of his search lingers in the name given to the rapids near Montreal: Lachine (French for *China*).

His timing for exploring and settling New France was good: the French government was now getting serious about building both a navy and colonies. Somehow Champlain managed year after year to find enough financial support to keep going. As he pushed westwards up the St. Lawrence, he looked for likely places to establish settlements and drew detailed maps, decorating their borders with the fruit and vegetables of the New World. His many published writings extolled the great promise of the vast unclaimed territories. At his first glimpse in 1603 of the site of the future Quebec City, he rhapsodized about the thick forests, the vines, and the fruit trees. The soil, he was sure, could bear rich crops, and he suspected that he had found diamonds in the local slate. Further upriver, towards Montreal, he noted: "There are plenty of grapes, pears, hazel-nuts, cherries, currants and gooseberries. They also have certain small roots, the size of a nut, that taste like truffles and are very good either roasted or boiled." Champlain, who was a keen gardener himself, dreamed of creating a thriving agriculture through "the ingenuity and skill of man." And if the St. Lawrence did indeed prove to be the route to Asia, as he confidently hoped, the French could make a fortune from tolls which could then fund further settlements. In 1618, he sketched out a vision of a series of flourishing colonies, growing ever richer from timber, furs, mining, and farming. One day, he hoped, there would a great city north of the settlement at Quebec, to be called Ludovica, in honour of Louis XIII.

Although he did not live to see his Ludovica or the cities growing along the St. Lawrence, Champlain did plant the colonies from which so much else followed. He was a skilled administrator and a leader who managed to cajole government into providing its own funds, or browbeat reluctant merchants into providing theirs. He could inspire his people as they faced the challenges of the Canadian climate and the threats from marauding English or Dutch, or attack by the Iroquois. In the winter of 1606, in the first of the French colonies at Acadia, now in Nova Scotia, Champlain kept up morale as supplies ran short by instituting the Company of Good Cheer to encourage the colonists to vie with each other to hunt and fish in order to produce a feast for them all. A good leader, Champlain once said, "should be liberal according to his opportunities, and courteous even to his enemies, granting them all the rights to which they are entitled. Moreover, he should not practice cruelty or vengeance, like those who are accustomed to inhumane acts, and show themselves to be barbarians rather than Christians, but if on the contrary he makes use of his success with courtesy and moderation, he will be esteemed by all, even by his enemies, who will pay him all honour and respect."

He always had to be a diplomat as well, and not just at the French court. To achieve his dreams — to explore and survive in the vast unknown territories — he relied utterly on building good relations with the Indians. Without food from the Indians, neither Champlain himself nor the tiny colonies he established would have survived those first long, harsh winters. He discovered that he had to manoeuvre within a complex network of alliances and enmities. His first contact was with an Algonquin-speaking group the French called the Montagnais, around the Saguenay River, which flows into the St. Lawrence where it is still wide. Further up the St. Lawrence were other Algonquin-speaking tribes and, north of Lake Ontario, the Algonquin allies of the Huron Confederacy. Opposed to this loose coalition was the five-nation Iroquois Confederacy, which controlled the whole area south of Lake Ontario, and the lands between Lake Ontario and Lake Erie, as well as many of the fur trading routes leading further to the west. The French had to decide between the two sides, and in 1603 they chose the Indians they already knew rather than the more distant Iroquois. Although Champlain reached out from time to time to the other side, and at times seemed close to brokering a peace, war kept breaking out again, with the French firmly committed to the Algonquins. In that one picture we have of him, he is firing his weapon at a war party of Iroquois.

Although he often sailed back to France in the autumns, Champlain also wintered over in Canada on several occasions. Some of his first reactions to the indigenous peoples of the Americas reflected the biases of his own times; he judged that they had no proper laws or religion of their own and longed for them to become Christian. He never assumed, however, that they were inferior in capacity or potential to the Europeans. In his first encounters with the Montagnais in 1603, he noted that they relied on fishing and hunting for their sustenance. But, he added, "I feel sure that if anyone showed them how to cultivate the soil they would learn quickly enough, for they are sensible and intelligent and ready to answer any questions you put to them." He and the French missionaries engaged in theological discussions with their chiefs, and occasionally he found himself at a loss to explain the advantages of his faith. "They couldn't always understand what it was we were trying to tell them," he wrote. "It wasn't always something you could put in words." The Indians suggested that the French should come with their families and settle among them so that they could show by example what Christianity meant. "This," wrote Champlain, "seemed sensible to me..."

Champlain approached the Indians from the start with an open mind and curiosity, and over time developed both a greater understanding of their society and made friends among them. In the winter of 1615–16 he lived with the Huron, not by his own choice. The Huron decided to keep him with them after an autumn campaign against the Iroquois had ended, partly as insurance against a fresh attack and partly for his advice. "Not being able to do anything," he wrote, "I had to resign myself to be patient." He took the opportunity to study the local flora and fauna and his hosts' "manners, customs, modes of life, the form of their assemblies."

Over the many years he spent in New France, he witnessed many Indian ceremonial gatherings and was struck by how their government worked. "Normally they act by majority vote, but sometimes they defer to someone they have special reason to respect." Did he ever compare that to the autocracy back in France? He also developed the discrimination to treat the Indians as individuals rather than merely types. "For the most part," he wrote in one account of his travels, "the people are cheerful and good-natured, although some are surly enough. Both men and women are strong and well-built. Many of the women and girls are attractive and have good figures, clear skin and regular features." He carefully noted down their customs, how for example when they were preparing a war party, the women stripped naked and danced towards canoes where they hit each other with their paddles. "They take care, I noticed, not to get hurt and are careful to ward off each other's blows." He described marriage customs, child-rearing, and burial practices, and gave detailed descriptions of Indian clothes and ornaments. He nicknamed the Outaouais the *Cheveux-Relevés* because of the way the men did their hair. "They comb it high on their head and arrange it more carefully than a French courtesan, for all her curlers and powder. They are a handsome people and go quite naked, armed with nothing but a club. To decorate their bodies they splash their skins and paint their faces in bright colours, pierce their nostrils and hang their ears with beads. I made friends with them and got to know some of them quite well."

The friendship seems to have been genuine on both sides. In May 1633, when Champlain came back to his settlement at Quebec after several years' absence (it had been briefly captured by the English), a large party of Montagnais arrived in their canoes to see him. Champlain gestured at the building works, including the fort, and said, "When that great house is built, our young men will marry your daughters, and henceforth we shall be one people." Later that summer, between five and six hundred Huron came down the river to welcome him, bearing presents, including valuable bundles of beaver robes. A Jesuit witnessed a council meeting with Champlain and some fifty to sixty Indian leaders; the priest recorded how one leader after another got up to say that they rejoiced in Champlain's return and that "they have all come to warm themselves by his fire." Sadly, although he was not to know it, Champlain and his colonists also brought the European diseases that were going to cut such a hideous swath through native societies. In the smallpox epidemic of the 1630s, two-thirds of the population of the Huron Confederacy died.

In 1635 Champlain suffered a severe stroke and started to prepare for his death. He died on Christmas day, and the whole population of Quebec turned out for his funeral. Delegations from the Hurons subsequently arrived with large gifts of wampum, in the hopes that the French would "dry their tears and more easily swallow the sorrow that they had suffered on the death of Monsieur de Champlain." His settlements along the upper St. Lawrence, such as Quebec and Montreal, were finally starting to take off and become self-sustaining. In 1633 Champlain brought 150 settlers with him, and more came in the following years in their hundreds and then thousands. Between 1630 and 1680 over a thousand French women arrived; it has been estimated that more than two-thirds of the long-established French in North America are descended from them. Although Champlain could not know it when he died, he had successfully laid the foundations of the French presence in Canada.

RISKS, AS WE KNOW, can pay off, but that is by no means all that motivates those who take them. Curiosity, ambition, determination — these drive certain people to take chances even against daunting odds. It helps too to have a disregard for convention or for the views of others. Above all, risk-takers are prepared to accept sacrifices, even failure, while others of us prefer to stay comfortably at home. In *The Lord of the Rings* the hobbits are content with the quotidian and cosy world of the Shire; most do not want to know about the great world outside, with its dangers and its excitements. Yet where would we be without those who do take risks, in science, politics, or business? Whether they are driven by simple curiosity, a longing for adventure, greed or ambition the world moves on because of such men and women.

FOUR

CURIOSITY

IN 1841 A YOUNG, well-born Englishwoman wrote to her mother, "Owing to some peculiarity in my nervous system, I have perceptions of some things, which no one else has... an intuitive perception of hidden things: — that is of things hidden away from eyes, ears and the ordinary senses. This alone would advantage me little, in the discovery line, but there is, secondly, my immense reasoning faculties, and my concentrative faculty." Ada Lovelace came from a complicated background. Her deeply religious mother had married the romantic and doomed Lord Byron, a leading poet and reprobate. It seems to have been a love match (although it must have helped that his large debts were matched by her large fortune), but by the time Ada was born they had separated. Lady Byron was determined to counteract the dangerous heritage of Ada's father and set her daughter to studying mathematics in the hopes that it would bring out her calm and rational side. Ada fell passionately in love with the subject.

Although she too married, to a man who became the Earl of Lovelace, she managed somehow to combine being a wife and mother with using her mind. She had the good fortune to meet Charles Babbage, a brilliant mathematician and inventor, in 1832, when she was seventeen, and the two became fast friends. He had spent much of his life building mechanical calculators, and by the 1840s, when Ada was searching for something to occupy herself, he was trying to create what he called an Analytical Engine — an early form of computer — which would use punched cards to carry out complex mathematical computations. He had a vision of a central processing unit, software, and random access memory a hundred years before they became reality, but the technology of the time was not sufficiently advanced to allow him to realize it. Ada was fascinated by the prospect and, in an extraordinary leap of the imagination, saw the Analytical Engine as being able to do more than mathematics: "The engine can arrange and combine its numerical quantities exactly as if they were letters or any other general symbols." She went still further, envisaging that machines could be built one day that would be capable of tasks such as composing music. She wrote to Babbage, "If I could be worth or capable of being used by you, my head will be yours." The two worked together for a number of years, in the course of which she wrote sets of instructions on how the Analytical Engine could be programmed to carry out calculations. In other words, she created the first software in history. In 1980 the United States Defense Department named a computer language after her.

When I started to compile a list of those characters in history who possessed to an exceptional degree the quality of curiosity, I was intrigued to notice that most of the names I came up with were women. This, I suspect, is not that women are naturally more curious than men, but because so often it has been more difficult for them to follow their own paths. Women throughout history have had to defy rigid conventions about what is and is not expected of them. The first women who went to medical schools encountered male professors who refused to teach them or who tried to horrify them into abandoning the subject. The British women who went out to India to join their husbands when it was part of the British Empire were frequently reminded that they had to behave in ways that upheld the Raj; they must not take too close an interest in Indian arts or customs, or the Indians themselves. The intrepid women travellers who explored Africa or the Middle East faced disapproval from their own kind and as often misapprehension from those they travelled among. In most societies women's ambitions were discouraged. Those women such as Queen Elizabeth I, Catherine the Great, or the Empress Wu who through birth or marriage came to exercise great power were, it was suggested, somehow imperfect or indeed monstrous. Elizabeth was the Virgin Queen and therefore unfulfilled as a woman, while Catherine and Empress Wu were said to have outlandish sexual appetites, consuming and throwing aside dozens of lovers — like a male ruler might. It has changed, of course, but perhaps not as much as we sometimes like to think. No one would call a male politician shrill, as they so often did Margaret Thatcher and still do with Hillary Clinton. Women in business are "domineering" where men are "forceful."

Nevertheless women, especially in developed societies, now have far more choice of careers than their mothers or grandmothers. We no longer hear that women don't have the heads or the stamina for business or law, that they are not strong enough to be firefighters or mountain guides. Or if we do hear such things, we wonder where that particular Neanderthal has been hiding. And the study of women in the present and in the past, and from different perspectives, such as sociology or economics, is now a serious subject. When I was a student at the University of Toronto in the 1960s, there was no women's history (just as there was little black or aboriginal or gay history, and not that much working-class history either). The indexes of our textbooks usually did not have an entry for "women." Since the questions we ask of history often reflect what interests us in the present, it was not until the 1970s, with the sudden growth of the women's movement, that historians, many of them women, started to examine women's lives over the centuries.

This was often a challenge, because the records of the past have been largely kept by men and there are far fewer women's voices available, especially the further back you go. There are some, of course: the wonderful letters about society in Paris or life at Louis XIV's court which the elegant and well-connected Madame de Sévigné wrote to amuse her beloved daughter in the seventeenth century; or the poems of Sappho from antiquity. In the twelfth century, the Abbess Hildegard of Bingen, who founded and ran convents near the Rhine River, wrote copiously about theology but also about botany and medicine, and the doomed lovers Héloïse and Abelard exchanged letters after the great catastrophe which befell them. He was one of Europe's leading philosophers and drew students from all over the continent to learn from him in Paris. She was younger, clever, and, unusually for a woman in the twelfth century, highly educated. The two met in the house of her uncle and fell in love. She became pregnant with Abelard's child and married him, secretly so as not to jeopardize his career. Her enraged uncle had Abelard castrated and forced them both into different abbeys. In the letters, the couple discuss language, theology, and ethics, and recent scholars have argued not only that Héloïse wrote the letters attributed to her but that she was a significant thinker in her own right who exerted intellectual influence on Abelard. I would like to think that the passionate statement of her love is also genuine: "If Augustus, as ruler of the whole world, deigned to honour me with marriage and conferred the whole world on me to possess in perpetuity, it seem to me dearer and more worthy to be called your prostitute than his empress." Two centuries later, an elderly and independent-minded Englishwoman named Margery Kempe dictated memoirs describing her spiritual quest and her adventures when she left her family — she had fourteen children — to go on pilgrimage to the Holy Land.

Historians have also found that they can sometimes use other sources to deepen and fill out women's history. The ways in which the Virgin Mary and the Infant Jesus have been depicted in painting and sculpture over the centuries, for example, say something about motherhood in different times. Old court records, whether of disputes over property or crime, have been used to get at an understanding of marriage and the status of women. Popular literature can add nuances; the fact that classical Chinese civilization produced so many stories and poems about domineering mothers and mothers-in-law strongly suggests that Chinese women were not the meek creatures subject to male rule that they were meant to be. When I tried to understand, for my first book, the lives of British women during the Raj, I was fortunate to have many of their own memoirs and letters, but I could also look at the government of India's records, where I found that officials worried about European women not getting proper education or medical attention or behaving badly, at least by official standards, whether that meant female missionaries standing in the bazaars to preach, or women marrying Indian men. I read treatises by gynaecologists advising women how to preserve their health and purity in the dangerous environment of India, guides for housekeeping for women in India, and many more novels than I now can remember.

Thanks to the explosion in women's history, we now have a better sense and a greater appreciation of the ways in which women worked within the constraints of their own time, class, and place and managed nevertheless to carve out spaces where they could be themselves and pursue their own interests. Like the risk-takers I talked about in my previous chapter, such women possessed determination and a capacity to endure. I want to single out here their curiosity, that appetite they had for wanting to know more, about people, places, flora and fauna, or the past. They were open to new ideas and new experiences, however alien or troubling those might be. As Fanny Parkes, who roamed through much of India in the first half of the nineteenth century, once said after witnessing a group of devout Hindus swinging from hooks they had inserted in their flesh, "I was much disgusted, but greatly fascinated."

AS THE BRITISH EMPIRE expanded and settled into an organized set of colonies in the course of the eighteenth and nineteenth centuries, women from the British Isles found themselves accompanying their husbands to all corners of the world. They wrote copious letters home, and many published memoirs with titles such as *Roughing It in the Bush* or *Trekking in Kashmir,* most of which sit unread on library shelves, echoes from a vanished world. We should not regard their authors merely as sepia-tinted curiosities dressed in funny clothes. These were flesh-and-blood women who dealt with challenges many of us would find overwhelming: being tossed about in rickety ships; jolting miles on horseback or in primitive carriages; facing childbirth with, if they were lucky, rudimentary medical care, and succumbing to illnesses such as typhoid or cholera in an age before antibiotics; being stung by wasps or bitten by mad dogs. Yet somehow they managed to keep a sense of humour and take an active interest in their new surroundings.

"Accustomed to fashionable life," wrote the anonymous author of *Canadian Letters* in the early 1790s about one such woman, "she submits with cheerfulness to the inevitable inconvenience of an infant colony." Elizabeth Simcoe was a considerable heiress, the chatelaine of a large and comfortable house in the west of England, and already at twenty-five the mother of six children. When she was only sixteen, she had fallen in love with and married the much older Colonel John Graves Simcoe. She was, even at that age, strong-willed.

Her husband had fought the Americans when the Thirteen Colonies rebelled, and he came out of that experience more committed a high Tory than ever, with a deep hatred of revolution in any form, whether American or, after 1789, French.

In 1790 he was appointed lieutenant-governor of the newly formed colony of Upper Canada. This was not as grand a post as it sounded; the colony's population was around ten thousand, and its farms and few small towns were widely dispersed along the lakes and rivers. (Lower Canada, by contrast, had a population of 150,000 and the well-established cities of Quebec and Montreal.) Many of Upper Canada's inhabitants were relative newcomers, Loyalist refugees from the United States, and Simcoe was to encourage thousands more to come with the promise of free farmland. In the next decades the wilderness slowly receded as the land was cleared, farms were started, and the foundations of what would one day be the prosperous province of Ontario were laid. Yet the new colony also faced a very real threat from the south; the Americans might well join in a war against Britain with revolutionary France, and Simcoe had only a handful of troops at his disposal.

On her husband's urging, Mrs. Simcoe left the four eldest children behind to be cared for by family and friends. She accepted that it was best for their education and was relieved that a close and trusted friend agreed to oversee the children's care. From a distance she welcomed every scrap of news that arrived from England and sent much advice and anxious admonitions about the details of their lives. The two youngest children, including a three-month-old boy, as well as servants, travelled to Canada with the Simcoes. Her mounds of luggage included children's clothes, toys, ball gowns, linen, china, folding chairs, cots, mosquito nets, her precious sketching materials, and a canvas "house" which they had bought from the estate of the explorer Captain James Cook. Because her husband's commission was delayed in coming, their ship did not set sail until the end of September, dangerously late for a safe crossing. Almost immediately they ran into stormy weather. "I am rather diverted at the difficulties we meet with at dinner," Mrs. Simcoe wrote, "when in spite of all care the dishes are often tossed to every corner of the Room." Sometimes it was too rough to cook and they subsisted on dry biscuits. The portholes leaked, leaving them wet and cold. The little Mrs. Simcoe was also covered with bruises from being dashed against the sides of the ship. On October 14 they hit a particularly bad gale which blew for several days. The waves were "like mountains," she reported, and when she ventured onto the deck she had to cling to a cannon. Matters were not helped by the purser, who with considerable relish and much harrowing detail recounted how this particular day was the anniversary of his two previous shipwrecks. "The account of such perils during such weather," remarked Mrs. Simcoe, "was not very amusing to me." She occupied herself by learning a new hymn and copying sketches of ships.

By the end of the month they had made land in Nova Scotia and picked up a much needed guide to the St. Lawrence River. Now it was cold, and the ropes froze as the ship made its way slowly up the river through snow and fog. On November 11 they finally arrived at Quebec City, their destination for the winter. Mrs. Simcoe was disappointed — "so dismal looking a Town" — but once on dry land she threw herself into its very active social life. The winter went pleasantly fast with balls, concerts, sightseeing, and visiting. She drove across the frozen St. Lawrence in a carriole, as the local sleighs were known. "The Scene on the River," she wrote at the end of February, "is now a very gay one. Numbers are skating; Carrioles driven furiously (as the Canadians usually do) & wooden huts are built on the Ice where Cakes and Liquor are sold, and they have stoves in their huts."

With some reluctance but with her usual determination to make the best of matters, she set out in the spring for her husband's colony. With one of the rapid weather changes that Canadians know so well, she found herself by June in Montreal in a heat wave and noted with amusement the sentry who complained, "There is but a sheet of brown paper between this place and hell." The party made its way upriver by boat or on foot and horseback along the shore when the rapids were too rough. She slept in farmhouses, inns, tents, on top of her trunks, and once on a table when the bed seemed too dirty. By the start of July they had reached Upper Canada's main town of Kingston, which comprised some fifty wooden houses. Its streets were muddy tracks and dotted with the stumps of the trees so recently cleared. Although Kingston had been considered as a possible capital for Upper Canada, Simcoe decided that it was too flat and too close to the American border to be defensible.

The party headed south and west across Lake Ontario on an armed government schooner to the town of Niagara, at the mouth of the river of the same name, which emptied Lake Erie into Lake Ontario. Simcoe preferred to call it Newark, which he thought more civilized, but there was little civilization to be seen beyond some twenty log cabins and a few dilapidated government buildings grandly called the Navy Yard. They spent the summer in tents, and Mrs. Simcoe had a bower made out of fresh branches, where she sat during the day writing letters, entertaining visitors, or helping her husband. "She is bashful, and speaks little," reported the Duke of Rochefoucauld-Liancourt, an exiled French aristocrat who was touring North America, "but she is a woman of sense, handsome and amiable, and fulfils all the duties of the mother and wife with the most scrupulous exactness. The performance of the latter she carries so far as to act the part of a private secretary to her husband. Her talents for drawing, the practice of which she confines to maps and plans, enable her to be extremely useful to the Governor." (She was less kind, writing in her diary about the Duke and his party, "Their appearance is perfectly democratic & dirty.")

That winter the Simcoes lived in their canvas house, which had two wallpapered rooms with stoves. One room was where they slept and received guests, the other the nursery. In January she gave birth to a daughter there. Shortly afterwards she was left on her own when her husband set off with a small party to walk south to Detroit, on the border

with the United States. She made light of the dangers — from
the weather, the rough country, or the Americans — he might
face. "I am so persuaded," she claimed, "that the Journey will
be of service to the Gov.'s health that I rejoice he has under-
taken it." She would, she wrote to a friend in England, be so
busy that the time was bound to pass quickly. The unexpected
death of her last-born the following year was one of the few
times she allowed herself to be downcast. "The recollection of
the loss of so promising a Child," she wrote to a close friend
in England, "must long be a painful thing."

For the most part she was determinedly cheerful, even
when insect bites left her unable to move an arm, when a
fire in her temporary wooden kitchen smashed her fragile
china, when a trunk full of her clothes fell into the water,
or when she had to move to Quebec City with the children
during the winter of 1794–95 because a war with the United
States looked likely. And social life cannot have been easy in
such a small, intimate society as Upper Canada's, where her
every move was scrutinized and mean whispers went about.
She was said to be interfering in matters of government. "I
am sorry the Governor did not come out solo as the People
seem not to like Petecoat Laws," Hannah Jarvis, the wife of
an official, complained. Mrs. Jarvis found fault constantly;
Mrs. Simcoe had missed two public balls, for example, "the
first in childbirth the second in a Fevor as *reported*." When
Colonel Simcoe decided, on the perfectly reasonable grounds
of security, to establish the colony's new capital, York, at a
good harbour on the north side of Lake Ontario, Mrs. Jarvis
pounced again: "Everybody are sick at York — but no matter —
the Lady likes the place — therefore everyone must — Money
is a God *many* worship."

Mrs. Simcoe had her own circle of friends and had more

than enough interests to keep her occupied. Like so many inhabitants of Canada then and since, she was both overwhelmed and drawn by the sheer scale and majesty of the land itself. As she said of herself, she had "the picturesque eye" and found much to sketch on paper and birchbark, from Niagara Falls, "the grandest sight imaginable," to her little son Frank. She described with pleasure how she watched maple sugar being made in the spring or walked through clouds of butterflies in the summer. Once, at dusk, she went into a woods where there had just been a forest fire: the smoke kept the mosquitoes away, and the trees shot out flares of flame, "a little like Tasso's enchanted wood."

When the government moved to York, there was almost nothing there beyond a few farms. Simcoe's men did surveys and laid out roads and started to clear the trees. Now, over two centuries later, where thick forests once stood, are the skyscrapers of Toronto. From the canvas house, which was now pitched on a rise east of the present Fort York, Mrs. Simcoe explored her new neighbourhood. Loons uttered their unearthly cry on the crystal-clear waters, deer foraged in the woods, and the skies filled with game birds and the spring and autumn migrations. She walked through oak groves and open grasslands, along the beaches and a spit of land which used to join the east end of the Toronto islands to the mainland. She saw the fish leaping and watched while the Indians speared salmon by torchlight. She rode along the shores to the creeks that emptied into Lake Ontario. The lowlands of one, "which is to be called the river Don," were covered with rushes and abounding with wild ducks and red-winged blackbirds. When tree trunks blocked the shoreline to the east, she got into a small boat and was rowed under white cliffs. "They appeared so well we talked of building a summer Residence there & calling it Scarborough." And build they did, a log cabin "on the plan of a Grecian Temple," with the giant white pines to make the columns of the porticos. They called it, however, Castle Frank, after their son. All that remains today is the name — of a subway stop.

She was endlessly curious, quizzing visitors such as Alexander Mackenzie, who had just crossed the continent to the Pacific. She noted down the details of the unfamiliar animals she encountered, from elk to skunks. Raccoons, she wrote back to England "resemble a Fox, are an exceedingly fat animal with a bushy tail." She made lists of trees and plants. "I send you May apple seeds," she wrote to a friend, "I think it the prettiest plant I have seen." She also collected local remedies: some plants were good for coughs; herbal tea cured headaches; sassafras was an antidote against the fevers they all came down with; and the boiled roots of a type of viburnum bush helped with stomach upsets. She willingly tried new foods: watermelons, blueberries, or Indian corn. Local Indians gave her a cake of dried blueberries, which reminded her of "Irwin's patent Currant Lozenges," although it tasted rather too strongly of smoke. She didn't much like bear, but raccoon was not bad with mint sauce, while black squirrel was "as good to eat as young rabbit." She barbequed venison over fires in the winter. Whitefish from Lake Ontario were "most exquisitely good & we all think them better than any other fresh or salt water fish." She reported proudly after a ball, "Some small Tortoises cut up & dressed like Oysters in Scallop Shells were very good at Supper."

Like many Europeans, she was intrigued and impressed by the Indians and, like Champlain two centuries earlier, was prepared to see them not as alien beings but as fellow humans whose values and practices were as worthy of respect as her own. They held lengthy councils, she reported: "I have seen some translation of speeches full of well-expressed fine sentiments, & marking their reliance on the Great Spirit." Many of the Indians reminded her of the ancient Greeks and Romans and looked "like figures painted by the Old Masters." She found the Ojibway in particular very handsome, "& have a superior air to any I have seen." Joseph Brant, the distinguished Iroquois leader who moved his people north when the American colonies became independent, dined with her from time to time. She came to enjoy travelling in canoes. "To see a Birch Canoe managed with that inexpressible ease & composure which is the characteristic of an Indian is the prettiest sight imaginable."

In 1796 the Simcoes left Canada, never to return. At her first sight of England, Mrs. Simcoe wrote, "the fields looked so cold, so damp, so cheerless, so uncomfortable from the want of our bright Canadian Sun." The family retired to their estate with the bows and arrows and canoes they had brought back. When there was enough snow in the winter, they would travel about the neighbourhood on their Canadian sleigh. Simcoe died in 1806, but his wife lived on until 1850, always, it was said, curious to hear news of Canada.

FROM NEW ZEALAND TO the Cape Colony, from Newfoundland to Ceylon, the challenges that women faced in the British Empire were often the same: adapting to new environments, coping with illness or homesickness, managing their households, or amusing themselves. India, the jewel in the crown of the empire, presented all that and more. It was so big, so old, so complicated with all its different peoples and religions.

The British presence there went back to the reign of the

first Elizabeth. What had started out as a trading company had turned over the centuries into a government, the Raj, controlling more and more of the subcontinent. Until the nineteenth century, however, the East India Company was only one power among several. The British, women included, who went there were frequently adventurers (or worse) and were obliged to make their way among the local societies. It also helped that the newcomers came from a Europe which was not yet the dominant and self-satisfied one of the later nineteenth century. Their Europe was that of the Enlightenment and was open and curious about other civilizations rather than judgemental. Sir William Jones, a high court judge in Calcutta in the 1780s and a distinguished scholar of Sanskrit, was by no means alone in thinking Asia "the nurse of the sciences." Mrs. Maria Graham, who travelled widely in India in the early 1800s, wrote approvingly in her memoirs that "Everywhere in the ancient Hindu books we find the maxims of that pure and sound morality which is founded on the nature of man as a rational and social being." Elizabeth Plowden, whose husband worked as an officer for the ruler of the still independent state of Awadh in the 1780s, lived for a time in the cosmopolitan city of Lucknow, with its mingling of Hindus, Muslims, and Christians. She was a regular guest at the court, studied Persian and Hindustani, and developed an enthusiasm for Indian music.

There were many friendships among British and Indians, and it was not at all unusual for British men to take Indian wives (although the converse was much rarer). Nor were the children of such unions shunned by the British, as they later would be. As late as 1848, when the young Emily Metcalfe rejoined her father in Delhi, where he was the Resident (in other words the leading British official), he took her to call on his friends, who included many of mixed race. She was amused but not, I like to think, patronizing when she described the very stout old sisters, Mrs. Foster and Mrs. Fuller, dressed in white cotton dresses "made very like bed-gowns," who were "dark in complexion and spoke English with a very curious accent." They were, she added, "excellent old ladies, and their sons and daughters were all connected with the British Army in India." By the second half of the nineteenth century, when the British had consolidated their rule over the Indians, it was no longer as easy for the two peoples to mix. An assumption of superiority on the one side and unease or resentment on the other did not make for comfortable relations, much less friendship on an equal basis.

The beautiful and energetic — and, by the time she reached middle age, stout — Fanny Parkes, who arrived in Calcutta in 1822, was fortunate to arrive at a time of transition, when there were still strong and independent Indian rulers. She was at first inclined to disdain India and the Indians. Indian fruits, she pronounced in her journal, were all tasteless; Indian singing was "curious." Indians themselves only appear in her writings in those early years as troublesome servants or as picturesque figures such as fakirs or dancing girls. Gradually her natural curiosity led her to look closer. After four years in Calcutta she realized she had never met any Indian women except servants or shopkeepers, so she had herself invited to the women's quarters, the *zenana*, of a rich local Hindu. While she did not find the women she encountered on this occasion particularly interesting, it was to be the first of many such visits. Over time, as she became better acquainted with India and more fluent in Indian languages, she moved from seeing Indian women as curiosities to making friends among them.

Her husband, who is a shadowy figure in the journals, managed to get a post upcountry, and for the next ten years they lived in Allahabad and Cawnpore. She coped with much aplomb with the scorching summer heat, fevers, earthquakes, plagues of locusts, snakes in the bathing rooms, or white ants eating a cupboard full of her linen. She no longer found India dull, and as she explored the countryside on horseback, she started to appreciate its beauty. Although the sociable Mrs. Parkes became part of the small local British communities, she also began to make contact with Indians, playing chess with a local notable in Cawnpore and visiting the *zenanas*. She spent much time with the ex-queen of Gwalior, pitching her tent for weeks on end in the queen's camp and gossiping with her and her female court. She entertained them by demonstrating how to ride side-saddle and then putting on Mahratta dress and trying one of the queen's horses. When she finally parted from the camp, she recorded in her journal, "I had passed so many happy hours, amused with beholding native life and customs, and witnessing their religious ceremonies." On a visit to Delhi, where the last remnants of the once-great Mughal dynasty lived, she had an introduction to an elderly Mughal princess living out her days among the decaying splendours of the palace. Mrs. Parkes was dismayed by the "wretched poverty of these descendants of the emperors," and bowed her head to receive a simple wreath of flowers, so she recorded, "with as much respect as if she had been Queen of the Universe."

Her journals are filled with vivid details because she was interested in everything she came upon: the colour of the Indian clothes, the jewels of the women, elephants fighting each other, tiger hunts, the acrobats and jugglers who came to her bungalow, or the religious processions and festivals.

What makes her journals more than a superior travelogue
is that she has the instincts of an anthropologist who wants
to understand other societies from within. She watched the
annual Muharram ceremonies — when Muslims, especially
the Shia, commemorate and mourn the death of the Prophet's
grandson Hussein — and explained the symbolism of each ele-
ment. In Allahabad she went to the great annual fair, where
pilgrims gathered to perform ritual prayers, the *pooja*, and
bathe in the Ganges, and she analyzed the beliefs that surrounded the event and the differences among the holy men
who arrived in great numbers. When she attended a performance of the great Hindu epic the *Ramlila*, it encouraged her
to learn about Hindu mythology. She applied herself with
such eagerness to studying the customs and beliefs of Hindus,
she reported, that her friends laughed and said, "We expect
some day to see you at *pooja* in the river." She also studied the
Koran. She learned Persian and Hindustani and acquainted
herself with Indian history.

Her enthusiasm did not prevent her from criticizing what
she felt to be unfair or unjust practices. She was horrified
when she saw a widow being forced onto her husband's funeral
pyre — so his relatives could get their hands on her property,
Mrs. Parkes believed — and she cited Hindu scriptures to back
up her objections to the practice. She thought the British were
right to outlaw sati but reminded her readers that it was not
only in India that women were treated badly: "Women in all
countries are considered such dust in the balance, when their
interests are pitted against those of the men, that I rejoice no
more widows are to be grilled to ensure the whole of the property passing to the sons of the deceased."

On her morning rides she collected plants and flowers and
followed local custom in planting a peepul, the "holy tree,"

near her bungalow. She also put in an avenue of neem trees because they were said to make the air wholesome. According to one of the local proverbs she loved collecting and perhaps believed herself, the act of planting these trees also took the planter one step closer to heaven. She now found Indian dancing graceful and the music "very pretty." She took lessons on the sitar. She described Indian women in their saris as "remarkably graceful," while European women by contrast were awkward and ungainly, their corsets making them "as stiff as a lobster in its shell." She developed a taste for Indian food. When she stayed with her great friend Colonel William Linnaeus Gardner (his middle name came from his godfather, the famous Swedish botanist), she asked that they have only Indian dishes because she found it so much more interesting than European-style food. She tried a *pan*, that mix of betel leaf, betel nut, and spices which Indians use as a digestive, and pronounced it "very refreshing." When she had a headache she took the opium offered by an Indian friend. She felt instantly much better, she noted, "and talked incessantly."

In Cawnpore, she had herself rowed on the Ganges at night to enjoy the "fairyland" of the annual Diwali festival: "On every temple, on every *ghāt*, and on the steps down to the river's side, thousands of small lamps were placed, from the foundation to the highest pinnacle, tracing the architecture in lines of light.'" She could never have imagined, she writes, that "the dreary looking station of Cawnpore contained so much beauty." She grew to appreciate the variety and beauty of Indian architecture and was appalled when the governor general proposed to sell the Taj Mahal for its marble and precious stones: "To sell the tomb raised over an empress, which from its extraordinary beauty is the wonder of the world?" It would be, she remarked, like the British government selling the exquisite chapel in Westminster Abbey where Henry VII is buried.

Mrs. Parkes spent much of her time travelling on her own with her servants. "How much there is to delight the eye in this bright, this beautiful world!" she exclaimed. "Roaming about with a good tent and a good Arab, one might be happy for ever in India." And perhaps she had another reason for enjoying her adventures.

Emily Eden, the sister of Lord Auckland, the governor general in the late 1830s, reported Mrs. Parkes' explanation for her travels: "She has a husband who always goes mad in the cold season, so she says it is her duty to herself to leave him and travel about." (Emily and her sister, also called Fanny, found Mrs. Parkes rather tiresome, as she insisted on following the governor general's progress through upper India and pitching her tent in their encampment.)

Wherever Mrs. Parkes went, she sought out the local sights: mosques, temples, tombs, ruined forts, palaces. She stood in awe at the great Qutb Minar tower in Delhi and found it especially striking at night: "I could not withdraw my eyes from it; the ornaments, beautiful as they are by day, shadowed as they were into the mass of the building, only added to its grandeur. We roamed through the colonnades, in the court of the beautiful arches, and returned most unwillingly to our tents." She made good use of her sketching materials, and the first edition of her journals is filled with her illustrations. She was enchanted by a scene along the Ganges: "a perfect crowd of beautiful Hindu temples clustered together." And she comments with relief, "no Europeans are there — a place is spoiled by European residence." On one trip she went by boat up the Ganges to see the Taj Mahal, which she found even more wonderful than she had expected. She arrived during Eid, the festival to mark the end of Ramadan. The large crowds of gaily dressed locals added great beauty to the scene, she writes, "whilst the eye of taste turned away pained and annoyed by the vile round hats and stiff attire of the European gentlemen, and the equally ugly bonnets and stiff and graceless dresses of the English ladies." She was shocked to learn that the Europeans held dances on the marble platform in front of the Taj Mahal.

It was during this trip that she met the man — a "kindly, mild, gentlemanly, polished, entertaining companion" — who was to become her great friend, and through him his half-Indian family. Colonel Gardner was the son of a British army officer, and his mother was the daughter of an old upper-class American family. His parents chose the British side in the American War of Independence, and when the war ended, the family joined the Loyalists who went into exile around the world. William, who was then only thirteen, went into the army in Britain but a few years later made his way to India as an officer. He never left. While he was helping to settle a complex dispute over an Indian princely inheritance, he caught sight of the "most beautiful black eyes in the world" peeping out of where the women sat in purdah. On the strength of the eyes alone, he proposed marriage and obtained what turned out to be a lovely young princess as his devoted wife. The two were to live happily together for many years until his death. She died a month afterwards. Their children were given a mix of Indian and English names but were brought up largely as Indians. Mrs. Parkes was delighted when she was invited to stay on Colonel Gardner's estate near Agra and take part in the wedding of one of his granddaughters to a Mughal prince. Again she provides a detailed description of what she sees, from the wedding clothes to the rituals themselves.

In 1839 she left India. When she arrived back in England, her disappointment echoed that of Mrs. Simcoe. "Everything on landing looked so wretchedly mean, especially the houses, which are built of slate stone, and also slated down the sides — no wonder on first landing I felt a little disgusted." She brought with her as much as she could of India — the "curiosities" of which she was so proud, including her collection of Hindu idols. There was nothing as good in the British Museum, she said proudly, "and as for Ganesh, they never beheld such a one as mine, even in a dream!" When she published her journals, she prefaced them with an invocation to the elephant-headed god, who is patron of the arts and sciences.

FANNY PARKES AND MEN such as Gardner and Sir Thomas Metcalfe, with his hookah and his deep love of Delhi (he had a wonderful series of paintings done by Indian artists of its buildings, monuments, and peoples), were the last of an old order which was rapidly disappearing. There was a growing gulf between the rulers and the ruled, and finding a way to bridge it was difficult. The British women who were coming to India in increasing numbers, thanks to steamships and the Suez Canal, have often been blamed for this — unfairly, in my view. As Britain and Europe came to dominate the world through their formal and informal empires, their peoples increasingly mistook power — temporary, as it turned out — for a superiority across the board, whether in science and technology or values and institutions. Britain was changing in other ways too; it was becoming more straitlaced, more prudish, and less tolerant of other cultures. Fanny Parkes regarded the newly discovered enthusiasm for evangelism among the servants of the East India

Company with cynicism. "Religious meetings are held continually in Calcutta, frequented by people to pray themselves into high salaries, who never thought of praying before." Yet the growing influence of evangelical Christianity was real, and it brought with it both a disdain for what were seen as heathen religions and a mission to convert those who, it was assumed, were sunk in darkness.

By the mid-nineteenth century the British working in India for the Raj were sober and judgemental officials, quite different from their more rackety and adventurous predecessors. More, they had a conviction that they were entitled to rule India for its own benefit. For the most part, the new men had little interest in mingling with Indians, and after the East India Company finally lost control of India in 1858, the Government of India effectively banned its employees from marrying Indian women. Increasingly the British took to describing themselves as a ruling caste which needed for reasons of prestige to remain aloof from its subjects. That helped to shape expectations of how British women should behave. In a novel by Maud Diver, a popular Anglo-Indian writer, the hero, an army officer, shouts at his wife as they stand on a raft in a raging river: "Remember that you're an Englishwoman in a boat full of natives and our women are *not cowards*." Somewhere in the attitudes of British men towards their women in India was a fear that they might be fallible and weak, susceptible even to the attractions of handsome Indian men. Or that the Indians might suddenly rise up and attack them as they had done in 1857 and ravish their women.

Now seen by Indian nationalists as India's first war of independence, that year saw a mutiny by parts of the East India Company's own army, supported by Indians who opposed British rule, which shook the Raj. The British restored order but they never forgot their officers who were cut down by their own men; or their women and children who were thrown down wells or hunted across the countryside. Even though order was restored, the British were never able thereafter to forget that the Indians were so many and they so few. When the first India-wide census was taken in 1881, out of a total population of 250 million, only 145,000 were counted as European. From time to time, especially around the anniversary of the mutiny, rumours would sweep through the British community in India that something was brewing, that posters urging Indians to rape European women were going up in the bazaars.

Usually the challenges were more quotidian, such as behaving with the appropriate dignity and aloofness. The Raj discouraged British women from getting involved in any form of social work among Indians; it might lower them in the eyes of Indian men and, equally important, stir up trouble by ruffling Indian sensibilities. The British community in India also got exercised by anything that might suggest that European women were immoral or easy. They worried about the new media of photography and film, and when Maud Allan, a music hall entertainer famous for her interpretation of the Dance of the Seven Veils, wanted to tour India before the First World War, the petitions from men and women poured in, begging the government of India to prevent it. (The government was sympathetic but found itself powerless.)

Still there remained British women, fewer perhaps than in the past, who resisted such pressures to conform and who engaged with India and the Indians. Some came as missionaries, teachers, or medical women, specifically to work with Indians. A handful more radical still, such as the British admiral's daughter who wore only Indian dress and served as one of Mahatma Gandhi's workers, chose to abjure their own society. Yet others managed to steer their own course between two worlds. Flora Annie Steel, married to a member of the Indian Civil Service, had many Indian friends, and when she returned to India to research her major novel on the Indian mutiny, she stayed with many of them in preference to her British friends. Annette Akroyd came to India in the 1870s to work with liberal Indians on education for women. Although she eventually married Henry Beveridge, also a member of the Indian Civil Service, she refused to become part of the endless social round, preferring instead to learn Bengali and study Persian. Her translation brought the wonderful memoirs of Babur, the first Mughal emperor in India, to the attention of the English-speaking world for the first time. (Her son, William, was to become the father of the British Welfare State.)

Towards the end of the Raj, Ursula Graham Bower found herself leading local scouts on the frontier between India and Burma during the Second World War to collect and pass on information about the Japanese. Described with justification by *Time* magazine as looking like a movie actress, Graham Bower, who came from a well-connected family in Britain, had come to India in the 1930s to visit a friend and her Indian Civil Service brother at his post in the northeast. They took a trip into the hilly country near Kohima, the capital of a province in the northeast, and something happened to her as she caught her first glimpse of the local Naga people and the hills and mountain peaks in the distance: "That landscape drew me as I had never known anything do before, with a power transcending the body, a force not of this world at all." She felt that she had rejoined a world from which she had unaccountably become estranged.

The local British community and most of the officials thought she was mad to want to live in the hills alone, but she paid little attention. With encouragement from anthropologists in Britain, she became an anthropologist and photographer, recording the lives and customs of the Nagas. The tribal people, as the government described them, had the reputation of being wild and difficult, possibly headhunters, but gradually she won their confidence and eventually their friendship — in part by running a small dispensary, but more, I suspect, because she so clearly showed that she liked and trusted them. Some came to see her as the reincarnation of a local goddess.

In 1942, as the Japanese forces were sweeping across Asia and through Burma towards India, she was asked to lead a group made up of local tribespeople to collect much-needed intelligence. Their work was invaluable and helped the British forces prepare for the great 1944 Japanese offensive towards Kohima. If Kohima had fallen, the crucial supply routes from India to free China under Chiang Kai-shek would have been cut. Chiang might well have sued for peace. India too would have been threatened and, so the Japanese hoped, seen the nationalists rising up against the British. Graham Bower and her team helped to provide the information that the British command so badly needed about the size of the Japanese forces, their disposition, and their equipment. (The Japanese paid her the compliment of placing a bounty on her head.) When the war ended, she was recognized with several honours, including the Lawrence of Arabia Memorial Medal. She had also met and married an Englishman who was as unconventional as she was and loved the hills as much. They had a wedding in a church in Shillong, but it wasn't until they had been married by Naga rites that her friends in the tribes finally approved.

Women have been some of the great adventurers of the nineteenth and twentieth centuries, perhaps because they were tempered and toughened by overcoming the obstacles society placed in the way of their sex. Think of Gertrude Bell, nicknamed "the Desert Queen," who travelled through much of modern Syria and Iraq before the First World War, when they were still parts of the Ottoman Empire; of Dervla Murphy, who bicycled overland to India from Europe by herself in the 1960s (and has had many other adventures since); of Dorothy Carrington, daughter of a British major general, who settled on Corsica in the 1950s and explored the island and its dark side when that was still daring and dangerous to do; or of Freya Stark, who travelled widely in the Middle East and Afghanistan. She drove across Afghanistan and then Iran in a Land Rover in her late seventies and rode by horseback to Annapurna in her eighties. Curiously such intrepid women have not always been great feminists: on the occasion of her seventieth birthday, Freya Stark invited only men for a celebratory dinner, while Gertrude Bell opposed votes for women and despised most she knew. "It is such a pity," she once exclaimed loudly in front of a new bride, "that promising young Englishmen go and marry such fools of women."

While some women travellers were content to explore and observe, others, such as Bell herself, became passionately committed to the other worlds they encountered, in her case the Arab Middle East. Thanks to a rich and indulgent father, she had spent much time there before the First World War and had made crucial contacts both among Arabs and among those British, such as T. E. Lawrence, who were going to play their part alongside her in creating the new map of the region in the aftermath of the war. The authorities had the good sense to recognize her exceptional knowledge and expertise, and in 1915 she was given an appointment in British military intelligence. She was highly intelligent, sure of herself, and domineering. What she hoped to do was create new Arab states out of the wreckage of the Ottoman Empire, in par-ticular a great one centred on Mesopotamia, in the lands of the Tigris and Euphrates. And she got at least a part of what she wanted. As virtually the only woman to play a part in the peace settlements at the end of the war, she lobbied the pow-erful statesmen in Paris and played a key role in the creation of what came to be known as Iraq ("the well-founded coun-try"). She wrote much of the constitution of the new country on her carved wooden table in Baghdad and handpicked as its new ruler, Faisal, the Hashemite prince who had fought with Lawrence in the Arab revolt against the Ottomans. She did not get all she wished for, however. The establishment of the new state did not serve to contain Arab nationalism or strengthen British influence over the Arabs as she had hoped. If anything, the converse happened. Arab national-ists increasingly turned on Britain as their chief opponent, and Faisal proved to have a mind of his own. He gradually sidelined Bell, and in 1926 she committed suicide. In recent years Gertrude Bell has been rediscovered through new biog-raphies and now in a movie, *Queen of the Desert*, starring Nicole Kidman.

EDITH DURHAM WAS ALSO in Paris at the end of the First World War, and she too lobbied the world's statesmen about a part of the world she loved and knew, but they did not lis-ten to her as they did to Gertrude Bell. She did not have the same connections, influence, or glamour, and her chosen cause was not the Middle East, with its oil and great strategic importance, but the impoverished little Balkan country of Albania. While Durham has one biography written about her and is mentioned occasionally in histories of the Balkans, it is unlikely that a movie will ever be made of her life. She and her cause were simply not as important, yet as an individual she is equally fascinating.

Like Bell, she ignored convention and the expectations of her family and risked dangers to travel throughout a part of the world unfamiliar to most outsiders. The Balkans (generally taken to include the mountainous area stretching southwards from Serbia, Rumania, and Bulgaria to the Aegean) were on the southeastern flank of Europe, but the region was backward, with poor communications, which discouraged travellers. And since most of the Balkans had been under the rule of the Ottoman Empire since the sixteenth century, its peoples were considered somehow different and slightly alien. It was only in the nineteenth century, as one by one the Balkan nations gradually freed themselves from Ottoman rule and started to modernize, that Europeans from elsewhere discovered them. Edith Durham was among them. Like Bell further east, she too fell in love with the local cultures and immersed herself in learning about the peoples she encountered and, so she hoped, in helping them.

Like many explorers, including Bell herself, Durham was brave, self-willed, loyal to her friends, and curious. She was also rude, intolerant, and maddening. She loved deeply — sadly, for her — a man who was not interested in her, and a people, the Albanians, whom she was never able to help as much as she wanted. An early photograph shows a very handsome young woman with a lovely profile, sensuous mouth, and thick dark hair, but as she grew older she lost her looks. Not that she much cared. Unlike Gertrude Bell, who had to have the latest fashions from London, Edith Durham wore whatever came to hand and was serviceable. Aubrey Herbert, the younger son of the Earl of Carnarvon, met her first in the summer of 1913, when they were both carrying out relief work among refugees in the Balkans. He described her in a letter to his wife: "She cuts her hair short like a man, has a cockney accent and a roving eye, is clever, aggressive and competitive but she has really done a lot for these people." The charismatic young aristocrat (he was the model for the hero in John Buchan's *Greenmantle*) and the ungracious middle-aged Englishwoman were to develop a grudging mutual respect and a sort of friendship as they worked together in the cause of the Albanians.

Born in London in 1863 and the eldest of nine children, Durham came from a solidly middle-class background. For some reason, all the children except Edith received good educations. While she dabbled in art, her brothers became doctors and engineers, and two of her sisters went to Girton College in Cambridge. When her father, a distinguished surgeon, died unexpectedly, the family seems to have agreed that Edith was the best suited to staying at home to look after their mother, who was now an invalid. Edith said later that she felt trapped: "The future stretched before me as endless years of grey monotony, and escape seemed hopeless." She became increasingly depressed and in 1900 suffered a collapse. Her doctor recommended that she travel for relaxation, and the family agreed that she should have two months every year away from her mother. They cannot have expected that Edith would choose the Balkans, the most lawless and turbulent part of Europe, for her recuperation.

She seems to have gone partly in a spirit of desperate bravado — "a bullet would have been a sort of way out" — but more importantly because she found the region exotic, mysterious, and exciting, somewhere that seemed to belong to a much earlier time in history. It was also a complete contrast to her staid and stifling life in London. Although she was disappointed at her first glimpses of the coast of Dalmatia, where the Austrians had imposed law and order and were busy bringing such joys of civilization as orderly streets and drains, she soon discovered the hills and mountains of Montenegro, "such utter desolation and barren wilderness," and then the high and remote country of northern Albania. The song she puts at the start of her best-known book, *High Albania*, sums up the attraction of the Balkans for her:

> Oh, we're back to the Balkans again,
> Back to the joy and the pain —
> What if it burns or it blows or it snows!
> We're back to the Balkans again.
> Back, where tomorrow the quick may be dead,
> With a hole in his heart or a ball in his head —
> Back, where the passions are rapid and red —
> Oh, we're back to the Balkans again!

By the time her mother died in 1906, finally freeing her to stay in the Balkans as long as she wanted, Durham had already established a reputation as a formidable traveller and writer who was one of the leading experts on the Balkans. Often on her own with only a guide, she explored the remaining European parts of the Ottoman Empire, such as Macedonia and the Albanian lands, the Austrian provinces of Bosnia Herzegovina, and the independent states of Serbia and Montenegro. She was sometimes the first foreigner, and certainly the first foreign woman, to visit remote monasteries and churches. As she jogged along muddy tracks on a mule, she accepted and even welcomed discomfort and danger. She slept in fields, barns, or filthy inns. She made light of reports of bandits or hostile locals. "Savage as are the Albanians," she wrote airily in one of her books, "I have been told repeatedly that they never assault women." Wherever she went, she attracted curious crowds who bombarded her with questions. Why wasn't she married? Was it true that she was a cousin of the King of England?

Although her first book was on Serbia, she never really warmed to the Serbs, whom she found short and plain — not like the handsome Montenegrin "giants" — and dull as well, always drinking glasses of water. In 1904 she got to know Macedonia when she ran a hospital and relief operation there for Albanian refugees who had been savagely displaced in the aftermath of an abortive rebellion against the Ottomans. In the end, she found the Macedonians intensely irritating and their superstitions infuriating. For a while Montenegro was her favourite part of the Balkans. She became friendly with its devious old king, Nicholas, and would sit gossiping with him in his little palace, although she regretted the signs of modernity that were creeping in — the electric lights along the main street of the capital, Cetinje, and the appearance of a newspaper. "Montenegro will now be less happy," she said. The happiest Balkan states, in her view, were the ones with the fewest newspapers.

By 1911 she was becoming disillusioned with Nicholas and suspicious of his attempts to increase the power and the lands of his dynasty. She was working in Montenegro at the time on a relief effort to clothe and feed the largely Albanian refugees who had fled from Kosovo after the Ottomans had put down a rebellion there with great brutality. She made shirts and turned out shoes in her hotel room, which came to reek of imperfectly cured hides in the summer heat. She was shocked when Nicholas seemed ready to abandon the refugees and seize as much Albanian land as possible from the Ottomans. During the Balkan wars of 1912 and 1913, she grew to hate him and his kingdom for their cruelties towards the Albanians. According to one observer, what finished her for good was when she looked into the bag of a Montenegrin warrior and found his booty of sixty noses. She transferred her devotion and considerable energies to the cause of Albanian independence.

The Albanians themselves had attracted her from the time of her first visits to the Balkans. In 1900 she had seen the mountains of northern Albania in the distance and longed to explore them. The following year, she joined a party of Frenchmen travelling across Lake Ohrid to Scutari, an important trading city by the mountains and one which few foreigners had visited. Her French companions disappeared when their ship landed, and with only a small boy to guide her she set off through narrow streets to find a hotel. "The swarming seething mass of savages I can give you no idea of," she wrote. She saw ferocious men from the mountains, "heavily armed with magnificent silver weapons" and Christian women belonging to the town dressed in "white and scarlet, masses of coins, silver buttons and embroidery." She felt overwhelmed: "The unutterable rags, the squalor and the gorgeousness, the heaps of newly flayed hides sizzling in the sun, the clatter and slither of pack animals, the goats, the cattle, the oxcarts and the dust." She loved it all.

In 1904 she finally made a prolonged expedition up into the mountains of northern Albania. Her one companion was an Albanian Christian who was distributing bibles, a potentially perilous activity in what was still the Ottoman Empire and where many of the Albanians themselves were Muslim. "I am the first Englishwoman here in the memory of man," she said proudly of one town, "where very few strangers of any kind have been." She received a warm welcome from the Albanians, who thought she must be both rich and powerful. And she responded with a deepening affection for them. She was fascinated by the remote villages and a way of life unchanged for centuries, especially in what she called High Albania. She came to share their resentment that they, the original Illyrian inhabitants of the Balkans, had been crowded out by the incoming Slavs over the centuries. And she wanted to explain them to the outside world in the hopes of gathering support for the cause of Albanian independence from the Ottoman Empire. She also feared, as did the early Albanian nationalists, that the already independent Balkan states of Serbia, Greece, and Montenegro would grab for themselves the territories inhabited by Albanians as the Ottoman Empire weakened still further.

In 1908 she made a series of trips into the mountains to gather material for the book that she would publish as *High Albania*. It provided, almost for the first time, a history of Albania, and it also is a work of serious ethnography, examining as it does the laws, tribes, myths, and customs of northern Albania. It is illustrated by her photographs and sketches of the peoples, their ornaments, even the different ways the men shave their heads. She writes about the elaborate tattoos that the women have, which she believes is an ancient Illyrian custom, and tries to understand the deep-rooted practice of blood feuds. The book was controversial; she was accused of either exaggerating the brutality of life in the Balkans or not sufficiently condemning it. "On almost every page," said one reviewer, "there are tales of men shot, men about to shoot, of men who glory in the tales of murders to their credit. Miss Durham seems to share their exultation in the glory of man-slaying."

Durham was not deterred. Increasingly she felt that her destiny lay with helping the Albanians, who were to her both romantic and underdogs. They were a friendless people with too many enemies and too many internal divisions. Their neighbours had designs on their lands. Yet the Albanians themselves, divided between Christian and Muslim, north and south, and bloody clan rivalries, were incapable of speaking with one voice. This infuriated and disheartened Durham, who feared that their own disunity would deliver the Albanians into the hands of their predatory neighbours. It was gratifying for her too to be called the Queen of Albania and welcomed with such reverence wherever she went. She made it her mission to free the Albanians from Ottoman rule and get them their own country. She recognized that the mix of populations in the Balkans made drawing borders difficult but hoped, optimistically, that the different nationalities and religions could work together.

She joined forces with Aubrey Herbert to set up the Anglo-Albanian Society. In 1912, when the first Balkan War left thousands of Albanians within Greece, Serbia, and Montenegro, the odd couple lobbied in London for an independent Albania. When the Great Powers, for their own reasons, concurred, the Anglo-Albanian Society successfully agitated to keep Greece from seizing too much Albanian territory in the south.

In 1914 the outbreak of the First World War forced Edith Durham back to England. As her ship sailed away from the Albanian port of Vlorë, she felt isolated among the other passengers. "It was years since I'd been with a large crowd of English," she wrote. "They seemed to me a strange race." Back home she was depressed that Britain was fighting on the side of the hated Serbia. She spent the war years writing her book *Twenty Years of Balkan Tangle* to explain the region to outsiders. When the war ended, she and Herbert did what they could to promote Albania's interests in the peace settlements. They demanded, unsuccessfully, that representatives of the Albanian people be allowed to travel to Paris to address the peace conference there. They were more successful with another demand, that Albania be admitted to the League of Nations.

In 1921 Durham, whose health had been shattered by long years of hard travelling, made one last trip to Albania. She had a warm welcome and saw some of the places that had been named after her, but her feelings were mixed. She didn't like the many signs of change and the outsiders who were arriving to live and work there. "Albania," she wrote, "is not like Albania with foreigners in it." She never returned. She continued to work for Albania as best she could for the rest of her life, but in the small circles that cared about the Balkans in Britain, she was increasingly seen as a crank and out of step with British opinion. She died in 1944, optimistic that the end of the war might bring better days for Albania. Fortunately she was not to see Albania's long agony under the rule of one of the more bizarre and dreadful of the Communist leaders.

At the time of her death the exiled King Zog of Albania, whom she had never liked, gave her a generous epitaph: "Albanians have never forgotten — and will never forget — this Englishwoman. In the mountains she knew so well, her death will echo from peak to peak." In the Communist period, the government ensured that she was forgotten, but with the coming of democracy again in the 1990s, her name is now remembered and is appearing again on Albania's streets and schools.

IF HISTORY IS A house, it is one where the portraits of some of our forebears are displayed prominently on the walls while others are relegated to dusty boxrooms and attics. We remember Gertrude Bell today because she helped to shape Iraq and the modern Middle East — even though that legacy is now falling to pieces. Edith Durham played a minor role in the emergence of an independent Albania in 1912, and that has earned her a modest place in recent Balkan history. Curiosity, daring, the desire to explore strange worlds — these admirable qualities do not in themselves guarantee lasting fame. Mrs. Simcoe was largely forgotten in Canada until the 1960s, when her diary was rediscovered and published. She did not leave a lasting influence on Canadian society. Fanny Parkes's memoirs, which were published in 1850, were out of print until the 1970s, and she was known only to handful of people, such as myself, who researched the British in India. What each did, however, whether they were famous or obscure, was leave a record of themselves and of the worlds they moved through. For this, we owe them much. They pop out of the past to catch our attention and remind us that they were human just as we are, and through the legacy of their writings they enable us to write history.

FIVE

OBSERVERS

ON MAY 17, 1824, a group of men gathered around a fireplace
in the large upstairs drawing room of the publishers John
Murray. The firm, which still exists today, was then relatively new but already had a reputation for publishing out-
standing writers, among them Jane Austen and Sir Walter
Scott. It also published the notorious Lord Byron, and his
memoirs had brought these men here on that spring day.
Byron, whose profligate behaviour had already driven him
from England, had dashed off the manuscript a few years earlier in "my finest, ferocious Caravaggio style" and then sent
it to his friend the Irish poet Thomas Moore for safekeeping.
With Byron having died earlier that month at Messolonghi
during a lull in the Greek War of Independence, Moore, as
his literary executor, now had to decide what to do with the
papers left in his charge.

He and a few others had already read the memoirs. Lady
Caroline Lamb, one of Byron's many mistresses, dismissed
them as "no value — a mere copy-book." Lord John Russell, a
leading Liberal politician, thought Byron's depictions of his
youth and his time in Greece "were strikingly described,"

although he admitted that "three or four pages were too gross and indelicate for publication." It was the obscenity and potential for scandal that worried John Hobhouse, a close friend of Byron's from his youth and an aspiring poet himself. While Byron's reputation had continued to go from bad to worse, Hobhouse had become a member of Parliament and grown increasingly respectable. Perhaps he feared for his reputation should the memoirs become public; perhaps he had come to resent Byron's much greater accomplishments as a poet. "After my first access of grief was over," Hobhouse later wrote, "I then determined to lose no time in doing my duty by preserving all that was left to me of my dear friend — his fame." He knew that he had the support of two determined women: Byron's estranged wife, Annabella, and his half-sister Augusta Leigh, widely believed to have had an affair with Byron. They had sent representatives to the meeting. Moore had tried to hold out for preserving the memoirs, even if they had to be locked up for years to come, but he was now alone, for John Murray had buckled under pressure from the Byron family and their friends. So Moore watched the other men tear the manuscript apart and throw the pages on the fire. Biographers, literary historians, and the merely prurient have regretted the loss ever since.

History has many such examples of the records being destroyed or carefully winnowed and adjusted, whether to protect the reputation of the deceased or to spare the living. Jane Austen's sister burned her letters; why has never been clear. The widow of another famous rake, the great explorer Sir Richard Burton, claimed to have seen a vision of her deceased husband in 1891 as she sat in front of the hearth wondering what to do with his writings, which contained among much else graphic descriptions of sexual practices encountered on his explorations of the Middle East and India. "Burn it!" the vision told her, and so she did. The poet Ted Hughes destroyed Sylvia Plath's last journal because he did not want their children to read it. Thomas Hardy burned what he called "the diabolical diaries" of his first wife and dictated his own biography to his second wife, to be published after his death as her own work. The Chinese government seized the memoir the infamous Madame Mao wrote while she was in prison in her last years. It is not known what has happened to it. Sometimes archives and libraries — the collective memory of a people — are deliberately targeted in war. When Yugoslavia broke up in violence in the 1990s, Serbian nationalists shelled the National Library of Bosnia in Sarajevo. Those who were there have told me of seeing priceless Ottoman manuscripts whirling through the air as they disintegrated into ash before their eyes.

Mice, white ants, fire, and flood destroy the records as much as humans. The switch to cheap pulp paper brought books and newspapers within the price range of poorer members of society (and made fortunes for Canadian timber barons) but has been a headache for archivists ever since. I have sat in libraries going through the yellowing pages of nineteenth-century newspapers and found them starting to disintegrate in my hands. And even when valuable sets of personal papers survive, the trustees, who are often family members, restrict access or refuse to let anyone see them at all. For years James Joyce's grandson, Stephen, has campaigned aggressively to keep control of anything written by his grandfather, even published works. He has sued or threatened lawsuits to prevent biographers or literary critics quoting from Joyce; anthologies could not use passages; and it has been nearly impossible to adapt Joyce's works for stage or even to have public readings. He also horrified a conference of scholars in Venice when he proudly announced that he had destroyed all the letters he and his wife had received from Lucia, Joyce's sad and troubled daughter. There was general relief when much of the copyright ran out in 2012 and most of Joyce's work came into the public domain.

Sometimes, and it is fortunate for posterity, executors such as Mackenzie King's ignore the expressed wishes. Canadian history would be much the poorer if his diaries had vanished. And to balance the sad list of the records that have been destroyed or simply vanished without trace, there are examples of those that were saved or discovered through good fortune. In 1967 an American professor visited an Italian baron in his family house near Florence to ask whether he might have any papers belonging to his great uncle Sidney Sonnino, Italy's foreign minister during much of the First World War and in the first years of the peace. The baron offered the professor a glass of Chianti and suggested that they might look in a neglected store cupboard. Inside were fourteen old trunks which turned out to contain Sidney Sonnino's official correspondence, diaries, letters, and other writings. Paul Mantoux, the chief French interpreter at the Paris Peace Conference, defied orders and kept a full record of the conversations between the world's four leading statesmen: President Woodrow Wilson of the United States, and Georges Clemenceau, David Lloyd George, and Vittorio Orlando, the prime ministers respectively of France, Britain, and Italy. He deposited two copies with the French Foreign Ministry, but those were part of the great stack of documents that were burned in the courtyard at the Quai d'Orsay as the Germans were advancing on Paris in 1940. Mantoux himself fled southwards, along with much of the French government, leaving the only remaining copy in his apartment. He managed to get a friend to retrieve it and hide it in the cellars at the faculty of law, where it remained until Paris was liberated. Without that record of the crucial conversations of 1919, we would not understand the negotiations that shaped the world of the twentieth century.

The material from which historians construct the past has become increasingly eclectic — we use the findings of archaeology, biology, or anthropology. We look at inscriptions and effigies on tombs, at coins, or at paintings. We study court records, tax rolls, or government reports. For more recent history we make use of everything from newspapers to film to Twitter. Yet we still need the individual voices who can give us the feel and texture of the past and the descriptions and stories of its people — what the American historian Barbara Tuchman once called the "corroborative detail" which fixes a person or a moment for us. And what such observers record, although they often did not intend it, gives us a greater understanding of the assumptions and values of a particular time, class, family, or place. Many of history's greatest observers, such as the duc de Saint-Simon at the court of Louis xiv, watched from the sidelines, while others — the Mughal emperor Babur, for example — changed history. What they all shared was an insatiable curiosity about their world and its inhabitants, a sharp eye for the telling detail, an appreciation of the absurdity of much of human affairs, a sense of irony, and, yes, a love of gossip. Even more important, they were determined to record what they saw. Without their records, our knowledge of the past would be so much the poorer. (And, I must confess, there is always something pleasurable in doing what one ought not to do in ordinary life, and that is read the private letters and diaries of others, all in the name of research.)

THE GREATEST DIARIES AND memoirs were often written by minor players who had fewer axes to grind than the powerful, and perhaps cared less about what posterity would think of them. Samuel Pepys, the English civil servant who started his diary in 1660, apparently never meant anyone to read it. He unselfconsciously talks about himself and the pattern of his days. He catalogues and describes everything — his emotions, illnesses, meals, clothes, friends, servants, wife, and cat. Sometimes he drinks too much; he quarrels with his wife and is rude to her friends. Although it makes him feel guilty, he is unfaithful to her. He also is a witness to the end of the Commonwealth and the re-establishment of the monarchy. He notes down the court gossip and keeps an eye on who in the government is up and who is down. He is in London in 1665, when it suffers the last great outbreak of plague, and there again the following year, when the Great Fire reduces much of it to ashes. Without Pepys's diaries we would not have nearly as complete a picture of life in the reign of Charles II. And we would not be able to make the acquaintance of this fascinating, infuriating, engaging human being.

Across the Channel, in a later generation, the duc de Saint-Simon assiduously collected the gossip of the court of Louis XIV. His lengthy memoirs are often unkind and acerbic, but they provide an unparalleled account of life in the great new palace at Versailles, with its rumours and endless speculations about who had the Sun King's favour and who did not. There were absurd quarrels over precedence, over who was allowed a seat in the king's presence or who would hand around the bag at mass to collect alms for the poor. Saint-Simon closely observed the king himself and those close to him. He was charmed by the little princess from Savoy brought to France as a twelve-year-old to be married to Louis's grandson and heir. (The king graciously stipulated that the consummation was to be delayed for a couple of years.) "In appearance she was plain," Saint-Simon wrote, "with cheeks that sagged, a forehead too prominent for beauty, an insignificant nose, and thick sensual lips, but the line of her chestnut hair and eyebrows was well marked and she had the prettiest, most eloquent eyes in all the world. Her few remaining teeth were badly decayed, which she was the first to laugh at and remark on." He was amused when she was in the king's chamber, chatting gaily to him and his attendants, while her old nurse lifted her dress from behind to give her an enema. When the princess died suddenly of an illness, Saint-Simon also recorded the rumours that she has been poisoned.

Saint-Simon hated Louis XIV and took pleasure in recounting his many acts of selfishness, as when he insisted that his favourite granddaughter accompany him on an excursion even though she was having a difficult pregnancy. When she miscarried, the king, Saint-Simon noted, was typically unrepentant. Saint-Simon also loathed Versailles, which he found inconvenient and unhealthy: "Beauty and ugliness; spaciousness and meanness were roughly tacked together." He described courtiers urinating in the corridors and a desperate duchess relieving herself in a chapel. He saw that Louis had used Versailles and the magnificence of his court to emasculate and tame the aristocracy: "He used this means deliberately and successfully to impoverish everyone, for he made luxury meritorious in all men." He warned that the competition to spend money on useless luxuries was like a disease spreading out from Versailles through France: "This cancer, kept alive by confusion of ranks, pride, even by good manners, and encouraged by the folly of the great, is having

incalculable results that will lead to nothing less than ruin
and general disaster."

MEMOIRS AND DIARIES ALSO act as a corrective to the ste-
reotypes we all form without realizing. In the West we can
grow up with a particular view of the Crusades, shaped by
popular literature and film, with noble knights heading off
to the Middle East to recover the Christian holy places from
the barbaric Muslims, and that can influence how we think
about the Middle East today. You will get a very different
picture if you read Amin Maalouf's wonderful little book
The Crusades through Arab Eyes or the memoirs of Anna
Comnena, who was born in 1083 and was the daughter of
a Byzantine emperor. Comnena's writings show the peoples of Constantinople and the Levant looking with dismay and disdain at the boorish, quarrelling, and greedy
Westerners who seemed far more interested in looting and
pillaging than in religion, and whose ideas of medicine or
basic hygiene were so primitive.

When we look at the exquisite miniature portraits of
Babur, the first Mughal emperor of India, we may first be
struck by the exotic: the bearded man in a jewelled turban,
with strings of pearls around his neck, seated on a marble
throne, lying in a palanquin or astride a horse, sometimes
with a hawk on his wrist. Yet he has left us a way of getting
below that glittering surface so that we discover a complicated and interesting human being.

Born in 1483, Babur was a minor Central Asian prince who
after many tribulations set up a kingdom at Kabul and then in
1526 became emperor of India and founded a dynasty which
lasted until 1857. His memoirs recount both the difficult road

he followed and his own reactions and reflections, including the moments when he despaired and thought of giving it all up and running away. "With such difficulties," he said to himself, "it would be better to go off on my own so long as I am alive...even to the ends of the earth." Yet he rallied again and again: "When one has pretensions to rule and a desire for conquest, one cannot sit back and just watch if events don't go right once or twice." He tells himself that persistence will eventually pay off: "It is important, when opportunity knocks, not to waver in determination. Regrets later on are useless." We know he thought this, and we have his own words for it, because, most unusually for someone of his time and rank, he wrote his memoirs.

Sadly they are not complete. There are gaps of several years at a time; during Babur's many and difficult wanderings, his luggage was repeatedly swept away or lost. And his son and heir Humayun may have lost more of the manuscripts after his father's death. Yet what remains is extraordinary, both for what it is and for the fact that it was written at all. The memoirs show a world with many interconnections and influences: Turkic-speaking warriors from Central Asia spreading outwards in all directions; Persian speakers moving eastwards; peoples from Afghanistan sweeping down towards India; and traders, artists, and scholars criss-crossing the whole. Babur himself, with his men and often with family members, travelled great distances, from Samarkand to Herat and Kabul, and in the end to Delhi, where he established the Mughal dynasty. So his memoirs constitute an invaluable record of the Mughals and of the peoples they conquered. Above all, however, they are the intensely personal observations, musings, and views of a warrior, poet, and man. They speak to us across centuries. At the time of their writing and for many years later, there was nothing in Islamic literature remotely like the *Baburnama*, as it is known. And I cannot think of any European ruler who has written such an autobiography.

Like so many other memoirists, Babur claimed that he had no axes to grind, that he was just recording what he saw and experienced. "I have not written this to complain," he remarks. "I have simply written the truth. I do not intend by what I have written to compliment myself: I have simply set down exactly what happened. Since I have made it a point in this history to write the truth of every matter and to set down no more than the reality of every event, as a consequence I have reported every good and evil I have seen of father and brother and set down the actuality of every fault and virtue of relative or stranger. May the reader excuse me; may the listener take me not to task." In fact Babur says much about his own reactions, his likes and his dislikes. He records his moments of doubt and his fits of melancholy. When, for example, he nearly died in a snowstorm on his way from Herat to Kabul, he wrote in a poem, "Does there remain for me unseen any cruelty or oppression of fate? / Shall my wounded heart yet know unknown pain or suffering?" From time to time he also expresses shame and regret. In his later years he wished that he had not written silly and obscene verses and wondered if that was why he was suffering from a serious fever and cough which left him spitting up blood: "What am I do to with you, O tongue? On your account my innards are bloody / No matter how gracefully you compose humorous poetry, part of it is obscene and part is false / If you wish not to burn for this crime, turn your reins from this field."

Babur also boasts, about his battles and his physical feats, including his epic drinking parties. Because he was a warrior who spent most of his life dealing with enemies, he carefully noted every battle, skirmish, and raiding party (he proudly notes that he drew the line at raiding his own subjects). He tried to assess what went wrong or right and in his memoirs he reflects on his mistakes. In his early years, he admitted, he was wrong to allow his men to plunder a newly acquired town, which needlessly alienated the locals at a time when enemies were close at hand: "From our issuing this order without reflection, how much contention and strife arose!"

Babur's father was a Mongol (in India the term became Mughal), one of the many descendants of Timur the Lame (Tamburlaine to the English). The family held a small territory in what is today's Uzbekistan, to the east of Samarkand, in the lush and fertile Ferghana Valley. Babur has left a vivid description of his father: "He was short in stature, had a round beard and a fleshy face and was fat. He wore his tunic so tight that to fasten the ties, he had to hold in his stomach; if he let himself go, it often happened that the ties broke. He was unceremonious in both dress and speech." When Babur was still a boy, his father died in a freak accident as he was looking after his beloved doves: the dovecote perched on the high walls of his fort suddenly broke loose and tumbled into the ravine below. Babur cannot resist an elegant pun in the original Turkic. His father, he writes, "became a falcon," which is also a synonym for dying.

At age twelve, Babur now found himself a ruler. Predators — many of them his Timurid relatives, including his half-brother — were gathering to seize his inheritance. Babur spent the next ten years on the move, attempting to secure a firm base. He took Samarkand twice but each time was forced out. On occasion he and his dwindling band of supporters came close to starvation. "It passed through my mind," he later wrote, "that to wander from mountain to mountain, homeless and houseless, had nothing to recommend it." He found his weakness humiliating and bitterly resented having to swallow repeated insults. "Except my soul no trustworthy friend have I found / Except my heart no intimate confidante have I found," he wrote in an early poem and concluded, "Babur, teach thyself to be loveless."

In 1502 he threw himself on the mercy of an uncle in Tashkent but found himself treated like the poor relation he was. "I endured much hardship and misery. I had no realm — and no hope of any realm — to rule." He decided — for a brief moment — to run away to China: "From my childhood I had had a desire to go to Cathay, but because of having to rule and other obstacles, it had never been possible." In the end, being Babur, he chose to pursue his long-standing goal of acquiring his own kingdom.

Throughout his life, Babur remained intensely proud of his lineage (he was descended from both Timur and Genghis Khan), but the memoirs show a relaxed attitude to etiquette. He notes, it is true, when he has not been greeted properly; a cousin gets to his feet "quite sluggishly" and one of his own attendants tugs on Babur's belt so that he doesn't advance too quickly. Yet when two others of his many cousins do not come far enough out from their camp to meet him, he records merely: "Their delay was probably due to a hangover, after having indulged in revelry and pleasure, not to arrogance or a desire to offend." He notices with approval when food is served properly in line with traditional rules, but then adds, "It is necessary to act in accordance with a good rule when someone leaves one behind; if an ancestor has set a bad precedent, however, it should be replaced by a good one."

When his relatives plotted against him, as they frequently

did, he spared them for the sake of family, but he was careful after his early years not to trust them too far. He revered his mother and treated her with great respect, but he did not always obey her. When he was seventeen, she arranged a marriage for him, but he was unenthusiastic about his bride. Every month or so, his mother, he complained, "drove me to her with all the severity of a quartermaster." Part of the trouble may have been that he had fallen madly in love with a boy. "I made myself miserable over him." Babur wrote him poetry, but when he met the object of his passion, "I was so bashful that I could not look him in the face, much less converse freely with him."

In his later years Babur had several wives and fathered a number of children. He took great pride in his eldest son, Humayun, a good warrior and competent administrator, but also worried about him. In one letter Babur wrote after he had seized India, he told Humayun that he needed to consult more and take advice: "In kingship it is improper to seek solitude." He also criticized his son's letters: "Although your writing can be read with difficulty, it is excessively obscure. Who has ever heard of prose designed to be an enigma?" Moreover his son's spelling was sloppy. He also worried that Humayun might be casting greedy eyes on Kabul, which was still in Babur's possession, and warned him off: "I consider Kabul my lucky piece."

The memoirs also show a man who found time to enjoy hunting, writing poetry, and making gardens. Babur loved beauty, whether in nature, people, or the arts. In 1519 he took a three-day trip into the mountains near Kabul to look at the autumn colours. He was enchanted by Herat, which he visited for the first time in 1504: "a fabulous city... where all the implements of pleasure and revelry were ready and present, all the devices of entertainment and enjoyment were close at hand." He delighted in new tastes and sensations. A kind of melon from a town near Samarkand had "a yellow skin as soft as glove leather, seeds like an apple's, and flesh four fingers thick; it is amazingly delicious." He enjoyed practical jokes, once telling a companion that a bitter gourd was a delicious apple: "It took him until that evening to get the bitterness out of his mouth."

When he took Kabul and its surrounding territories in 1504, Babur noted with pleasure that his new kingdom had an excellent climate. He made copious notes about the local fruits, trees, and animals. He counted the varieties of tulips, planted fruit trees, and laid out formal gardens. He was deeply curious about the people who now came under his rule: their customs, trades, and skills; how they hunted and farmed and captured birds; or how they threw herbs into the water in autumn to drug the fish. He was also critical of their lack of proper Islamic religious observances and of the local superstitions. When he discovered that the attendants at a shrine had a trick for making it appear as though the building was moving, he forbade them to do it ever again, on pain of death.

While he had at first been reluctant on religious grounds to taste alcohol, Babur later discovered "the delight and pleasure of being drunk." His drinking parties often lasted for days, frequently starting on boats on the river and ending on dry land. He also took a mild narcotic he called *majun*, which seems to have been a form of cannabis. He described taking a strong draft on his first foray into the Punjab, and how he sat on a hill, gazing at the scene that presented itself: "How strange the fields of flowers appeared under its influence. Nothing but purple flowers were blooming in some places, and only yellow ones in the others. Sometimes the yellow and the purple blossomed together like gold fleck." On occasion he took something stronger, perhaps opium, and found himself unable to come out of his tent for a council. "These days," he wrote wistfully towards the end of his life, "I don't know if it would produce half the high."

He noted that drugs and alcohol do not mix well, but that did not prevent him from taking both at once. Always competitive, he boasted in his memoirs of how intoxicated he had been. On one occasion he left a party and got on his horse: "I took a torch in my hand and, reeling to one side and then the other, let the horse gallop free-reined along the riverbank all the way to camp. I must have been really drunk." He didn't, he said proudly, remember a thing, "except that when I got to my tent, I vomited a lot." Occasionally he felt some uneasiness that he, as a devout Muslim, was taking alcohol and indulging to excess, but he found excuses for himself, writing in 1520, for example, "Having vowed to give up drinking at age forty, with only one year left to my fortieth year I was drinking to excess out of anxiety." In fact he did not give it up for another seven years, and then as a political move as much as anything else.

Babur could get very angry, but he tended to forgive people the next moment. He was remarkably generous to his enemies; when a leader who had once rebelled against him arrived starving and in rags in Kabul, Babur notes, "Now he was humbled by his past deeds, ashamed of the way he had gone off, and distraught. I, for my part, did not berate him in the slightest but received him warmly and soothed his distress." Such generosity was also good policy, for it might show others that they were better off sticking with Babur than joining with his enemies.

On the other hand he could be casually brutal, and the

reader realizes with a jolt that his values are not always the same as ours. He and his allies send each other severed heads as tokens of success. After one victory he remarks in an off-hand way, "A tower of dead Afghan skulls was erected." He then goes on to write an admiring description of a lovely local lake. When he has trouble with local Afghan bandits, "several of them were impaled to set an example." On another occasion his forces take a fort in western Afghanistan. "Since the people," he remarks, "were rebels, and infidel customs had spread among them, and the religion of Islam had been lost, they were put to massacre and their women and children taken captive." When the mother of the deposed sultan of Delhi tries to poison him by suborning some of his servants, he deals briskly with the guilty: "I ordered the taster to be hacked to pieces and the cook to be skinned alive. One of the two women I had thrown under the elephants' feet, and the other I had shot."

Babur would have preferred to establish a kingdom where his Mongol ancestors had once held sway, in the territories that stretch across the Central Asian republics of today, but he and his quarrelling Timurid relatives now faced a formidable opponent in the shape of the powerful leader Shibani Khan, who had welded separate Uzbek tribes into a formidable fighting force. Babur regarded the man he nicknamed Wormwood as an uncultivated, illiterate boor. When Wormwood took Herat briefly in 1507, he made a fool of himself according to Babur, presuming to give lessons in the interpretation of the Koran to leading mullahs, and correcting the calligraphy and paintings of famous artists in that sophisticated and cultured city. "Moreover every few days he would compose insipid poetry and have it recited from the pulpit and hung in the marketplace to receive accolades from the population." Wormwood, it was true, did pray five times a day and could recite the Koran, "but he nonetheless did and said a multitude of stupid, imbecilic, audacious, and heathenish things."

Nevertheless Wormwood and the Uzbeks consolidated their hold on Central Asia, and that as well as a new threat in the west from the Safavids of Persia, drove Babur southwards into Afghanistan. "The foe was powerful and we were weak," he said. "There was neither the possibility for coming to terms nor any scope for resisting." After he established his kingdom in Kabul, he faced the choice between expanding his sway into northeast Afghanistan or moving south towards India, the land he called Hindustan. India proved to be the greater temptation. In 1519 Babur crossed the Indus (in present-day Pakistan) for the first time and entered the rich settled plains of the subcontinent. On that occasion he contented himself with collecting loot. Increasingly, though, he was claiming and receiving tribute from peoples between Kabul and the Indus.

In 1525 he was ready for an all-out assault on the major power in the northwest of India, the Afghan Sultanate of Delhi. Armed with matchlock guns and cannon he had obtained from the Ottoman Turks, Babur marched into India. At first his opponents laughed at the new weapons, but they rapidly learned how deadly they could be. Step by step, as he describes, Babur and his forces prised away the subordinates of the Delhi sultan and defeated the armies sent against them. In the spring of 1526 he won a decisive victory at Panipat, to the north of Delhi, and the road to the city itself lay open. Babur's forces took Delhi and then Agra to the south, and he proclaimed himself the emperor of Hindustan. Among the loot the armies seized were piles of gold and silver and jewels.

Humayun found a huge diamond, which he handed over to his father, who in turn made him a present of it. By a circuitous route, what came to be known as the Koh-i-Noor eventually made its way into the British crown jewels.

By the following year many of Babur's troops were unhappy and homesick. They hated the summer heat of the plains and longed for the cooler air of Kabul. While Babur shared their longing, he was not prepared to relinquish his conquests, and he urged them to remain: "What now compels us to throw away for no reason at all the realms we have taken at such cost? Shall we go back to Kabul and remain poverty-stricken?" As large and hostile Rajput forces gathered to the south and west of Agra, he solemnly broke up all his gold and silver drinking vessels and made the dramatic announcement that he was renouncing drink forever. He exhorted his soldiers to do the same and swear on the Koran to become holy warriors for Islam. "It was a really good plan," wrote Babur, "and it had favourable propagandistic effect on friend and foe." (He still, however, allowed himself to take drugs.)

Babur's forces won another decisive victory over the Rajputs in February 1527. Again his guns gave him the advantage. Afterwards an astrologer who had predicted disaster showed up to congratulate Babur: "I cursed him roundly and made myself feel much better." Since the man had been useful in the past, however, Babur sent him off with a handsome pile of money.

Though he was not to know it, the new emperor of India had only two years to live. He continued to work on his memoirs and added detailed observations on India: "It is a strange country. Compared to ours, it is another world." He compares almost everything, from the flora and fauna to the

peoples, to his beloved Afghanistan and central Asia, usually to the disadvantage of his new realm. India's cities and
towns were "very unpleasant" and the land in most places "as
flat as boards." The humidity in the rainy season was dreadful
and ruined his archers' bows. The peacocks, he admits, were
very beautiful and the elephant "a huge and intelligent animal." He is intrigued by the parrots that could learn to talk,
although he finds it a pity that a beautiful red species has a
voice "as unpleasant and shrill as a piece of broken china being
dragged across a brass tray." He carefully describes the fruit
(although, apart from mangoes, he finds most of it tasteless)
and the flowers (he likes the hibiscus and oleanders). His
overall assessment is damning: "Hindustan is a place of little charm. There is no beauty in its people, no graceful social
intercourse, no poetic talent or understanding, no etiquette,
nobility or manliness. The arts and crafts have no harmony
or symmetry. There are no good horses, meat, grapes, mel-
ons or other fruit. There is no ice, cold water, good food or
bread in the markets. There are no baths and no madrasas."
He consoled himself by laying out properly symmetrical gardens with pools and running water. And he does note that
"the one nice aspect of Hindustan is that it is a large country
with lots of gold and money."

The extant memoirs end suddenly. Babur, who had been
complaining with increasing frequency about his health,
died at the end of 1530. There is a legend that since his son
Humayun was grievously ill, Babur walked around the young
man's bed and asked God to take him in his son's place. As
Humayun recovered, so it was said, Babur fell ill and died.
Humayun and his successors had the memoirs copied by the
best calligraphers and illustrated with marvellous minia-
tures. In the nineteenth century Annette Beveridge, one of

those intrepid and curious women I have talked about earlier, translated them into English. Her translation has in turn
been updated, and so we can peer into the mind and world of
an extraordinary man.

WHILE THE EARLY DAYS of European settlers in Canada are
not as distant in time as those of Babur — my own Canadian
grandfather heard stories from his grandfather about how the
family had to clear their own land near London, Ontario, in
the mid-nineteenth century — they can seem equally remote
to us today. The accounts of Mrs. Simcoe, who knew Toronto
when the very first buildings were going up, or of those
intrepid sisters Catharine Parr Traill and Susanna Moodie,
who went from the relative comforts of middle-class life in
Britain to being settlers in the bush, fortunately remain to
give us a sense of what life was like before cars or modern medicine or a social safety net, in a way that careful
social analysis with graphs and statistics cannot. Closer to
our own time, the memoirs of the leading Canadian feminist
Nellie McClung take us on the journey her family made by
train, boat, and horse-drawn wagon from Ontario to virgin
land on the prairies. Their first house was a rough-built log
shanty with a thatched roof. In the nights the winds whis-
tled through the chinks in the walls, and they could hear the
prairie wolves howling. Two years later the neighbours gathered to put up a new, weather-tight house for them. When
spring came, her mother planted maple seeds she had brought
from Ontario and made flowerbeds edged with buffalo bones,
all that remained of the great herds which had so recently
been exterminated by hunters. In the summers the newly
tilled prairies grew golden with wheat. In the long winters

the Northern Lights danced in the night sky, and the snow piled up around the house and kept them prisoner.

Everyday life in Quebec, where European settlement had started with Samuel de Champlain in the early seventeenth century, is captured for me in two memoirs: the first by Robert de Roquebrune, and the second by the great historian Marcel Trudel. The two men came from different social classes — the first was from an old seigneurial family, with its big stone manor house built in the seventeenth century, and the latter from a more modest background of artisans, trappers, and farmers — but both left a vivid record of a world that seems even further away than that of the prairie settlers.

"My childhood years in Canada," Roquebrune wrote, "were spent in a world that has vanished. Those years between 1890 and 1905 passed as if in a completely different universe — not only remote from us in time, but remote in the appearance of things, in the way people thought, and the way they acted. So entirely has the world of my childhood disappeared, so alien has it become, that I can scarcely even remember it." The family lived only two miles away from the main road to Montreal, bustling with commerce and industry, but they might have been on an island. They lived simply, and largely off the produce of their own land. In the winters they travelled in the horse-drawn sleighs that had given Mrs. Simcoe such pleasure. They took great pride in their ancestors, whose portraits — the men in frock coats or uniforms with powdered wigs, and the women in silk dresses — lined the walls. Their social life revolved mainly around their neighbours, although occasionally a relative came from Montreal or Quebec to bring news of the outside world. The idyll, for so it was to the children and their mother, came to an end when their father took a post with the government and moved them to

Quebec City. The manor house was sold and subsequently destroyed in a fire.

Trudel, born in 1917, was of a later generation, but he came from rural Quebec well north of the St. Lawrence River, where the old ways lingered longer than in the south. To the people of his village, those ways were best, while the outside world was exotic and full of dangers, especially spiritual ones. The British may have conquered New France in 1759, but the *ancien régime* still shaped a hierarchical and conservative society in which authority, particularly that of the church, was deeply respected. Trudel remembers the older women wearing panniers and crinolines, and men's high-heeled shoes were known as the "French" ones. People used the old weights and measures that had once been customary in Paris. And, as Trudel noted, "one had to be a practising Catholic to exist in civil society." Births, marriages, and deaths all had to be recognized by the church to be legal. Couples were married in accordance with the old laws, and the wife's property was to be administered solely by the husband, her "lord and master." The parish church was the spiritual and social centre of the community, and the regulations laid down by successive bishops — such as the ban on dancing in 1691 — were strictly enforced. The same bishop had also banned the play *Tartuffe*; it was not performed in Quebec until 1952.

Education was also according to the *ancien régime*. The sexes were strictly separated. Trudel's older brother became a priest, and Marcel himself went to a seminary where the students wore a uniform modelled on a seventeenth-century priest's cassock and studied the classics in Greek and Latin. Trudel's own dream was to teach in a university, which in those days normally meant he would have to take holy orders as well. After one year of advanced studies in the Grand

Seminary, he realized that he had no vocation, so he transferred to the University of Laval, hoping to get a doctorate,
which might allow him to teach.

Beneath the surface of what looked like an unchanging
French society in Quebec, new ideas and ways of thinking
were stirring. Trudel himself helped to push the boundaries of what the church would allow to be studied and written
about. With the support of a liberal-minded uncle who was
a bishop, he got permission from the religious authorities to
write about the influence of Voltaire on French literature in
Canada. As part of his special dispensation, he was allowed
to read Voltaire's works, which were kept under lock and key
in the university library, and in 1946 was able to publish his
thesis. He went on to a career of researching the founding
and development of New France, and again he pushed the
boundaries — writing, for example, about a French Catholic
priest who converted to Presbyterianism. In 1962 he became
president of a new movement promoting the separation of
church and state in Quebec, and this was the last straw for
the church hierarchy. He was demoted at Laval and three
years later moved to Ottawa to teach at a university there.
The church was fighting, and losing, a rearguard action; political, social, and intellectual changes were sweeping away the
old order. As Trudel put it, "The man of my generation was
therefore born and brought up in an extended version of the
Old Régime. Suddenly, without warning, he found himself
in another kind of society — a process that took place in the
1960s with Quebec's Quiet Revolution." A way of life that
had lasted for well over three hundred years disappeared in
a decade.

A keen eye for detail helps to make a good observer, and
so does a sense of the absurd, even or perhaps especially with

a touch of malice. In his series of diaries, Charles Ritchie, an elongated and elegant Canadian diplomat, skewers everyone, starting with himself. He grew up in yet another Canada from that of the early settlers or tradition-bound French Quebec. His was the cosy world of Halifax, where the old families who had been there for generations mixed only with each other, and where London rather than Toronto or Montreal was the metropolis. He shared their snobberies, dividing the world into those who could be invited to tea and those who couldn't because they were too "new."

Cosseted by his mother, whom he adored, he also longed to leave home. His dream was to get to Oxford and become wildly, even dangerously, sophisticated. "Not altogether lacking in intelligence," as he said of himself, he was acutely aware of his own deficiencies. "I want to be handsome and dashing and self-assured," he wrote in an early diary, "but I am angular, beak-nosed, narrow-chested, and wear glasses." He worries that people are laughing at him. He falls in love with one unobtainable girl after another. He carefully notes that he also has what his school masters call impure thoughts, "but I don't know if that is a vice or not." He admires the visitors who come through from Britain, their smart clothes, their worldliness, and their confidence.

In the late 1920s he got his wish and became a student at Oxford, where he gravitated effortlessly to the company of the more frivolous, moneyed undergraduates. He ran up bills at his tailors and gambled and drank too much. He discovered the pleasures of sex, thanks to an accommodating local woman. He also recounts one memorable evening when some of his friends take potshots with his air rifle at the busy thoroughfare below his windows. To their horror, they wing a passerby, who turns out to be a local councilwoman. It might have ended Ritchie's career, but in the Oxford of those days such matters could be hushed up.

In 1934, his awkward adolescence well behind him, he joined Canada's young Department of External Affairs. In 1939, on the eve of the Second World War, he was posted to London, where he stayed until the war's end in 1945. His diaries show life during the Blitz: "Our ears have grown sharp for the sounds of danger — the humming menace that sweeps from the sky, the long whistle like an indrawn breath as the bomb falls." London, he remarks, looks increasingly run down: houses are no longer painted and gaps appear where the bombs have done their damage. In the autumn of 1940, with the Blitz at its height, he comes out of a movie theatre to find the whole of Piccadilly, in the heart of London, on fire. He confesses to a strange sense of excitement: "Things one will forget when this is over — fumbling in the dark of the blackout for one's front door key, while bits of shrapnel fall on the pavement beside one — the way shrapnel seems to drift — almost like snow flakes through the air in an aimless, leisurely way, and the clink of it landing on the pavement." Eventually his own flat had a direct hit; he was annoyed at the loss of his expensive suits and books. Like so many in London, he kept wondering when the German invasion would come and then, when the war dragged on, whether the Allies could really win.

The war was a serious business, but he enjoyed a hectic social life, with weekends and dinners and lunches with "rococo Romanian princesses and baroque dilettantes." People found him charming and entertaining, and he became friendly with, among many others, the Sacheverell Sitwells, Princess Callimachi from Rumania ("lively … with the look of a lizard"), Miriam Rothschild, and Archduke Robert of Austria.

He spent Christmas with the Duchess of Westminster and dined with David Cecil. He went to parties with Nancy Mitford and met her sister Unity Mitford, who so admired Hitler that she tried to kill herself when the war broke out. At a lunch he listened as T. S. Eliot maliciously dissected another writer: "the closing in on the prey, the kill, so neat and so final, and the picking of the bones, the faint sound of licking of lips and the feast is over."

He also started a love affair that was going to last for over thirty years with the well-known writer Elizabeth Bowen. She was slightly older, married, and moved easily between literary London and the inbred world of the Anglo-Irish aristocracy in the newly independent Ireland. His first impression was restrained: "well dressed, middle aged with the air of being the somewhat worldly wife of a don, a narrow intelligent face, watching eyes and a cruel, witty mouth." Half a year later he was obsessed by her. "Naked, she becomes poetic, ruthless and young." He went with her to her beloved family house in Ireland, Bowen's Court, for brief days of happiness, but the affair became increasingly difficult and unhappy. She did not intend to leave her husband, and Ritchie was repeatedly unfaithful to her. He came to resent his dependence on her. As he wrote in his diary, "I don't want to have any more involved, shaming conversations over the Irish whiskey about my feelings. I am not an adolescent any more." As he tried to withdraw, he also decided, selfishly and cynically perhaps, that he needed to marry for the sake of his career, and did so in 1948. He and Elizabeth still managed to meet from time to time, but their chief communication was now through their letters. Bowen poured herself into them, and they contain some of her best writing. Unfortunately, and again selfishly, Ritchie edited them ruthlessly before he died, cutting or tearing out pages. He also destroyed some of her letters altogether, as well as virtually all his to her. Alive she may have expressed the greater love, but when she died he wrote, "I would give anything I have to give to talk to her again, just for an hour. If she ever thought that she loved me more than I did her, she is revenged."

Mrs. Simcoe, Susanna Moodie, Catharine Parr Traill, Nellie McClung, Robert de Roquebrune, Marcel Trudel, and Charles Ritchie all wrote about their own Canadas. The world of settlers struggling to clear the forests in Ontario or break the prairies is far removed from the more established one in French Canada, or the gentility of an anglophile Halifax. Yet there are similarities too: the clash between the Old World of Europe and the new one; the challenge of the land itself; the gradual and largely peaceful evolution from a collection of colonies to a nation; or the search for what it is to be Canadian. The stories these Canadians tell bring colour and depth to the large canvas of Canadian history as it slowly unrolls.

UNLIKE RITCHIE, COUNT HARRY Kessler, one of the greatest record-keepers of the nineteenth and twentieth centuries, did not dream of editing the record, but when he died in Majorca, an exile from Nazi Germany, the diaries that he had kept for over fifty years vanished along with his few remaining possessions. In 1983, however, the lease on a safe deposit box in a local bank ran out and the diaries were discovered intact. They provide an extraordinary, detailed account of a turbulent and rapidly changing period of European history. When a twelve-year-old Kessler started keeping them in 1880, Queen Victoria was on the throne of the world's largest empire, and the British navy ruled the waves. Germany and Italy — Canada too — were new countries, and the first was rapidly becoming the economic powerhouse of Europe. With a few exceptions, such as France and Switzerland, European countries were ruled by monarchs, and the old landed aristocracies dominated the upper ranks of society, from the church to the army. Austria-Hungary still controlled the centre of Europe, and the Ottoman Empire still ruled over the Arab world as well as parts of the Balkans and today's Turkey.

The continent taken as a whole was the most powerful, important, and prosperous part of the world. Much of the world, in Africa or the Far East, belonged to one European empire or another. No non-European country counted as a major power. Japan was just starting to modernize, while China looked as though it would fall to pieces. The United States was recovering from its Civil War and had a negligible army and only the rudiments of a navy. European society was changing rapidly under the impact of the industrial and scientific revolutions, the spread of capitalism, or of political movements, including liberalism and socialism. Yet large numbers of Europeans still lived in traditional ways, adhering to old values.

By the time Kessler died in 1937, Europe had impoverished itself and spent the lives of millions of men in a prolonged war. The old social and political order had been shaken, in some countries into pieces. Revolution had brought Russian tsardom down, and in its place a new political movement in the shape of Bolshevism ruled over what was now the Soviet Union. Austria-Hungary had vanished from the map, leaving in its place a collection of smaller ethnic states which quarrelled among themselves and with their neighbours. The Ottoman Empire too had gone, and new countries had

emerged, including Turkey and Iraq. Germany had under-
gone its own revolution, and the monarchy had been sup-
planted by a liberal and democratic regime which in turn
had been swept away by the Nazi revolution of 1933. Europe
still had its empires, but they were increasingly challenged
by nationalist movements from within and by new powers
from without, whether an aggressive Japan or an increasingly powerful United States. In his lifetime, Kessler witnessed and recorded these great political upheavals, but he
did far more. He experienced the death of an old order and
the difficult birth of a new as modernism clashed with tradition. He encountered new ideas coming from thinkers such
as Nietzsche and Einstein, saw new styles of painting and
sculpture, and listened to new forms of music.

Kessler was exceptionally well-suited to be an observer of
such great changes. He was clever, sensitive, curious, and avid
for new people and new experiences. He was also very well-
connected. The son of a rich German banker who had been
ennobled in the 1870s by the first German emperor, and of a
beautiful Anglo-Irish mother (there were rumours, which the
family always denied, that Alice, Kessler's mother, had been
the emperor's mistress), he had cousins across Europe — and
perhaps further afield, for one of Alice Kessler's grandfathers
had married a member of the Persian royal family. Educated
partly in England and partly in Germany, the boy grew up
fluent in several languages and was at home in the upper-
class circles of different European countries. Yet, unlike many
in that world, he adored the arts and sought out new ideas and
new styles both in Europe and around the world. When he
travelled to Japan, for example, he was struck by the economy
with which the Japanese artists drew and painted. Western
artists, he proclaimed, put in too much detail.

He was a neat and elegant man with small, carefully man-
icured hands, who dressed with great care. His manners were
impeccable. "Half diplomat, half Prussian officer," said the
Russian composer Nicolas Nabokov. Kessler was a snob and
quick to condemn vulgarity wherever he noticed it, which
was everywhere. At a grand court ball in Berlin he noted
that the empress in her gold dress with a red sash looked
"like a cheap party cracker." He was conscious of his rank as
a German nobleman and could, too often, echo the prejudices of his class, such as its anti-Semitism. In 1902 he wrote
in his diary that he was repelled by the Jews on account of
their remarkable mixture of cowardice and a will to power.
He also could make silly remarks, all too typical of his times,
about how the human races were fundamentally different.
The Jews and French, he claimed in one entry, were dominated by reason and had as a result impoverished emotional
lives, unlike his own Prussians, the English, or the Greeks.
Yet throughout his life he had many close Jewish friends, and
by his later years his views had altered. When an old friend
remarked in the troubled years of the 1920s that the important task facing Germany was to root out the Jewish spirit,
Kessler asked pointedly what spirit would then be left.

Kessler possessed both enormous energy and a great
capacity for social life. He went to premieres and the open-
ings of most of the major artistic events of his time, and he
was constantly lunching, dining, or having drinks with an
extraordinary range of people. Throughout his life he moved
easily across social and political lines. A gay man in an age
when that was frowned upon or worse, he saw first-hand the
injustice and cruelty of social conventions. And perhaps his
love affairs with young men from the working classes helped
to give him a greater awareness of the difficulties they faced

in their lives. Over the years he was to shift leftwards in his views until, by the 1920s, he was nicknamed the Red Count.

Kessler's address book contained over ten thousand names. Auguste Rodin, Friedrich Nietzsche, Wilhelm II, Henry Asquith, Cosima Wagner, Gustav Mahler, Isadora Duncan, George Bernard Shaw, Gustav Krupp, Otto von Bismarck, Erich Ludendorff, Sir Ernest Cassel, William Morris — it is hard to find anyone in Europe's cultural, political, or financial elites from the 1880s to the 1930s whom he did not meet. In a diary entry from before the Great War, which I took at random, he describes having tea with the painters Pierre Bonnard and Édouard Vuillard and then dinner with Pierre-Auguste Renoir. He becomes friends with the young Viennese poet Hugo von Hofmannsthal and suggests a plot to him which later becomes the Richard Strauss opera *Der Rosenkavalier*. Kessler spent holidays with the sculptor Aristide Maillol, talked to Rainer Maria Rilke about writing poetry, and exchanged views about the poor state of Germany's relations with Britain with the chancellor, Theobald von Bethmann-Hollweg.

"Sometimes he appeared German, sometimes English, sometimes French, so European was his character," wrote Thomas Mann after Kessler's death. "In truth the arts were his home." Kessler discussed painting light and shadow with Claude Monet, how to capture the movements of the human body with Edgar Degas, and the purpose of art with a young George Grosz. Edvard Munch, another acquaintance, painted his portrait. When Kessler created the scenario for a ballet, he persuaded Richard Strauss to write the music, Léon Bakst did the costumes and sets, and Sergei Diaghilev's Ballets Russes staged it.

Kessler's mother worried from time to time about his

extravagance — the flats in Berlin and Paris, the house in Weimar, his expensive projects in the arts, and his compulsive buying of paintings, drawings, and sculptures. (His collection included Van Goghs, Seurats, Maillols, Cézannes, and Gauguins.) Yet, until the First World War, his life was one of great privilege and freedom at the heart of the most powerful continent in the world. With no need to work he could choose to do whatever he wanted. Along with leading intellectual and artistic figures of his time, Kessler was a radical in the arts. He wanted to throw out the old forms and conventions and bring in a purer, more functional art, stripped of unnecessary ornamentation. More, he believed that European society was overdue for change. "Something very great," he wrote, "the old, cosmopolitan, still predominantly agrarian and feudal Europe, the world of beautiful women, gallant kings, and dynastic combinations, the Europe of the eighteenth century and the Holy Alliance was growing old and weak, dying out; and something new, young, energetic, and still unimaginable was in the offing." Kessler, like so many of his contemporaries, was fascinated by Nietzsche, whom he considered a genius, struggling to maintain the importance of the individual in the face of the rising tide of mass society. Nietzsche's call to rethink the moral and intellectual basis of European civilization was disturbing and challenging, promising an unknown new and perilous world. Kessler believed that some great change was in the offing (as indeed it was) but he hoped to unite the new and transformed Europe through culture.

He engaged seriously with the main new artistic movements of the pre-war era not just on aesthetic grounds — although those were always important to him — but because he felt that through new forms of art, new societies could be built. Kessler's great opportunity came when he was asked to advise

the duchy of Weimar on regenerating its artistic life. With the
modernist Belgian architect Henry van de Velde, he helped
to found a new school of arts and crafts which would become
the forerunner of the highly influential Bauhaus school of the
1920s and 1930s. Kessler himself took on the directorship of
the local art museum and determined to get rid of what he
saw as the uninspired clutter of the past, making the place
a showcase of modern functional design to educate the citizens of Weimar. He put on a major exhibition of French post-
impressionists and invited his friends, including André Gide
and the cutting-edge set designer Gordon Craig, to come as
visiting artists. At the same time, Kessler got involved in a
great struggle dividing the artistic world in Germany, between
the traditionalists, backed by Kaiser Wilhelm II himself, and
the modernists. Kessler helped to set up a Germany-wide organization of artists who were challenging the conventions and
the control of the establishment over the art. "The final goal,"
said Kessler, was "the liberation of all constraints in art, freedom of art, absolute toleration by the state."

This was too much for the volatile Kaiser, who saw all
forms of modernism as rubbish, and certainly too much for
the sleepy little town of Weimar and its archduke. Kessler was
eventually eased out when there was a row over an exhibition of Rodin watercolours of nude male dancers that Kessler's
enemies claimed were too sexual. Kessler had no intention of
backing away from the modernist cause, and he continued to
support modernism and innovation in the arts. Before 1914
he became a patron to some of the younger artists who were
developing what became German expressionism.

He also found a new enthusiasm in modern dance; he
became a fan of the American experimental dancer Ruth
St. Denis, who drew on Egyptian and Hindu mythology to

create new forms. "I have never seen," he wrote in 1906, "an art that so completely radiates outward like budding flowers, soft green, and the fresh pure April sky as her movements at that moment." By contrast he first found Isadora Duncan overly sentimental and striving too hard for effect. (He later changed his mind.) He became increasingly close to Diaghilev and the Ballets Russes and was enchanted by the brilliant young Vaslav Nijinsky. At their first meeting, Kessler was struck by how the dancer appeared smaller than when he was on stage: "The face is narrow and a little Mongolian, the eyes crooked, but very large and of a deep Italian brown." Kessler was there at the sensational first night of *The Rite of Spring,* danced by Nijinsky in Paris in 1913. He approved entirely of the new vision of what dance could be: "a new kind of wildness, both un-art and art at the same time. All forms laid waste and new ones emerging suddenly from the chaos." Many in the audience disagreed, and the performance was marked by shouts, whistles, loud arguments, and even fist fights. At three in the morning, Kessler recorded, he ended up in a taxi careening around Paris with Diaghilev, Nijinsky, Bakst, and Jean Cocteau.

Kessler's and Europe's golden age ended abruptly in the summer of 1914, with the outbreak of the First World War. At first he was caught up in the surge of patriotism which hit Germany (and indeed the other Great Powers). On August 3, as German troops were already marching into Belgium, Kessler wrote that the mood was one of calm confidence: "One knows that the war will be frightful, that we will suffer perhaps occasional setbacks, but trusts that the qualities of the German character — dutifulness, seriousness, and stubbornness — will in the end bring us victory. Everyone is clear that this war must result in Germany's world domination or its ruin." He agreed that the German army was right to take stern measures in Belgium, including shooting Belgian civilians as examples to the others and burning down Belgian towns. He blamed the Belgians for resisting: "Through the fault of the Belgian population, it is already much crueller and more barbaric than the war of 1870 or even the Napoleonic wars." Kessler was in Namur as it burned: "The glow, the shower of sparks, is terrible and grand." He was in favour of Germany annexing Belgium. When he was posted to join the German armies in the east, he got caught up in the grandiose dreams of a great German empire which would include large swaths of Russia. He watched approvingly as Ludendorff and his colleague General Paul von Hindenburg extended their control over the war effort, setting up by 1916 what was virtually a military dictatorship and forcing through disastrous policies, including the resumption of unrestricted submarine warfare on neutral shipping, which would bring the United States into the war on the Allied side in the spring of 1917. In his diaries Kessler depicts Ludendorff as a man of great talent, energy, and intelligence, while Hindenburg is a wonderfully reassuring grandfatherly figure.

As the war dragged on, Kessler's initial fervour waned and he came to despair of what the conflict was doing to Germany and to European society more generally. In November 1918, with Germany's capitulation to the Allies, he now placed his hopes in a revolution by the world's working classes which might usher in a new, more democratic age. As a German patriot he also hoped that such a revolution would lead to his country being treated more gently by the victors. In the confused aftermath of the war, as a new socialist government tried to establish order in Berlin, Kessler agreed to go as the first German ambassador to the newly emerged country of Poland (he already knew its leader, Józef Piłsudski). His attempts to negotiate an agreement with Poland were undercut both by Polish suspicions of German intentions and by the sweeping demands of the German high command. In December 1919 he returned to Berlin in time to see the attempt by the German Communists to seize power. His diary describes the crowds bearing the red flags of Communism and the counter-demonstrations of socialists. He watched the fighting in the streets and saw the soldiers moving in to seize key points and restore order. The days and nights were filled with the sound of machine guns, artillery fire, and exploding grenades. Yet the underground trains continued to run, and away from the fighting the cafés stayed open. He looked into one: "The band was playing, the tables were full, and the lady in the cigarette-booth smiled as winsomely at her customers as in the sunniest days of peace." An orchestra loyal to the government played *Lohengrin* in a courtyard outside the police headquarters, where there had been heavy fighting; the crowd had come, he noted, to see the damage as well as to enjoy the music. Like many Berliners, Kessler was horrified by the savagery of the reprisals on the revolutionaries, including the murder of their leaders, but was relieved that order had been restored.

In the 1920s, he witnessed first-hand the confused struggle over the future of Germany, between the forces of liberalism and constitutional democracy and their enemies on both the left and the right. His friend the intellectual industrialist Walter Rathenau, who became German foreign minister in 1922, dismissed his colleagues as nonentities and told Kessler that Bolshevism was "a splendid system" which would rule the world of the twenty-first century. Kessler reported that he found Rathenau's conversation sterile and his manner "a mixture of bitterness and conceit," but he was horrified when Rathenau was assassinated by right-wing extremists. As he himself moved leftwards, Kessler lost many of his old upper-class friends who were gravitating towards the Nazis. Although he never joined the socialist party formally, he became increasingly sympathetic to its policies and a strong supporter of the Weimar Republic. He made new friends among its leading figures, including Gustav Stresemann, who was foreign minister between 1923 and 1929 and who did much both to strengthen the Weimar Republic and to bring Germany back into the international community. Kessler himself worked to support the liberal coalition at home and a peaceful international order abroad, going, for example, to meetings of European pacifists with his good friend Albert Einstein. In 1924 he wrote, "Now I come at last to my real goal in life: to help, in the first place and in a practical way, to forge a united Europe. Before the war I tried it on the all too thin and fragile level of culture." Being Kessler, he continued to be fascinated by whatever was new: he notes with pleasure that he met Josephine Baker at a private party where, "naked except for a pink muslin apron," she danced for the guests. He found her bewitching, "but almost quite unerotic."

By the end of the decade he was watching the rise of the Nazis with horror. The younger generation, he believed, whether on the right or the left, were mistakenly looking for an escape into some sort of belief, and for a discipline which would give meaning and structure to their lives. After the death of Stresemann in 1929, no German leader was willing or able to stand up to Hitler. The right-wingers around the increasingly infirm Hindenburg, who had become president, allowed the Nazis to ignore the law and, in an act of folly, invited Hitler to become chancellor at the start of 1933. Kessler did not for a moment believe that the Reichstag fire the following month was an accident; he saw it correctly as an opportunity for the Nazis to consolidate their hold on the German state and society. That March he left for Paris on what he thought would be a visit, but while he was there he received warning not to return. He sent for his possessions and found out that his servant had become a Nazi supporter and had not only been denouncing him but stealing his possessions. "Sometimes," Kessler wrote, "I seem to be going through an evil dream from which I shall suddenly awake." That April he noted in his diary, "The abominable Jewish boycott has begun. This criminal piece of lunacy… It is difficult to say which feeling is stronger, loathing or pity for these brainless, malevolent creatures." His life went on: he continued to see friends, read, work on his memoirs, and go to the theatre and to concerts. Something had gone out of him, however: "All the time I am aware of a muffled pain throbbing like a double-bass."

His money was now running short, and his loyal sister, who had been subsidizing him for years, could no longer afford to give him much support. He lived for a time in Majorca — where he left his diaries in their safe deposit box — but his health was now deteriorating rapidly, so in 1935 he returned to France, hoping to find a cure. Although he did get better, briefly, the Spanish Civil War, which broke out in 1936, made it impossible for him to get back to Majorca. He lived his last months in a boarding house in the French provinces and died in November 1937. His funeral was small, and his death passed largely unremarked in the press.

If his diaries had not survived, Count Harry Kessler would be remembered now, if at all, as a minor figure, hanging around on the fringes of artistic circles and playing a small part in German politics. Instead we have discovered a perceptive and indefatigable eyewitness to some of the most important developments of modern European history.

AS KESSLER'S HEALTH WAS fading and his record-keeping was coming to its end, another German was partway through creating his own remarkable diary, a much grimmer one than Kessler's but with the same perceptiveness and acute awareness of the foibles and strangeness of humanity. Victor Klemperer, from an assimilated, cultivated German Jewish family (the conductor Otto Klemperer was a cousin), had tried a career in journalism but eventually became a professor of Romance languages in Dresden. Although he took his academic writing very seriously, we remember him now for his diary, which provides a detailed account of what it was like to live in the Germany of the 1930s, as the Nazi hold on power tightened, and then in the 1940s during Hitler's war. Because he was married to an Aryan, under the deranged Nazi bureaucratic rules he was not sent to the camps. Rather he and his wife were obliged to move into a special Jews' House for mixed couples.

The English translations of the diaries start in 1933 with the Nazis assuming power. Klemperer complains, as he is going to do throughout, about his health. He is, he notes, exhausted, lethargic, and depressed. He suffers from one ailment after another and constantly lives with the fear that his heart or eyes or kidneys are about to give out. He is sure, and says so repeatedly, that he will not live to see the end of the Third Reich. Yet he keeps researching and writing. He works on his biography and on studies of French writers. He also starts a project on Nazi language, noting the hyperbole, the frequent references to heroism or bravery, the many superlatives — the biggest victory, the greatest success — and the repeated use of military terms. He also notes how the Nazis dehumanize the objects of their hatred by referring to "the Jew" or "the Communist" or how they vaunt irrationality so that it now becomes praise to describe someone as a fanatic or possessed by blind rage. And Klemperer doggedly keeps his diary, noting down the daily details of his life: the growing restrictions that surround him; the petty humiliations; the happy moments that, in spite of all, he and his beloved wife enjoy; and his own thoughts and reactions as he sees Germany changing. He comments on politics and the war, but his purpose, as he says, is not to provide a history of his times but of himself and his own small world, of the view from below.

As the Nazis stamped out all opposition, it became increasingly dangerous to keep anything from a book to a drawing that could be interpreted as subversive or critical of the regime. The German secret police, the Gestapo, made unscheduled searches, and suspicious material or forbidden objects frequently meant death. "I shall go on writing," Klemperer wrote in 1942. "That is *my* heroism. I will bear witness, precise witness!" His wife, who as an Aryan was still allowed to travel freely, smuggled the pages out of the house and took them to a woman doctor friend, who risked her own life to keep them safe.

Klemperer, against all odds, did survive the Nazis and the war, and so did his diary. He was determined to keep going, partly by his deep love for his wife and the hope that one day he would see the end of the Nazi criminals. With many complaints, fears, and worries, he did indeed bear witness, week after week, month after month, and year after year. There is no account of life in Nazi Germany quite like it. What makes the diaries such a powerful and compelling record is that we go along with him step by step: from the first time when as a Jew he is singled out for persecution; through the grinding, unending series of privations, meannesses, and prohibitions; to the ever-growing fear of death, either at the hands of the Nazis or by Allied bombing. Like Klemperer himself, we move from being shocked at the first revelation of what is happening to Germany under the Third Reich to absorbing greater and greater horrors. Unlike him, however, we always know how much worse it is going to get.

The first signs of what was to come appeared early in 1933. Klemperer notes that more and more people were using the greeting "Heil Hitler," and then that it had become compulsory. The Klemperers' social circle started to narrow as some they knew joined the Nazi Party while others decided to leave Germany. Conversations became increasingly circumspect as people grew wary of uttering any criticism of the regime, and dissidents started to disappear into the first concentration camps. It was increasingly clear that the state itself was waging war on many of its own citizens. Jew-baiting had now become acceptable and open as the Nazi-controlled press filled with wild stories and accusations about Jews; signs started to appear throughout Dresden saying, "Who buys from a Jew is a traitor to the nation" or "No Jews wanted here." Klemperer resisted pressure to join the body known as the Jewish Community; he kept insisting that he was a Protestant by religion and a German by nationality. He gradually gave up hope that the German people would tire and overthrow the regime. As he noted in his diary, ordinary Germans might grumble about the Nazis, but many felt they were preferable to the Communists.

For a time his life went on relatively normally. He and his wife Eva continued to see the films they enjoyed so much. In evenings at home, as he had always done, he read out loud to her. Although he worried constantly about his finances, he also bowed to pressure from Eva and agreed to build a small house in the village of Dölzschen. He was touched and delighted by the pleasure she took in the house and its garden and pleasantly surprised that they were able to manage it at such a time. "Why," he asks in a moment of optimism, "should there not be further miracles?" He also decided to learn to drive and bought a small car in which he and Eva made a series of excursions around Germany.

In 1934 the first of what was to be a lengthening and increasingly punitive series of exclusions for Jews started as he learned that German clubs for owners of cats were now only for Aryans. At the university, his students dwindled and he was squeezed out of responsibilities. The following year, he was made redundant, but he was luckier than some of his colleagues because he still kept part of his pension. His money started to run short, however, and he started pawning his possessions. In Dölzschen the local police came to the house to carry out searches for radios or weapons to confiscate or cultural treasures of the German people which had to be removed to be "safeguarded." When they found the rusty sabre he had kept from his military service in the First World War, he was obliged to report to the police station, but at this stage he was still treated with courtesy. In September 1935 the government passed the Nuremberg Laws, for the "protection of German blood and German honour," which served further to isolate and exclude Jews from German society. In 1936 Klemperer celebrated what he described as "the worst birthday of my life." He was first banned from the reading room at the library and then told by a weeping librarian that he was no longer allowed to borrow books.

The petty humiliations and the more serious exclusions intensified. In 1938 the Klemperers' cleaning lady was summoned by an official and told it would harm her son's and daughter's prospects if she continued to work for a Jew. The couple unhappily took up housework; at first it took them three hours to wash the dishes. By this time Jews could not go to film theatres, nor were they allowed to have driving licences, so Klemperer was obliged to give up the car which had given them so much enjoyment. The first prohibitions on Jews practising certain professions were enacted: all Jewish doctors were struck from the medical register. Jews now had to carry special yellow cards if they wanted to visit the public baths, and all Jews had to have an identity card with a Jewish forename. Klemperer became Victor-Israel. He was disappointed in his fellow Germans for going along with the Nazis, but especially in the intellectuals — his colleagues who did not lift a finger to support him, or the professors who joined the Academic Society for Research into Jewry and wrote papers about the eternal engrained characteristics of the Jews, such as cruelty, violent emotion, adaptability, or ancient Asiatic hate. In his diary he wrote that he felt that he and his wife were being buried alive and that they were just waiting for the last shovelsful.

The Anschluss of March 1938, when Germany easily took over Austria, increased Nazi self-confidence and brutality — and anti-Semitism. Hitler repeatedly attacked what he called the Jewish-Bolshevist world enemy, and the Nazi press was filled with stories of Jewish wickedness. That November the Nazis attacked Jews and synagogues and Jewish businesses across Germany in what came to be called Kristallnacht, the night of broken glass. A friend of the Klemperers described what she saw in Leipzig, where storm troopers poured gasoline into a synagogue and a Jewish department store and then prevented the fire department from putting out the blaze. Klemperer was in despair over the supine reaction of the democracies. In Dölzschen someone stuck handbills with the Yellow Star of David on their fence.

More and more people were disappearing into the concentration camps. Klemperer picked up scraps of information coming out of Buchenwald, where, it was said, twenty to thirty people a day were dying. Increasingly he was hearing of others who were committing suicide. He and his wife talked of leaving — and they now knew many who had — but something always held them back. Eva did not think she could start another life in a strange land. She did not want to leave Germany or her house and garden, and Victor did not want to make her unhappy. "We are digging ourselves in," Klemperer wrote shortly before the war, "and shall perish here." And his pride was a factor as well. He did not want to be dependent on his relatives who had already left Germany, in particular his older, more successful brother Georg, who was established in the United States. Victor was obliged again and again to accept the money which Georg so freely offered, but resented being patronized, as he saw it. Nevertheless Klemperer made stabs at leaving, even if his heart was never really in it: he got the addresses of people abroad who might help him; he sent offers to come and teach or give lectures; he even tried, in a desultory fashion, to learn English. He and Eva discussed booking passage for Australia or Cuba, where it was still easy for Jews to be admitted. At one point they contemplated moving to Rhodesia (now Zimbabwe) and starting a mineral water factory. (He completely ruled out emigrating to Palestine: he was firmly anti-Zionist.) In a way he was relieved when it became clear by the summer of 1941 that there was no longer any chance of leaving. "That suits us entirely. All vacillation is now at an end." Either he and Eva would die or they would survive.

What also held him in Germany was that, as far as he was concerned, he remained German. As he wrote in April 1942, "I *think* German, I *am* German — I did not give it to myself, I cannot tear it out of *myself*." Although at times he felt that he would never belong in Germany or trust his fellow Germans again, at others he felt that it was all a bad dream. "I am German," he wrote, also in 1942, "and waiting for the Germans to return... They have gone into hiding somewhere."

On New Year's Day 1939, while the world was still at peace, Klemperer looked back at the dismal events of the previous year. Perhaps, he wondered, the lowest circle of hell had been reached. We the readers know of course that he was wrong. With the outbreak of war in the autumn, conditions became much worse for the Jews. In 1940 Klemperer received an order to leave his house, even though he was still obliged to pay the taxes and upkeep. Because his wife was Aryan, he was assigned two rooms, where most Jews would have had only one. The couple moved into their first Jews' House, a "superior concentration camp," as Klemperer described it, where they endured the pinpricks and frustrations of being forced to live at close quarters with others. Klemperer got tired of the quarrels over who was using too much hot water or who had taken someone's sugar ration. He was irritated by some of his fellow Jews who remained intensely patriotic, still hoping for a German victory. He himself believed that only defeat would end the Nazi regime. Klemperer was also snobbish about the lack of education of several of his fellow inmates and was driven to distraction by the good-hearted Frau Voss, the Jewish widow of an Aryan, whose house they now found themselves living in. She was endlessly talkative and given to popping in without being invited.

The inmates of the house also had to endure the mindless bullying and brutality of the Gestapo officers, such as those they nicknamed the Spitter and the Boxer. The secret police made repeated house searches, emptying cupboards and drawers, throwing powder and sugar about, and smashing everything from pills to Christmas decorations. After one search, the Klemperers found a head of garlic cut to pieces and hidden around their rooms. The Gestapo stole valuables, from bottles of wine to Klemperer's Service Cross from the First World War. (Klemperer notices that they did not usually take books.) They asked the Jews why they didn't hang themselves and slapped Aryan women such as Eva, calling them whores and pigs for marrying Jews. Often Jews were taken off to Gestapo headquarters to endure even more abuse; sometimes they never returned, and their families were told that they had died of a "heart attack."

The list of prohibitions and restrictions lengthens. Jews can no longer buy foods such as chocolate, gingerbread, coffee, certain fresh vegetables, oranges, eggs, or ice cream. They cannot buy flowers, tobacco, or newspapers. If they own furs, opera glasses, or typewriters they must surrender them to the authorities. They cannot have telephones or pets (the Klemperers have to put down their beloved cat). If they had military medals, as Klemperer does they could no longer wear them. As the months and years went by Jews were also forbidden to eat in restaurants, go to concerts, ride on trams, or walk in Dresden's main parks or along certain streets. They also had to observe a curfew. Shops were forbidden to deliver to Jews, so Klemperer now had to spend much of the day queuing for food or coal and dragging what he could find home in a knapsack or on a borrowed handcart. Jews were no longer eligible for clothing coupons but had to apply to the Jewish Community for clothes. At first Klemperer was appalled to receive second-hand clothes from dead men; later he was glad to get anything he could. Although he felt increasingly shabby, he never forgot he was a professor. When his shirts wore out, he continued to wear a detachable collar and a tie.

The diaries catalogue the dreary daily struggle to keep going, the disappointments when there is no food to be had, or the small triumphs — when, for example, he gets an extra piece of meat or sack of potatoes. Where once he felt shame borrowing money, his main feeling now was relief that they could survive for a bit longer. And fear was always very close to the surface. He and his wife never knew, when either went out, if they would see each other again. In March 1941 he had a close call when he was sentenced to a week in prison because there was a chink in their blackout. There he endured fresh degradation, having to hold up his trousers because his belt had been taken away and not being allowed his glasses or anything to read. He passed the time thinking about his work and wondering whether he had been a good husband to Eva. He was fortunate in that, unlike so many others, he did not die mysteriously in custody.

In September 1941 there came a fresh humiliation. All Jews now had to wear the Yellow Star when they went out in public. At first Klemperer could not bring himself to venture forth, but in time he got used to this, as he had to the other, earlier humiliations, even when members of the Hitler Youth shouted "Yid" at him on the street. On the other hand he notes down the acts of sympathy: the butcher who slipped him extra meat, the grocer who gave him chocolate, or the housewife who bought him vegetables, which as a Jew he could not purchase. Complete strangers greeted him courteously on the streets and said quietly that what was happening to the Jews was all wrong. In Dölzschen the trustee appointed by the authorities to look after his house did his best to keep it safe for him and talked frankly about how much he disliked the Nazis. Aryan friends brought the Klemperers food and passed on news from the BBC broadcasts that Germans were forbidden to listen to.

As the war went on, Klemperer, like other Germans, listened avidly to rumours and tried to read between the lines of the official Nazi bulletins. Soldiers back from the front, he reports, were talking of fierce fighting in the east and heavy German losses. By 1943 he started to hope that the end might be approaching. The Allied victories in North Africa, their landings in Italy and then the armistice with a new Italian government, and finally the Soviet victory at Stalingrad, all gave him hope. The question in his mind, however, was whether he and Eva would survive to see the end of the war.

By this point they had been moved into a smaller, more crowded Jews' House, where they had to share a kitchen and lavatory with several other families. Food was now much scarcer, and German cities, although not yet Dresden, were being destroyed by Allied bombing. Ominously more and more Jews were being taken away from Germany; to what fate was not yet clear.

The diaries show that the realization of the full meaning of the Final Solution dawned slowly on Klemperer. As early as 1941 he knew that Jews were being deported eastwards into Nazi-occupied Poland, but he still was inclined to believe that they were being used for labour, perhaps even getting good rations and decent treatment in the factories where they were forced to work. By 1942, however, he was hearing reports of Jews being shot on the way east. A nurse told him of the brutality of the evacuation, how the elderly, many of them sick, were crowded into trucks without any provision for their care. Klemperer started to suspect that those who could not work would secretly be disposed of in isolated camps such as Theresienstadt. He was relieved that his oldest sister, who was designated to be sent east, died before she could go. He heard too that Auschwitz was a particularly dreadful concentration camp where people were dying of overwork. He described it as "a swift-working slaughter-house" and no longer expected that anyone sent east would return, but he did not yet get the full horror of what the Nazis were doing. When he learned in 1944 that the BBC was reporting that Jews were being gassed, he still wondered if the report was wrong but gradually he became convinced that it was correct. A soldier back in Dresden from Poland spotted the Yellow Star on an acquaintance of Klemperer's and said to its wearer: "I've seen such awful things in Poland, such awful things! It will have to be paid for." Klemperer heard stories of German soldiers having to be given schnapps before they would carry out their orders, or committing suicide rather than obey.

In 1933 there had been 4,600 Jews, defined by religion, in Dresden; by 1945 198 were left. Klemperer had been spared to this point because of his marriage, but it now appeared that his end had come. On Tuesday, February 13, all remaining Jews in Dresden who were capable of working were told to report for deportation. That night the British bombed Dresden, and in the chaos of the ruined and burning city, the Klemperers left the Jews' House. He pulled off his Yellow Star and managed to obtain a ration card as an Aryan. Walking and occasionally finding rides on trams or carts, the couple wandered through the countryside, finding food and lodging as they could. On May 7 Germany surrendered and the Klemperers headed for Dölzschen by a roundabout route. On June 10 they walked up a hill into the town. Their house was waiting for them.

When the Cold War divided Germany, Klemperer chose to stay on in the East. He resumed teaching and published books on Voltaire and Rousseau as well as his work on Nazi language. He died in 1960 at the age of seventy-eight. His diaries survived the Communists just as they had the Nazis.

WE OWE SUCH GRATITUDE to those like Kessler and Klemperer who kept the records. They make it possible for us to see from inside the events, good and bad, of a particular time in the past. They help us to understand what it must have been like to be at the court of Louis XIV, on the Canadian frontier, or in Nazi Germany. They provide those wonderful, vivid details which stay with us and help to fix the personalities of the past: the size of Bismarck's chamber pot, for example, or the decaying teeth of the young princess in France.

If history is, as I believe, a feast, the savour comes from its people. Some I have considered in this book were at the heart of great events and changed the course of history and so shaped our world. Others I have chosen for qualities I admire, such as courage, open-mindedness, and curiosity, or simply because I find them interesting. Our understanding and enjoyment of the past would be impoverished without its individuals, even though we know that history's currents — its underlying forces and shifts, whether of technology or political structures or social values — must never be ignored. Without the work of historians to explain the context — the class structure in the *ancien régime*, the troubled nature of the world in the 1930s, or the evolution of Canadian society over several centuries — our appreciation of individual diaries, letters, or memories would be limited. Yet without those records we would have fewer means to develop a picture of the past and make it enjoyable for readers of history.

It is the interplay between individuals and their worlds that makes history and brings it to life for those of us in the present. And just as we need to free ourselves from our own limited perspectives and try through an act of imagination and empathy to understand those of our contemporaries who come from different backgrounds, races, or ethnicities, so we should strive for a many-faceted view of the past. If we only read the letters of a Madame de Sévigné or the diaries of a Charles Ritchie, we are missing out so much: what it was like, for example, to be a peasant or an artisan in eighteenth-century France or a worker or farmer in twentieth-century Canada. Historians have done much to recover those voices too and to give a fuller picture of past societies.

Is history, then, just a hobby? A rummaging around the past to find interesting people and curious tidbits? It is, in my view, much more. Without history we deprive ourselves of useful tools for understanding our own world. Canada was founded by the First Nations, the French, and the British, who were later joined by peoples from all over the world. The order in which they came and the ways in which they have mingled have made Canadian society what it is today. And the peaceable evolution of Canada from within the British Empire to full nationhood has helped to shape a society based on values and institutions such as respect for the law and representative government. We should be grateful that we do not have the burden of violent revolution or civil war, which still cast their shadows over countries such as France or the United States.

History can be dangerous when it is used to set peoples against each other or to justify foolish, destructive, or evil policies or courses of action. Partial, nationalist histories fuelled the horrors of the 1990s, when Yugoslavia broke into pieces and neighbours turned on each other because they were told that their peoples, whether Serb, Croat, or Bosnian Moslem, had always been enemies and always would be. History was called in, as it too often is, by the American and British governments in 2003 to give validity to the invasion and occupation of Iraq. If Saddam Hussein were not toppled, we were told, we would see a repeat of the 1930s, when the democracies failed to stop Hitler, Mussolini, and the Japanese militarists in time. The misuse of history is not an argument for ignoring it. Rather we must ensure that present generations learn about the past in its complexity and take from that the simple but crucial message that there is no single correct view of history. Rather history is a work in progress shaped by new material, new interpretations, and new questions. Understanding that can be an inoculation against those such as Hitler or Stalin who say with confidence that they are merely obeying the dictates of history.

The study of individuals in the past also makes us aware of the importance of contingency and timing. We must ask: What would have happened if people such as Churchill, Stalin, or Hitler had not been born or died before they could make a difference? If Babur had not conquered India, how might the history of the subcontinent have been different? What might the history of the 1930s have been if Woodrow Wilson had succeeded in getting his country to join the League of

Nations? If Champlain had not succeeded in establishing the first lasting French colony on the St. Lawrence — if instead the British had come first — would there be a French presence in Canada today? By raising such possibilities, history helps us to think about ourselves in our particular presents.

History does not, however, offer clear guidelines for us as we make decisions in the present or blueprints as we try to anticipate the future. We have seen what can happen when leaders and opinion-makers say confidently that they are drawing on the lessons of the past. The protean nature and scope of history means that people, for good or for evil, can find justification or prior examples for whatever they want to do. History and its people offer only a more modest insight and some modest encouragement: that we are all creatures to a certain extent of our own times, but that we can transcend or challenge what limits us. I hope that the individuals I have selected from the past will help to illuminate for us here in the present the complicated nature of humanity, its many contradictions, inconsistencies, its wickedness and follies but its virtues too. Above all, history's people can make us aware of the possibilities for good and evil we all possess.

NOTE ON READINGS

I HAVE TRIED TO provide key readings for each chapter for those who want to know more about the topics I raise or the people I describe. There is such a wealth of memoirs, diaries, and letters from the past, as well as first-rate biographies and histories, that I could give a very lengthy list indeed for those who want to explore the past further still. I will just pick out a few here that I have particularly enjoyed.

Suetonius's *The Twelve Caesars* remains a starting point for anyone interested in the early days of the Roman Empire, while Michael Psellus does something similar for the Byzantine Empire. For anyone interested in the court of Catherine the Great, the memoirs of the painter Louise Élisabeth Vigée-LeBrun give a vivid account of that and of revolutionary France. The many volumes of the Greville diaries are essential reading for anyone interested in the British court and British politics from the 1790s to the 1860s, as are the letters of the Princess Lieven, who, as the wife of the Russian ambassador, lived in London between 1812 and 1834.

Readers who are particularly interested in the encounters between Europeans and the rest of the world in the age of imperialism might want to look at Maya Jasanoff's *Edge of Empire: Lives, Culture, and Conquest in the East, 1750–1850* or Lesley Blanch's older *The Wilder Shores of Love*, which looks at four English women who fell in love with Arabia. In a later period, Arthur Grimble's *A Pattern of Islands* shows the meeting between a young and naïve English administrator and the inhabitants of remote South Sea islands, while *A Cure for Serpents* by Alberto Denti di Pirajno shows the encounter between an Italian doctor and the inhabitants of what was then the Italian colony of Libya.

Among travel writing, my favourites include Mark Twain's very amusing and perceptive 1869 *The Innocents Abroad*, about his travels through Europe and the Middle East, and *On Horseback through Asia Minor* by Captain Frederick Burnaby, who was said to be the handsomest man in the British army of the 1860s and 1870s. In a later period there are Robert Byron's *The Road to Oxiana*, about his adventures in Iran and on the borders of Afghanistan in the 1930s, or Patrick Leigh Fermor's *A Time of Gifts* and *Between the Woods and the Water*, about his trip from England to Istanbul in the 1930s.

SOURCES AND FURTHER READING

CHAPTER ONE: PERSUASION AND THE ART
OF LEADERSHIP

Bakewell, Sarah. *How to Live, or a Life of Montaigne in One Question and Twenty Attempts at an Answer*. London: Vintage, 2011.

Bliss, Michael. *Right Honourable Men: The Descent of Canadian Politics from Macdonald to Mulroney*. Toronto: HarperCollins, 1995.

Bothwell, Robert, Ian Drummond, and John English. *Canada, 1900–1945*. Toronto: University of Toronto Press, 1987.

Brands, H. W. *Traitor to His Class: The Privileged Life and Radical Presidency of Franklin Delano Roosevelt*. New York: Doubleday, 2008.

Brown, Archie. *The Myth of the Strong Leader: Political Leadership in Modern Politics*. New York: Basic Books, 2014.

Burns, James MacGregor. *Leadership*. New York: Harper and Row, 1978.

_____. *Roosevelt: The Lion and the Fox*. New York: Harcourt, Brace, 1956.

Cannadine, David, ed. *What Is History Now?* Basingstoke, UK: Palgrave Macmillan, 2002.

Carr, E. H. *What Is History?* 2nd ed. London: Penguin, 1990.

Clark, Christopher M. *Iron Kingdom: The Rise and Downfall of Prussia, 1600–1947*. London: Penguin, 2007.

Costigliola, Frank. *Roosevelt's Lost Alliances: How Personal Politics Helped Start the Cold War*. Princeton: Princeton University Press, 2012.

Craig, Gordon A. *Germany, 1866–1945*. Oxford: Oxford University Press, 1980.

Dawson, R. MacGregor. *William Lyon Mackenzie King: A Political Biography*. Toronto: University of Toronto Press, 1958.

Ferns, Henry, and Bernard Ostry. *The Age of Mackenzie King: The Rise of the Leader*. London: Heinemann, 1955.

Gildea, Robert. *Barricades and Borders: Europe 1800–1914*. Oxford: Oxford University Press, 2007.

Herring, George. *From Colony to Superpower: U.S. Foreign Relations since 1776*. New York: Oxford University Press, 2008.

Hutchison, Bruce. *The Incredible Canadian: A Candid Portrait of Mackenzie King, His Works, His Times, and His Nation*. Toronto: Longmans, Green, 1952.

King, William Lyon Mackenzie. The Diaries of William Lyon Mackenzie King. http://www.bac-lac.gc.ca/eng/discover/politics-government/prime-ministers/william-lyon-mackenzie-king/Pages/diaries-william-lyon-mackenzie-king.aspx.

Kissinger, Henry. *Diplomacy.* New York: Simon and Schuster, 1994.

Langer, Uli, ed. *The Cambridge Companion to Montaigne.* Cambridge: Cambridge University Press, 2005.

Lee, Hermione. *A Very Short Introduction to Biography.* Oxford: Oxford University Press, 2009.

Montaigne, Michel de. *The Complete Essays.* Translated by M. A. Screech. London: Penguin, 2003.

Psellus, Michael. *Fourteen Byzantine Rulers.* London: Penguin, 1966.

Reynolds, David. *From Munich to Pearl Harbor: Roosevelt's America and the Origins of the Second World War.* Chicago: Ivan R. Dee, 2001.

Robertson, Gordon. *Memoirs of a Very Civil Servant: Mackenzie King to Pierre Trudeau.* Toronto: University of Toronto Press, 2000.

Steinberg, Jonathan. *Bismarck: A Life.* Oxford: Oxford University Press, 2011.

Tour du Pin Gouvernet, Henriette Lucie, Marquise de la. *Memoirs of Madame de la Tour du Pin.* Translated and edited by Felice Harcourt. London: Harvill, 1971.

Watt, D. C. *Personalities and Politics: Studies in the Formulation of British Foreign Policy in the Twentieth Century.* London: Longmans, 1965.

Wills, Garry. *Certain Trumpets: The Call of Leaders.* New York: Simon and Schuster, 1994.

CHAPTER TWO: HUBRIS

Bullock, Alan. *Hitler and Stalin: Parallel Lives*. New York: Knopf, 1992.

Clark, Alan. *Diaries*. London: Weidenfeld and Nicolson, 1993.

Cooper, John Milton. *Woodrow Wilson: A Biography*. New York: Knopf, 2009.

Evans, Richard J. *Altered Pasts: Counterfactuals in History*. Waltham, MA: Brandeis University Press, 2013.

Kershaw, Ian. *Fateful Choices: Ten Decisions That Changed the World, 1940–1941*. London: Allen Lane, 2007 .

_____. *Hitler*. Vol. 1, *1889–1936: Hubris*. London: Allen Lane, 1998.

_____. *Hitler*. Vol. 2, *1936–1945: Nemesis*. London: Penguin, 2001.

_____. *Hitler, the Germans, and the Final Solution*. New Haven: Yale University Press, 2008.

King, Anthony. "The Outsider as Political Leader: The Case of Margaret Thatcher," *British Journal of Political Science* 32, no. 3 (July 2002): 435–54.

Kotkin, Stephen. *Stalin*. Vol. 1, *Paradoxes of Power, 1878-1928*. New York: Penguin, 2014.

Lebow, Richard Ned. *Archduke Franz Ferdinand Lives! A World without World War I*. New York: Palgrave Macmillan, 2013.

MacMillan, Margaret. *Paris 1919: Six Months That Changed the World*. New York: Random House, 2002.

Moore, Charles. *Margaret Thatcher: The Authorized Biography*. Vol. 1, *Not for Turning*. London: Allen Lane, 2013.

Snyder, Timothy. *Bloodlands: Europe between Hitler and Stalin*. New York: Basic Books, 2010.

Tucker, Robert C. *Stalin as Revolutionary, 1879–1929: A Study in History and Personality*. New York: Norton, 1973.

_____. *Stalin in Power: The Revolution from Above, 1928–1941*. New York: Norton, 1990.

Waldegrave, William. *A Different Kind of Weather: A Memoir*. London: Constable, 2015.

Weber, Max. *The Theory of Political and Social Organization*. Translated by A. M. Henderson and Talcott Parsons. New York: Oxford University Press, 1947.

Widenor, William C. *Henry Cabot Lodge and the Search for an American Foreign Policy*. Berkeley: University of California Press, 1983.

Young, Hugo. *One of Us: A Biography of Margaret Thatcher*. London: Macmillan, 1991.

CHAPTER THREE: DARING

Abulafia, David. *The Discovery of Mankind: Atlantic Encounters in the Age of Columbus*. New Haven: Yale University Press, 2008.

Alanbrooke, Field Marshal Lord. *War Diaries, 1939–1945*. Edited by Alex Danchev and Daniel Todman. London: Weidenfeld and Nicolson, 2001.

Ambrose, Stephen E. *Nixon*. Vol. 1, *The Education of a Politician, 1913–1962*. New York: Simon and Schuster, 1987.

_____. *Nixon*. Vol. 2, *The Triumph of a Politician, 1962–1972*. New York: Simon and Schuster, 1989.

Beaverbrook, Baron (Max Aitken). *Men and Power, 1917–1918*. London: Hutchinson, 1956.

Brooks, Timothy. *Vermeer's Hat: The Seventeenth Century and the Dawn of the Global World*. London: Profile, 2008.

Chisholm, Anne, and Michael Davie. *Beaverbrook: A Life*. London: Hutchinson, 1992.

Champlain, Samuel de. *Voyages, 1604–1618*. New York: Barnes & Noble, 1959.

_____. *Voyages to New France: being a narrative of the many remarkable things that happened in the West Indies in the years 1599–1601, with an account of the manners and customs of the savages of Canada and a description of that country in the year 1603*. Translated by Michael Macklem. Ottawa: Oberon, 1971.

_____. *Voyages to New France: being an account of the manners and customs of the savages and a description of the country, with a history of the many remarkable things that happened in the years 1615 to 1618*. Translated by Michael Macklem. Ottawa: Oberon, 1970.

Davis, Wade. *Into the Silence: The Great War, Mallory, and the Conquest of Everest*. New York: Knopf, 2011.

Fischer, David Hackett. *Champlain's Dream*. New York: Simon & Schuster, 2008.

Frank, Jeffrey. *Ike and Dick: Portrait of a Strange Political Marriage*. New York: Simon and Schuster, 2013.

Goh, Evelyn. *Constructing the U.S. Rapprochement with China, 1961–1974: From "Red Menace" to "Tacit Ally."* Cambridge: Cambridge University Press, 2005.

_____. "Nixon, Kissinger, and the 'Soviet Card' in the U.S. Opening to China, 1971–1974," *Diplomatic History* 29, no. 3 (June 2005): 475–502.

Heidenreich, Conrad, and K. Janet Ritch. *Samuel de Champlain before 1604: Des Sauvages and Other Documents Related to the Period*. Montreal: McGill-Queen's University Press, 2010.

Holmes, Richard. *Falling Upwards: How We Took to the Air*. New York: Pantheon, 2013.

Isaacson, Walter. *Kissinger: A Biography*. New York: Simon and Schuster, 1992.

Jenkins, Roy. *Churchill: A Biography*. New York: Farrar, Straus and Giroux, 2001.

Lewis, Michael. *The Big Short: Inside the Doomsday Machine*. New York: W. W. Norton, 2011.

Li, Zhisui. *The Private Life of Chairman Mao: The Memoirs of Mao's Personal Physician*. Translated by Tai Hung-Chao. New York: Random House, 1994.

Litalien, Raymonde. *Champlain: The Birth of French America*. Montreal: McGill-Queen's University Press, 2004.

Lukacs, John. *Five Days in London, May 1940*. New Haven: Yale University Press, 1999.

MacMillan, Margaret. *Nixon in China: The Week That Changed the World*. Toronto: Viking Canada, 2006.

Mann, James. *About Face: A History of America's Curious Relationship with China, from Nixon to Clinton*. New York: Knopf, 1999.

Marchildon, Gregory P. *Profits and Politics: Beaverbrook and the Gilded Age of Canadian Finance*. Toronto: University of Toronto Press, 1996.

Reith, Baron. *The Reith Diaries*. Edited by Charles Stuart. London: Collins, 1975.

Short, Philip. *Mao: A Life*. London: Hodder and Stoughton, 1999.

Sorkin, Andrew Ross. *Too Big to Fail: The Inside Story of How Wall Street and Washington Fought to Save the Financial System and Themselves*. New York: Viking, 2009.

Taylor, A. J. P. *Beaverbrook*. London: Hamish Hamilton, 1972.

Tett, Gillian. *Fool's Gold*. New York: Free Press, 2009.

Von Krockow, Christian. *Hour of the Women*. Boston: Faber and Faber, 1993.

Young, Kenneth. *Churchill and Beaverbrook: A Study in Friendship and Politics*. London: Eyre and Spottiswoode, 1966.

CHAPTER FOUR: CURIOSITY

Bayley, Emily, Lady Clive, and Sir Thomas Metcalfe. *The Golden Calm: An English Lady's Life in Moghul Delhi: Reminiscences.* Edited by M. M. Kaye. New York: Viking, 1980.

Carrington, Dorothy. *Granite Island: A Portrait of Corsica.* Harmondsworth, UK: Penguin, 1984.

Cheeseright, Paul. "Queen without a Throne: Ursula Graham Bower and the Burma Campaign," *Asian Affairs* 45, no. 2 (June 2014): 289–99.

Durham, Mary Edith. *Albania and the Albanians: Selected Articles and Letters 1903–1944.* Edited by Bejtullah Destani. London: Centre for Albanian Studies, 2001.

_____. *High Albania.* London: Virago, 1985.

_____. *Through the Lands of the Serb.* London: E. Arnold, 1904.

_____ *Twenty Years of Balkan Tangle.* London: Allen and Unwin, 1920.

Eden, Emily. *Up the Country: Letters Written to Her Sister from the Upper Provinces of India.* London: Virago, 1983.

Eden, Fanny. *Tigers, Durbars and Kings: Fanny Eden's Indian Journals, 1837–1838.* Transcribed and edited by Janet Dunbar. London: John Murray, 1988.

FitzHerbert, Margaret. *The Man Who Was Greenmantle: A Biography of Aubrey Herbert.* London: John Murray, 1983.

Graham Bower, Ursula. *Naga Path.* London: John Murray, 1952.

Jasanoff, Maya. *Liberty's Exiles: American Loyalists in the Revolutionary World*. New York: Knopf, 2011.

Moorehead, Caroline. *Freya Stark*. Harmondsworth, UK: Penguin, 1985.

Murphy, Dervla. *Full Tilt: From Dublin to Delhi with a Bicycle*. London: John Murray, 1965.

Parkes, Fanny. *Begums, Thugs & Englishmen: The Journals of Fanny Parkes*. Selected and edited by William Dalrymple. London: Penguin, 2003.

Simcoe, Elizabeth Posthuma. *Mrs. Simcoe's Diary*. Edited by Mary Quayle Innis. Toronto: Dundurn, 2007.

Taylor, Alan. *The Civil War of 1812: American Citizens, British Subjects, Irish Rebels, & Indian Allies*. New York: Knopf, 2012.

Tanner, Marcus. *Albania's Mountain Queen: Edith Durham and the Balkans*. London: I. B. Tauris, 2014.

Wallach, Janet. *Desert Queen: The Extraordinary Life of Gertrude Bell, Adventurer, Adviser to Kings, Ally of Lawrence of Arabia*. New York: Doubleday, 1996.

Winstone, H. V. F. *Gertrude Bell*. London: Quartet, 1980.

CHAPTER FIVE: OBSERVERS

Babur, Emperor of Hindustan. *The Baburnama: Memoirs of Babur, Prince and Emperor*. Translated by Wheeler M. Thackston. New York: Random House, 2002.

Cochran, Peter. *The Burning of Byron's Memoirs: New and Unpublished Essays and Papers.* Newcastle upon Tyne, UK: Cambridge Scholars Publishing, 2014.

Comnena, Anna. *The Alexiad of Anna Comnena.* Translated by E. R. A. Sewter. Middlesex, UK: Penguin, 1969.

Dale, Stephen F. "The Poetry and Autobiography of the Bâbur-nâma," *Journal of Asian Studies* 55, no. 3 (1996): 635–64.

Easton, Laird M. *The Red Count: The Life and Times of Harry Kessler.* Berkeley: University of California Press, 2002.

Gascoigne, Bamber. *The Great Moghuls.* London: Jonathan Cape, 1971.

Glendinning, Victoria, ed., with Judith Robertson, *Love's Civil War: Elizabeth Bowen and Charles Ritchie, Letters and Diaries, 1941–1973.* London: Simon and Schuster, 2009.

Gray, Charlotte. *Sisters in the Wilderness: The Lives of Susanna Moodie and Catharine Parr Traill.* Toronto: Viking, 1999.

Kessler, Count Harry. *Berlin in Lights: The Diaries of Count Harry Kessler (1918–1937).* Translated and edited by Charles Kessler. London: Weidenfeld and Nicolson, 1971.

_____. *Journey to the Abyss: The Diaries of Count Harry Kessler, 1880–1918.* Translated and edited by Laird M. Easton. New York: Random House, 1911.

Klemperer, Victor. *I Shall Bear Witness: The Diaries of Victor Klemperer, 1933–41.* Translated by Martin Chalmers. London: Weidenfeld and Nicolson, 1998.

_____. *I Will Bear Witness: A Diary of the Nazi Years 1942–1945*. Translated by Martin Chalmers. New York: Modern Library, 2001.

Maalouf, Amin. *The Crusades through Arab Eyes*. Translated by Jon Rothschild. London: Al Saqi, 1984.

McClung, Nellie. *The Complete Autobiography: Clearing in the West & The Stream Runs Fast*. Edited by Veronica Strong-Boag and Michelle Lynn Rosa. Peterborough, ON: Broadview, 2003.

Norton, Lucy. *Saint-Simon at Versailles*. London: Penguin, 1985.

Ritchie, Charles. *An Appetite for Life: The Education of a Young Diarist, 1924–1927*. Toronto: McClelland and Stewart, 2001.

_____. *The Siren Years: A Canadian Diplomat Abroad, 1937–1945*. Toronto: McClelland and Stewart, 2001.

Roquebrune, Robert de. *Testament of My Childhood*. Toronto: University of Toronto Press, 1964.

Ross, Alex. "Diary of an Aesthete: Count Harry Kessler Met Everyone and Saw Everything," *New Yorker*, April 23, 2012.

Sévigné, Marie de Rabutin-Chantal, marquise de. *Selected Letters*. Translated by Leonard Tancock. London: Penguin, 1982

Tomalin, Claire. *Samuel Pepys: The Unequalled Self*. London: Penguin, 2002.

Trudel, Marcel. *Memoirs of a Less Travelled Road: A Historian's Life*. Translated by Jane Brierley. Montreal: Véhicule, 2002.

Watt, D. C. *Personalities and Politics: Studies in the Formulation of British Foreign Policy in the Twentieth Century*. London: Longmans, 1965.

PERMISSIONS

ACKNOWLEDGEMENTS

THIS BOOK AND THE lectures on which it is based come out of many years of reading and of discussing history with too many people to name here, and I thank them all. I also want to thank my many students over the years, at Ryerson, the University of Toronto, and Oxford, for the ways in which they pushed me, perhaps without realizing it, to explain history as clearly as I could. I learned first and best from those at Ryerson who were instrumental in teaching me how to make history relevant and, so I hoped, entertaining. I still treasure the remark of a student in environmental engineering who said a particular lecture of mine — on Napoleon — was more interesting than the one he had just heard on industrial sludge.

I owe much to old friends and colleagues in Toronto at Ryerson University and the University of Toronto and my newer but equally valued ones in Oxford in the History Faculty, the Department of Politics and International Relations, and, in particular, to those at St Antony's, the best of intellectual communities.

While it is a difficult business to single out particular individuals, I must say a particular thanks to Bob Bothwell, Avi Shlaim, Gwyn Daniel, Paul Betts, Noah Richler, Hermione Lee, and John Barnard for their patience in discussing my ideas with me. I am also most grateful to Hermione for inviting me to give a lecture at her Life Writing Centre at Wolfson College where I was able to test out some of my ideas.

Caroline Dawnay is at once a great friend and agent, and I am equally fortunate in my publishers, Sarah MacLachlan at the House of Anansi and Andrew Franklin at Profile. All three helped me greatly with valuable ideas and suggestions. Both publishers have excellent teams which were a pleasure to work with: at Anansi Janie Yoon, the editor; Peter Norman, the copyeditor; Alysia Shewchuk, the designer; and Laura Meyer, Publicity Director; and at Profile Penny Daniel, the managing editor, Peter Dyer, the art director, and Valentina Zanca, Senior Publicity Manager. At the Canadian Broadcasting Corporation, Philip Coulter and Greg Kelly have done their usual magic of transforming a book into a series of lectures. I would also like to thank Hugh Segal, the Master of Massey College, and his able administrator Anna Luengo, for the support that the College continues to give to the lectures.

As always, I end by thanking my large and much-loved family, who are always ready to talk over my ideas, read my manuscripts, suggest titles, come to my lectures, or cheer me up when I get stuck. I hope they know already how much I owe them and how grateful I am. I will not list them all except for one — my mother Eluned who has always been until now the reader I have in mind when I write and who read this book in manuscript and, as always, made my work much better with her kind but firm comments.

A NOTE ON TERMINOLOGY

I have chosen to refer to the native peoples of Canada as Indians, partly to reflect the terminology of those such as Mrs. Simcoe whom I quote, and partly because we have as yet no single agreed designation from among the various possibilities of First Nations, aboriginals, natives, or indigenous peoples.

INDEX

Iroquois Confederacy, 138, 142, 143
Irvine, Sandy, 107
Islam, 2, 194, 198, 202
isolationism, 42–43, 45, 48
Italy, 46, 47, 98, 212

Japan, 2, 28, 44, 45, 46, 51, 55, 57, 91, 93–94, 98, 100, 129, 212, 213
Jarvis, Hannah, 158
Jewish Community, 225, 231
Jewish refugees, 44
Jews' House, 223, 229, 232, 233
Jobs, Steve, 114
John Murray (publishing co), 185, 186
Johns Hopkins University, 61
Joll, James, 5
Jones, Sir William, 162
Joseph, Keith, 73
Joyce, James, 187–88
Joyce, Lucia, 188
Julius Caesar, 57
Junker class, 16–17, 52, 110, 134

Kazakhstan, 90
Keane, Molly, 135
Kempe, Margery, 152
Kennedy, John F., 11, 124, 126
Kennedy, Joseph, 40
Kershaw, Ian, 55, 86, 88, 97
Kessler, Alice, 213, 215–16
Kessler, Count Harry, 211–23

Kidman, Nicole, 175
King, Anthony, 71
King, William Lyon Mackenzie, 4, 13, 23–35, 36, 40, 47, 49, 52–53, 59, 188
Kingsmere (W. L. King's country house), 31
Kipling, Rudyard, 120
Kissinger, Henry, 129, 131–32, 133
Kitchen Debate, 128
Klemperer, Eva, 226–32
Klemperer, Georg, 228
Klemperer, Otto, 223
Klemperer, Victor, 231–34
Knox, Frank, 40
Koh-i-Noor, 202
Kohl, Helmut, 16
Königgratz, 22
Korean War, 127
Kosovo, battle of, 56
Kotkin, Stephen, 55–56
Kristallnacht (1938), 46, 227–28
Krupp, Gustav, 215
Khrushchev, Nikita, 128

Labour Party (UK), 72, 73, 74
Lachine Rapids, 141
Lamb, Lady Caroline, 185
Landon, Alf, 52
Lapointe, Ernest, 29
Laurier House, 30
Laurier, Wilfrid, 28, 30, 31
Law, Bonar, 120, 121, 122

THE MASSEY LECTURES SERIES

The Massey Lecture series was created in honour of the Right Honourable Vincent Massey, former Governor General of Canada, and was inaugurated in 1961 to provide a forum on radio where major contemporary thinkers could address important issues of our time.

This book comprises the 2015 Massey Lectures, "History's People: Personalities and the Past," broadcast in November 2015.